THE CASE OF THE
Slave-Child, Med

A VOLUME IN THE SERIES
Childhoods: Interdisciplinary Perspectives on Children and Youth
Edited by
Karen Sánchez-Eppler, Rachel Conrad, Laura L. Lovett, and Alice Hearst

THE CASE OF THE
Slave-Child, Med

FREE SOIL IN ANTISLAVERY BOSTON

KAREN WOODS WEIERMAN

UNIVERSITY OF MASSACHUSETTS PRESS
Amherst & Boston

Copyright © 2019 by University of Massachusetts Press
All rights reserved
Printed in the United States of America

ISBN 978-1-62534-476-2 (paper); 475-5 (hardcover)

Designed by Jen Jackowitz
Set in Adobe Jenson Pro and Mrs Eaves

Cover design by adam b. bohannon
Cover art: *View of the new court house, Court Street, Boston*, 1836. Boston Pictorial Archive, Boston Public Library, digitalcommonwealth.org. This work is licensed for use under a Creative Commons Attribution Non-Commerical No Derivatives License (CC BY-NC-ND).

Library of Congress Cataloging-in-Publication Data
Names: Weierman, Karen Woods, 1971– author.
Title: The case of the slave-child, Med : free soil in antislavery Boston / Karen Woods Weierman.
Description: Amherst : University of Massachusetts Press, 2019. | Includes bibliographical references and index. | Summary: "In 1836, an enslaved six-year-old girl named Med was brought to Boston by a woman from New Orleans who claimed her as property. Learning of the girl's arrival in the city, the Boston Female Anti-Slavery Society (BFASS) waged a legal fight to secure her freedom and affirm the free soil of Massachusetts. While Chief Justice Lemuel Shaw ruled quite narrowly in the case that enslaved people brought to Massachusetts could not be held against their will, BFASS claimed a broad victory for the abolitionist cause, and Med was released to the care of a local institution. When she died two years later, celebration quickly turned to silence, and her story was soon forgotten. As a result, Commonwealth v. Aves is little known outside of legal scholarship. In this book, Karen Woods Weierman complicates Boston's identity as the birthplace of abolition and the cradle of liberty, and restores Med to her rightful place in antislavery history by situating her story in the context of other writings on slavery, childhood, and the law"—Provided by publisher.
Identifiers: LCCN 2019019896 | ISBN 9781625344755 (hardcover) | ISBN 9781625344762 (paper) | ISBN 9781613767191 (ebook) | ISBN 9781613767184 (ebook)
Subjects: LCSH: Med (Slave), 1830–1838. | Free African Americans—Massachusetts—Boston—Biography. | Child slaves—Massachusetts—Boston—Biography. | Antislavery movements—Massachusetts—Boston. | Slavery—Massachusetts—History. | Slaves—Legal status, laws, etc. —Massachusetts. | African Americans—Legal status, laws, etc. —Massachusetts.
Classification: LCC E450 .W44 2019 | DDC 306.3/62092 [B] —dc23
LC record available at https://lccn.loc.gov/2019019896

British Library Cataloguing-in-Publication Data
A catalog record for this book is available from the British Library.

For two little girls:
Med, *requiescat in pace*
Ryan, my dear heart

For Dr. Thea K. Hunter, in memoriam.

Slaves cannot breathe in England; if their lungs
Receive our air, that moment they are free;
They touch our country, and their shackles fall.
—William Cowper

If we should succeed, a decision would be obtained of greater importance than any within the last half century.
—Boston Female Anti-Slavery Society

They never saw a child.
—Ruby Bridges

CONTENTS

PREFACE xi

INTRODUCTION
The Said Med 1

CHAPTER 1
Before Med: James Somerset and Phillis Wheatley 13

CHAPTER 2
Slaves Cannot Breathe in Boston 29

CHAPTER 3
All Girls Are Bound to Someone 54

CHAPTER 4
Maria Sommersett, the American Stewart, and Dred Scott 76

CHAPTER 5
Free Soil Fictions 98

CONCLUSION
Sarah, Ruby, and Med 117

NOTES 127
INDEX 153

PREFACE

In 1836, the Boston Female Anti-Slavery Society (BFASS) celebrated "the case of the slave-child, Med," the successful freedom suit that affirmed the free soil of Massachusetts (figure 1). While the ruling in actuality did no such thing—Chief Justice Lemuel Shaw ruled quite narrowly that enslaved people brought to Massachusetts by their enslavers could not be held against their will—BFASS nevertheless claimed a broad victory for the abolitionist cause.[1] But little Med did not live to enjoy her new life in freedom: she died two years later in a Boston institution, and the celebration quickly turned to silence. As a result, *Commonwealth v. Aves* is little known outside of legal scholarship. The historical record is full of gaps and erasures, but I believe that Med's story, however incomplete, is worth telling. This book restores Med to her rightful place in Boston's antislavery history and contends that her minor status is the key to understanding her fate and the outcomes of other freedom suits involving children.

I first encountered the Med case while reading Lydia Maria Child's *Letters* and then learned about her death in Child's *Collected Correspondence*. I was stunned by this tragic outcome and wondered why I had never heard of this case before, despite years of scholarly work in the field. In my profound shock, I was determined to find the "romance of resistance" in a case of what, in my mind, had to be good intentions gone awry. After much consideration and extensive research, however, I could only conclude that my abolitionist heroes had used and abandoned a child. Following the lead of other scholars such as Britt Rusert and Saidiya Hartman, I went on to acknowledge my disappointment and use it productively to ask better questions about "freedom's

[3d] ANNUAL REPORT

OF THE

BOSTON FEMALE

ANTI-SLAVERY SOCIETY;

BEING A CONCISE HISTORY OF THE CASES OF

THE SLAVE CHILD, MED,

AND OF THE

WOMEN DEMANDED AS SLAVES

OF THE

SUPREME JUDICIAL COURT OF MASS.

WITH ALL THE OTHER

PROCEEDINGS OF THE SOCIETY.

BOSTON:
PUBLISHED BY THE SOCIETY.
ISAAC KNAPP, PRINTER.
1836.

FIGURE 1. *Third Annual Report of the Boston Female Anti-Slavery Society, Being a Concise History of the Cases of the Slave Child, Med, and of the Women Demanded as Slaves.* Courtesy of the Library of Congress.

vexed, ambivalent archive."[2] My research questions have thus evolved over time: What happened to Med? How could this have happened to Med? What did it mean to use a little girl as a test case? What did it mean to be the emancipated child of an enslaved mother? And how might I find this child in the archives, who died too young to leave even the slightest trace?

Classic legal scholarship about slavery, comity, and slave transit by Don E. Fehrenbacher, Paul Finkelman, and Leonard Levy form an essential foundation for this work. More recently, T. K. Hunter offers a useful comparative study of *Somerset's Case* and *Commonwealth v. Aves*, and Stuart Streichler's judicial biography of Benjamin Robbins Curtis offers essential analysis of both *Aves* and *Dred Scott*. Sue Peabody, whose work has been influential on this project, reminds us that "free soil was formulated, advanced, contested, and manipulated in specific and varied historical contexts." The project is also indebted to Edlie Wong, who complicates our readings of slave transit suits by asserting the power of family ties and their impact on the agency of enslaved people. Carolyn Karcher and Lee Chambers have helped me track BFASS activism and the influence of Lydia Maria Child and Maria Weston Chapman. Carolyn Karcher's *The First Woman in the Republic: A Cultural Biography of Lydia Maria Child* is as essential to my scholarly life now as it was at the time of its publication in 1994, and Lee Chambers's more recent *The Weston Sisters: An American Abolitionist Family* has helped me understand the public and covert activities of this influential family.[3]

Recent developments in childhood studies have helped me ask the right questions. Through this scholarship, I have come to understand how children disrupt the free soil model. In particular, Anna Mae Duane's new edited collection, *Child Slavery before and after Emancipation: An Argument for Child-Centered Slavery Studies*, has been fundamental to this project. Karen Sánchez-Eppler's *Dependent States: The Child's Part in Nineteenth-Century American Culture* helped me consider the questions of dependency and consent at the heart of freedom suits. Robin Bernstein's *Racial Innocence: Performing American Childhood from Slavery to Civil Rights* and Nazera Sadiq Wright's *Black Girlhood in the Nineteenth Century* have been especially useful to the project, while Katharine Capshaw's *Civil Rights Childhood: Picturing Liberation in African American Photobooks* has shaped my thinking about children, young girls in particular, as test cases.[4]

❖ ❖ ❖

I am fortunate to have had a lot of help along the way as I followed Med's archival trail. This book was made possible by the support of Worcester State University. I conducted the original archival research and drafted the manuscript during sabbatical leaves and during several summers with the support of Faculty Mini-Grants and a Faculty Scholarship/Creative Activity Grant. I also launched this project as an African American Studies Fellow at the Massachusetts Historical Society. I am grateful to Conrad Wright and the entire staff at the Massachusetts Historical Society for encouraging and supporting this project in its infancy.

Many generous scholars and librarians have assisted me in my research. I especially thank the staff at the American Antiquarian Society for cheering on my archival detective hunt, pointing me in the right direction, and finding impossibly hidden items. Special thanks to Ashley Cataldo, Thomas Knoles, and Marie E. Lamoureux. I am also indebted to the staff at the Boston Public Library, the Wellesley College Library, the Houghton Library, the Schlesinger Library, the Morse Institute Library, and the New Orleans Notarial Archives Research Center. Author Susan Goodman generously shared her research notes about the Sarah Roberts case and antebellum Boston. The Beacon Hill Scholars, especially the late National Park Service ranger and activist Horace Seldon, embraced this project and gave me a personal tour of the neighborhood.

I have presented early versions of this research at many conferences, including the Society of Early Americanists; Society for the History of Authorship, Reading, and Publishing; Society for the Study of American Women Writers; New England American Studies Association; Sedgwick Society Symposium; Historians Against Slavery; C19; and the American Studies Association. I am grateful to respondents and audience members for their thoughtful questions and feedback, which have vastly improved the project.

Writers need readers, and I am fortunate to have generous, insightful colleagues at Worcester State who have seen this project through its various iterations. Charlotte Haller, Tona Hangen, Matthew Ortoleva, and Heather Treseler, brilliant writers and rigorous critics all, have read the manuscript in its entirety over the years, and their faith in its value and my ability to tell Med's story have meant everything. Lisa Krissoff Boehm has supported the project from near and far. More recently, Anna Mae Duane reminded me that it was Med's minor status that shaped all the events and that I needed to put childhood at the center of "the case of the slave-child, Med." Karen Sánchez-Eppler, Carolyn Karcher, the Lydia Maria Child Society, and the Northeast Nineteenth-Century American Women Writers Study Group have offered continued support for the project. At the University of Massachusetts Press, Brian Halley, Rachael DeShano, and Susan Ferentinos have guided me through every step of the publishing process, and my anonymous readers have pushed me to write a better book.

Finally, I remain grateful to my family and friends for their interest in Med, and, more importantly, for the life they give me outside of my books. My parents, Susan and John Woods, taught me to love reading, to pursue history, and to write with precision; they also taught me to seek and value community. I have found that community in my adopted hometown of Natick, Massachusetts, and my vast network of Hoyas has offered enthusiastic support for the project and asserted its continued relevance. Most of all, I am deeply grateful to Bob, Dylan, and Ryan for the creative chaos that is the stuff of living. My daughter Ryan and this book have grown together, and this book is dedicated to her and to the memory of the little girl whose life was cut short.

THE CASE OF THE
Slave-Child, Med

INTRODUCTION

The Said Med

We do not know much about Med's short life. We do know that she accompanied her enslaver, Mary Aves Slater, on a summer journey from New Orleans to Boston in 1836. She was about six years old and must have missed her mother, who remained behind in the Slater household in New Orleans. Her legal status on this journey was unclear: while Massachusetts was a free state, the status of enslaved people in free jurisdictions had not been definitively settled by the courts. Previously state courts had made a careful distinction between domicile, sojourn, and transit, effectively permitting enslavers to travel with the people they claimed as property as long as they were just visiting or passing through. But by the 1830s, northern courts became increasingly unwilling to accept any slavery within their jurisdictions, and the regional compromises were beginning to break down.[1]

The members of the Boston Female Anti-Slavery Society (BFASS) learned about Med's presence on Beacon Hill and decided to take action. This decision would change the course of little Med's life. Lydia Maria Child, Maria Weston Chapman, and their BFASS colleagues believed that all slavery was unlawful in the free state of Massachusetts, and they went "undercover" to investigate Med's situation: one account suggested that they accessed the home of Thomas Aves, a watchman and Mary Aves Slater's father, under the pretense of recruiting children for Sunday school. Samuel Slater, Mary's husband, would later express his fury at this subterfuge in the newspapers: "It is much to be regretted that some two or three *females* (for I cannot call them Ladies), should lend their aid to these men, and intrude themselves into a private house in the absence of the family, to act the part of spies for the Abolitionists."[2] The BFASS women concluded that Med's unique situation—an enslaved child brought to Massachusetts by her enslaver—presented them with an important test case, and they decided to file suit on her behalf. As Child wrote to her friend:

> When in Boston I was entreated to exert myself concerning a little child, supposed to be a slave, brought from New Orleans, and kept shut up at No. 21 Pinckney Street. The object was to persuade the child's mistress to leave her at the colored asylum, and failing to effect [sic] this object, to ascertain beyond doubt whether the child was a slave, whether there was intention to carry her back to New Orleans, and to obtain sight of her in order to be able to prove her identity.... We obtained all the evidence we wanted, carried it to a lawyer, who petitioned for a writ of habeas corpus; the judge granted the petition; and the man who held little Med in custody was brought up for trial.[3]

The writ of habeas corpus was actually filed by Levin H. Harris, an African American "Mariner of Boston" on August 16, 1836. The writ lays out the circumstances of the case and his concerns for Med's safety:

> A certain female colored child named Med, of New Orleans in the State of Louisiana, an infant under the age of twenty-one years is now unlawfully restrained of her liberty by Thomas Aves of said Boston, Watchman.... And your petitioner fears that the said Med, who is free by the law of Massachusetts, may be unlawfully carried back to New-Orleans, and there made a slave, unless this honorable Court will interfere for her protection. Wherefore your petitioner prays, that your honors will grant a writ of *habeas corpus*, to bring the said Med before you, and to compel the said Aves to shew the cause of her detention. Your petitioner applies in behalf of the said Med, who is about six years old, not knowing that the said Med has any relative in this place.[4]

It is not clear how Harris became involved with the case: he might have brought the case to BFASS or have been recruited to petition for the writ. In any event, Harris initiated the legal proceedings and then mostly disappears from the historical record. The following day, Deputy Sheriff H. H. Huggeford brought Med before the court and summoned Thomas Aves "to appear and show the cause of the detaining of the said Med." Aves, as a watchman, was part of Boston's early law enforcement community; the watchmen patrolled the streets at night to protect public safety.[5]

It must have been frightening for Med to be far from home and to hear strangers discuss her future. We can find insights about this age from the experience of other writers, reflecting back on their enslaved childhoods. We know Frederick Douglass was separated from his grandmother at about age six and sent to live with his enslaver, where he was exposed to the violence of slavery for the first time. In his famous *Narrative*, he recounts how he saw his owner whip his Aunt Hester: "I was quite a child, but I well remember it.... It was the blood-stained gate, the entrance to the hell of slavery, through which I was about to pass.... It was all new to me. I had never seen anything like it before." Harriet Jacobs also reports the moment of bitter childhood revelation at this age: "I was born a slave; but I never knew it till six years of happy childhood had passed away." We might speculate that this was that moment for Med: she may have learned about her status through her journey north or through the legal proceedings; at the very least, she may have gained a new understanding of what it meant to be at the mercy of others. The fact that Med is described as "an infant of the age of six or thereabouts" is also a familiar generic convention; previously enslaved people often reported that their birthdays and exact ages were unknown. Frederick Douglass explains that this is part of the dehumanizing process: "I have no accurate knowledge of my age, never having seen any authentic record containing it. By far the larger part of the slaves know as little of their ages as horses know of theirs, and it is the wish of most masters within my knowledge to keep their slaves thus ignorant. I do not remember to have ever met a slave who could tell of his birthday."[6]

Thomas Aves's "return to the writ"—his explanation for the detention—offers glimpses into Med's biography and the events of that summer. He recounted that his son-in-law Samuel Slater purchased Med and her mother around June 1, 1833, when Med was about three years old, and a few months after the birth of Slater's first son Thomas Aves Slater, born in February 1833. The Slater family continued to grow with the birth of their second son, Samuel N. Slater in January 1836. The return goes on to explain that Med and her mother lived in New Orleans with the Slater family until around May 1, 1836, when "Mary Slater, the lawful wife of the said Samuel Slater, left the said City of New Orleans for the purpose of coming to Boston in this Commonwealth and visiting the said Thomas Aves, her father, intending to return to the said city of New Orleans, ... after an absence of four or five months." It is unclear whether the Slater boys remained home or traveled north with their mother, but we do know that Med's mother, whose name we never learn, remained behind in New Orleans with Samuel Slater "in the said state of slavery." At the time of the lawsuit, Med was "confided [sic] to the custody and care of the said Thomas Aves by the said Mary Slater, to be by him kept and nurtured during the absence of the said Mary Slater from the said City of Boston for a few days, she having gone to Roxbury in the county of Norfolk, there to remain for that period on account of ill health."[7]

The document also offers a tantalizing clue about Med's family life: Thomas Aves asserted that in Louisiana, "the marriage of a slave is in law wholly void," which meant that Med was a "natural child," that is, born out of wedlock, and that her mother was her legal guardian. This argument suggests that Med's parents were married in some fashion; otherwise, it is difficult to understand why Aves and his attorney would discuss questions of marital status. It is the only hint of Med's father in the entire case. The argument about Med's custody continued, somewhat convolutedly, as follows:

> Such right of guardianship over the infant children of a slave, where such children are not themselves slaves, devolves upon the owner of the mother of such infant children. That if the said child is by force of the Laws of Massachusetts, now emancipated and a free person, that the said Samuel Slater, as the owner of the mother of this natural child is entitled to the custody of the person of this child as its legal guardian, and the said Aves is the agent and legally authorized representative of the said Samuel Slater in this behalf.[8]

In other words, Slater contended that because he claimed Med's mother as property, he remained Med's guardian, *even if* she were declared free in Massachusetts. This was a provocative conclusion: that the free child of an enslaved mother should remain under the control of the mother's enslaver. This argument about marriage and the custody of the free children of enslaved women does not appear again in the proceedings, but this complicated defensive posture—that Med was a slave, but that even if she were not a slave in Massachusetts, her parents' "null and void" marriage made her an illegitimate child in the custody of her mother's enslaver—is certainly suggestive. Finally, the return of the writ concluded that Aves had been a proper guardian: "Thomas Aves continues to use that possession and custody, only for the purpose of benefiting the said child, and only restraining it of its liberty, so far as is necessary for the safety and health of the said child."[9]

Despite these efforts, Thomas Aves and the Slaters would not prevail in court. In *Commonwealth v. Aves*, Chief Justice Lemuel Shaw of the Massachusetts Supreme Judicial Court ruled that enslaved people brought to Massachusetts by their enslavers could not be held against their will. This narrow ruling did not apply to fugitives from slavery: had Med been a fugitive from slavery, Justice Shaw would have returned her to the Slaters. The case had a significant and lasting impact: Shaw's decision became the determining precedent in most free states, and a wave of freedom suits followed.[10] But this antislavery triumph was devastating for little Med: just two years later she died in the Samaritan Asylum for Indigent Children in Boston. No longer a poster child for abolitionist benevolence, Med became a ghostly presence who would haunt the antislavery community.

The Med case began as a neighborhood matter, taking place in a small geographic space in the neighborhoods surrounding Boston Common (figure 2). Mary Aves Slater was visiting her father, Thomas Aves, at 21 Pinckney Street in Beacon Hill, the cross street that separated the elite section of Beacon Hill from the North Slope, one of the largest antebellum free black communities. Today, Beacon Hill still resembles antebellum Boston, with its brick sidewalks, street lamps, and Greek Revival red brick homes.[11] This was a site where wealthy whites, some with abolitionist sympathies, and the organized African American community on the North Slope lived, interacted,

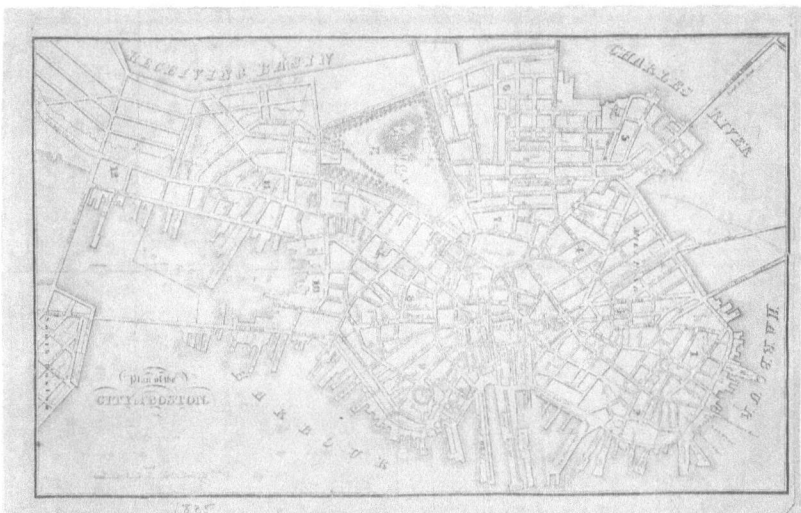

FIGURE 2. *Plan of the City of Boston*, 1835. Courtesy of the American Antiquarian Society.

and sometimes even collaborated. Today, this neighborhood is part of the Black Heritage Trail and a National Historic Site, and National Park Service rangers lead groups down Pinckney Street on a daily basis. As they walk down this street, tourists learn about African American heroes such as George Middleton, the Revolutionary War veteran, and the Underground Railroad rendezvous spot in John J. Smith's barbershop, but the Aves house and Med's story are not part of the official history (figure 3).

Back in 1836, the cast of characters in the Med drama included stars of the legal community, such as attorneys Ellis Gray Loring, Samuel Sewall, Rufus Choate, Benjamin Robbins Curtis, and Charles P. Curtis, as well as Chief Justice Lemuel Shaw; BFASS members, such as Lydia Maria Child, Maria Weston Chapman, Henrietta Sargent, and Nancy Prince; the Slater-Aves family; private citizens such as Levin Harris, the mariner who initiated the legal proceedings; and the African American residents who probably brought the case to BFASS, watched developments carefully, and protested the slow

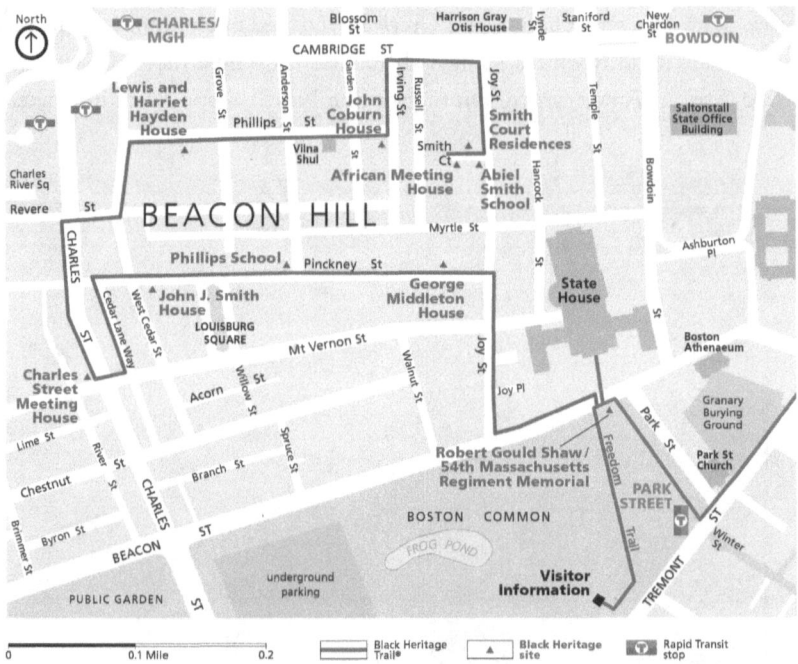

FIGURE 3. Black Heritage Trail Map, Boston African American National Historic Site. Courtesy of the National Park Service.

implementation of the ruling. The central character was Med herself, the six-year-old girl whose voice was never heard and whose name has been erased by time and the subsequent silence of her legal advocates.

Both Samuel Slater and his attorney Benjamin Robbins Curtis had complicated relationships with slavery and antislavery. Slater, born in Massachusetts, began his mercantile career embedded in the antislavery community in Alton, Illinois, the site of the murder of abolitionist editor Elijah Lovejoy. Slater went on to enslave people in New Orleans; was charged with abolitionist insurrection during the Texas Troubles, the slave insurrection panic of 1860 that contributed to the secession movement in the South; and late in life served as quartermaster in the Union Army. His young attorney Benjamin Robbins Curtis had a family secret: his father had sailed to the coast of Africa to trade in enslaved people for the South Carolina slavery market, one of the last Massachusetts men to do so before the closing of the Atlantic slave trade in 1808.[12] In his own career, Curtis became a leading expert on issues of slavery and comity, that is, the conflict of laws between slave and free states. He was praised for his legal acumen in *Commonwealth v. Aves* and would go on to defend the Compromise of 1850, but he is best known as the Supreme Court justice who dissented in the *Dred Scott* decision.

These figures emerge, albeit incompletely, from a variety of sources. The entire record of the legal proceedings can be found in *The Case of the Slave-Child, Med*, a pamphlet published soon after the ruling by Isaac Knapp, William Lloyd Garrison's business partner (figure 4). The title of this book alludes to the pamphlet of the legal proceedings published that year; it is also meant to evoke the mystery of Med's life and the archival detective work it has inspired. While the official case title was *Commonwealth v. Aves*, "the case of the slave-child Med" was commonly used in publications at the time.[13] Other accounts of the events can be gathered from BFASS reports, newspapers, and personal letters.

Writing about a young child poses a particular challenge: we have no access to her interior life, and we can only catch brief mentions of her in the historical record.[14] The words of fugitives from slavery who lived to adulthood, such as Frederick Douglass and Harriet Jacobs, as well as the reflections of twentieth-century civil rights children, offer some psychological insight through their parallel experiences. My chapter title, "The Said Med," refers to the legal expression (a reference back to something that was previously mentioned), but it also reminds us that we only know this child

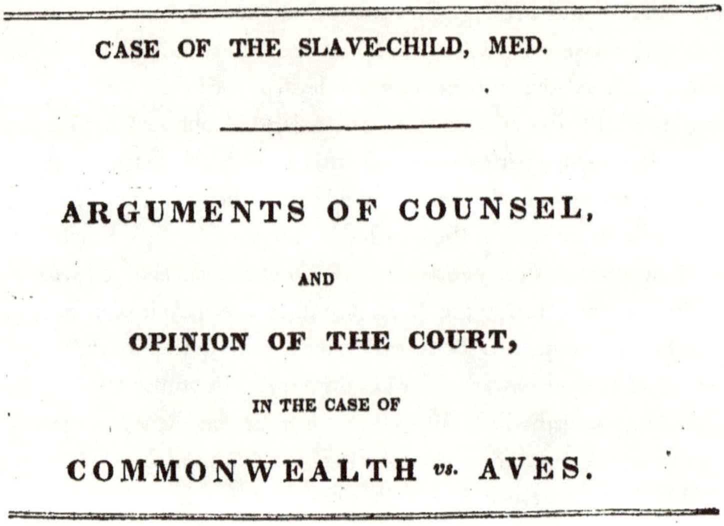

CASE OF THE SLAVE-CHILD, MED.

ARGUMENTS OF COUNSEL,

AND

OPINION OF THE COURT,

IN THE CASE OF

COMMONWEALTH vs. AVES.

FIGURE 4. *The Case of the Slave-Child, Med.* Courtesy of the Library of Congress.

through *what was said about her* by others and that we need to glean the facts with caution.

It is also challenging to find the words to write about enslavement; our language and historical understanding continue to evolve. This book will use the nineteenth-century descriptors—such as "the slave-child Med"—in context, but will use twenty-first-century usages in the remainder of the text. For example, scholars in slavery studies argue for the use of *enslaved* as an adjective and for the use of *enslaver* rather than *master, owner,* or *slaveholder* in order to more accurately name the practice of enslavement and the active work done to maintain that status.[15]

Legal scholars and historians have long established the importance of *Commonwealth v. Aves* as a legal precedent, but our understanding of the case remains incomplete; the child at the center of the lawsuit is generally unknown. Unlike other slave transit litigants such as James Somerset and Dred Scott, Med's name does not even appear in her own case title. This book redirects attention to her case and contends that she is as important as the more well-known African Americans who appeared in Shaw's court, such as Sarah Roberts, who unsuccessfully challenged Boston's segregated school system, and the fugitives from slavery Shadrach Wilkins and Thomas

Sims. Today, we lament Justice Shaw's "separate but equal" ruling on school segregation and his fugitive renditions as failures to uphold American ideals. In Med's case, while Justice Shaw's legal philosophy led him to rule in favor of freedom, her subsequent death in an institution was a failure that overwhelmed the legal victory. *The Case of the Slave-Child, Med* restores the tangled history of antislavery Boston's greatest success and darkest failure: following the affirmation of free soil, Med became a trope, discarded when no longer useful as a test case and erased when her death disrupted the triumphant antislavery narrative.

WHAT HAPPENED TO MED?

Med was unusual in that she became a test case, and yet she was very typical in demographic terms. Most enslaved people were children, as American studies scholar Karen Sánchez-Eppler reminds us, and more than 30 percent of antebellum enslaved people were under ten years of age. One in three enslaved children were separated from one or both parents. While children made some contribution to household or plantation labor, they were "more valuable as goods themselves than as workers." In addition to considering their demographic and economic importance, American studies scholar Anna Mae Duane makes a compelling argument for putting children at the center of the study of enslavement: "Thinking about children as a fundamental element within slavery forces us to confront questions about power and dependence, about authority and force that structure how we think about rights, about power, about citizenship, and about human development. Because slavery and childhood have been defined in relation to one another since antiquity, enslaved children are a paradox for analysts who wish to engage the complex relationship between slavery and freedom."[16]

Med's case reveals that emancipated children were part of this paradox as well. If "all boys are bound to someone," as Frederick Douglass famously noted in his *Narrative*, equating freedom with adulthood, then what does it mean to be a free child? And "how free is a free child whose parents are still in bondage?" as Sarah L. H. Gronningsater asks. Med was not alone in this no-man's land: her anomalous status was also experienced by children under gradual emancipation laws in the North, which typically freed children born to enslaved parents after a particular date. These laws focused on infant children because enslavers would be more likely to give up this demographic and because binding out poor children was already common practice. Children were "problematic as subjects of emancipation" because they could not provide for their own sustenance and education, and so binding them out under the existing overseers of the poor frameworks seemed the practical solution.[17] Med's future would likely have been similar had she regained her health.

In addition, Med's case raises important questions about consent and agency in freedom suits. A key difference between *Somerset's Case*, a key precedent in Med's case, and *Commonwealth v. Aves* was the fact that Med lacked the autonomy of the adult James Somerset, who made the decision to self-emancipate and then sought his own legal representation. Med's fate can be partially explained by her minor status: children disrupted the free soil model in which enslaved people were transformed into free people by crossing a border (or, as the courts would rule, that enslaved people brought to free states could not be removed without their consent). This scenario became complicated for minors who were enslaved: Could a child consent for herself? And if a child were to choose freedom, what would that really mean? Is the free child of enslaved parents really free? This irregular status explains the events that would follow: Med, as a six-year-old child, could not consent or speak for herself and was reduced to her usefulness as a test case for antislavery activists. Med initially served the cause well, allowing the abolitionists to portray themselves as protectors of children, but her early death was a public relations disaster for her advocates who had proclaimed that she would "never want a friend" as a free citizen of Massachusetts. While she died at a time when child mortality was not unusual, a child martyr, who died in northern freedom, hurt the cause and disrupted the antislavery narrative. Every detail of the case can be found in the newspapers of the day, but I have found no report of her death outside of personal correspondence.

Chapter 1 explores the eighteenth-century origins of Med's case, from the *Somerset* precedent to the life of Phillis Wheatley to the court rulings from Pennsylvania's free soil borderland. If "slaves cannot breathe in England," as the poet William Cowper wrote in commemoration of the *Somerset* ruling, then it followed, for Med's advocates, that slaves could not breathe in Boston either.

Chapter 2 establishes the immediate Boston context for Med's case and describes the courtroom proceedings. *Commonwealth v. Aves* was a gathering of the usual suspects: the attorneys, activists, and judges had appeared together in court many times before to argue slave transit suits and fugitive cases. Med's attorneys relied on both the *Somerset* precedent and the popular belief in free soil. In their savvy embrace of vernacular law, they argued that New England shared the unique moral geography of the mother country.

Chapter 3 focuses on the complicated questions following Med's emancipation: What did it mean to be the free child of an enslaved mother? Boston's abolitionists continued to pursue slave transit cases involving children, but despite the authority of the Med legal precedent, not a single subsequent case followed the Med script, to the confusion of the abolitionists and the delight of many proslavery observers. In the midst of it all, Med's death seemed to have no impact on the abolitionists' legal strategies, and the meaning of freedom for emancipated children remained unsettled.

Chapter 4 turns to three subsequent strands of the Med story. It first traces the commemoration and erasure of "Maria Med Sommersett" in the immediate aftermath of the case. It goes on to describe Slater's second brush with history, when he was charged with abolitionist collaboration during the Texas Troubles. Finally, the chapter notes Med's historical cameo in the 1850s, when Boston grappled with the impact of the Fugitive Slave Act and the *Dred Scott* decision. With remarkable historical irony, Supreme Court Justice Benjamin Robbins Curtis, who as a young lawyer had argued against Med's freedom, now found himself siding with Dred Scott and sparring with Chief Justice Roger Taney on the issues of citizenship and the Missouri Compromise.

Despite the brief Med references during the turbulent 1850s, her status as child martyr remained too rhetorically untouchable and too historically unusable for Boston's abolitionists. In various "free soil fictions," the deceased Med was replaced with adult characters, thus avoiding all the complications of emancipated childhood and tragic early death. Chapter 5 examines how in the decades following the case, Maria Weston Chapman, Lydia Maria Child, and Herman Melville—who were all personally linked to Justice Shaw's slave transit rulings—rewrote the Med precedent and its outcome with an adult protagonist.

The practice of using little girls as test cases never ended, however, and the concluding chapter returns us to the ethics and implications of these decisions, using the adult voice of the civil rights icon Ruby Bridges to access the experiences of Sarah Roberts and Med in antebellum Boston.

My search for Med has forced me to "stretch the field of view," and I have found that the origins and aftermath of her 1836 case span three centuries.[18] We will begin with the arrival of another young enslaved girl in Boston Harbor, seventy-five years before Med's journey north.

CHAPTER 1

Before Med

JAMES SOMERSET AND PHILLIS WHEATLEY

When does Med's story begin? In many ways, it originates in the life stories of James Somerset and Phillis Wheatley, two of the most famous enslaved people in the eighteenth-century British Atlantic world.

PHILLIS AND MED

On July 11, 1761, the enslaved child who became Phillis Wheatley arrived in Boston Harbor, several years before James Somerset and seventy-five years before Med. She was probably seven or eight years old, an estimated age based on her missing front teeth. She had survived the Middle Passage on a ship in which 25 percent of the enslaved Africans died, nearly twice the average death rate for these voyages. She was purchased by John and Susannah Wheatley and callously renamed after the slaving ship *Phillis* that brought her from Africa to Boston. Like Med, she was torn away from her family of origin and claimed by her enslavers as "one of the family," a description commonly used to mask the power dynamics of enslavement.[1]

We have no images or even a physical description of Med, but our historical memory of Wheatley survives through three items: a written description of a nearly naked child arriving in Boston, the frontispiece portrait from her 1773 book by the enslaved artist Scipio Moorhead, and the 2003 statue in the Boston Women's Memorial based on the frontispiece image (figure 5). Unlike Med, Wheatley lived to adulthood, leaving behind a body of work revealing a shrewd engagement with her Revolutionary era. And yet her fame in many

FIGURE 5. Phillis Wheatley, frontispiece to *Poems on Various Subjects, Religious and Moral*. Courtesy of the Library of Congress.

ways depended on her continued infantilization: the "slave-child, Med" was preceded by the "infant muse."[2]

In one of the rare mentions of her childhood, Wheatley attributes her love of liberty to her childhood kidnapping and notes her father's sorrow:

> Should you, my lord, while you peruse my song,
> Wonder from whence my love of *Freedom* sprung,
> Whence flow these wishes for the common good,

> By feeling hearts alone best understood,
> I, young in life, by seeming cruel fate
> Was snatch d from *Afric's* fancy'd happy seat:
> What pangs excruciating must molest,
> What sorrows labour in my parent's breast?
> Steel'd was that soul and by no misery mov'd
> That from a father seiz'd his babe belov'd:
> Such, such my case. And can I then but pray
> Others may never feel tyrannic sway?[3]

With careful reading, we might find glimpses of Med's experience in Wheatley's account of her life. Med's voyage from the slave state of Louisiana to the free state of Massachusetts cannot be compared to Wheatley's experience of the Middle Passage, but she was about the same age as Wheatley when she was separated from her family. As such, we might imagine similar fear and grief. Wheatley would go on to reverse her Middle Passage when she left for London in June 1773, one year after the ruling in the *Somerset* case, the precedent that would change everything for both Phillis and Med.

SOMERSET'S CASE

No one doubted in 1836 that Massachusetts was a free state, but there was no such legal certainty in eighteenth-century England. During Somerset's day, the legal status of slavery in England was muddled at best. For example, in 1701, Chief Justice John Holt ruled that "as soon as a negro comes into England he is free," and in 1705, he affirmed that "the common law takes no notice of negroes being different from other men. By the common law no man can have a property in another. . . . There is no such thing as a slave by the law of England."[4] But these antislavery rulings were countered by the 1729 proslavery Yorke-Talbot opinion, which posited that "a slave did not automatically become free when he was brought to Britain from the West Indies . . . and that his master could legally compel him to return to the plantations." Later in the century, William Blackstone, in his *Commentaries on the Laws of England* (1765), disagreed with Yorke-Talbot: "A slave or negro, the moment he lands in England, falls under the protection of the laws, and with regard to all natural rights becomes [in that instant] a freeman." But in his 1766 second edition, Blackstone qualified this freedom by adding "though the master's right to his service may still continue."[5]

The confused state of slave law meant that *Somerset's Case* was about much more than one man's freedom: as historian T. K. Hunter explains, "At stake was nothing less than the legitimacy of slavery in England, despite the fact that the court arguments were framed around the much more narrow and specific question of wrongful detainment." *Somerset* also required the court to face some difficult questions about the relationship between colonial and metropolitan law: Did Somerset's enslaved status depend upon his geographic location? Did a colonial slave's status change upon arrival in England? And, more broadly, how was slavery itself impacted by the imperial conflict of laws?[6]

For Somerset's advocates, it was clear that an enslaved person's arrival in England was indeed liberatory. They endorsed the free soil principle articulated by Holt and Blackstone and proclaimed their belief in the moral geography of England. "A moral geography," as geographer Tim Cresswell explains, "is the idea that certain people, things, and practices belong in certain spaces, places, and landscapes and not in others." In antislavery terms, the moral geography of England dictated that enslaved people were decidedly "out of place" and "non-compliant" with England's local values. It is important to note, however, that the free soil principle was not unique to the common law tradition. Historian Sue Peabody has found considerable evidence throughout the Atlantic world that "local, popular traditions, dating back at least as far as the sixteenth century, freed people in bondage when they crossed particular state borders." Leading British abolitionist Granville Sharp and Somerset's legal team invoked this tradition, citing French and Dutch case law to establish a long history of European free soil. Against the backdrop of this broader European custom, the moral geography of England—the free soil and pure air which "conferred the gift of liberty in its entirety"—took center stage in *Somerset's Case*.[7]

The case was heard by William Murray, first Earl of Mansfield, who served as Lord Chief Justice of the King's Bench, one of the highest courts in England. Speaking for Somerset, lawyer Francis Hargrave warned that the liberty of all English citizens was at risk if enslaved people could be brought to England, "a soil whose air is deemed too pure for slaves to breathe in it." In the case that launched his career, he went on to argue that "the laws, the genius and spirit of the constitution, forbid the approach of slavery; will not suffer its existence here." Lawyer John Dunning, speaking for Stewart as well as the West India interest, which lobbied for the Caribbean sugar trade, dismissed both the free soil tradition and the constitutional arguments: "Let me take notice, neither the air of England is too pure for a slave to breathe in, nor the laws of England have rejected servitude." But Somerset's lawyer William Davy had the last word about England's "pure air": "For the air of England ... has been gradually purifying ever since the reign of Elizabeth ... it has been asserted, and is now repeated by me, this air is too pure for a slave to breathe in: I trust, I shall not quit this Court without certain conviction of the truth of that assertion."[8]

While Somerset's legal team won the case, Lord Mansfield did not endorse Davy's conviction about the "pure air" of England in his ruling, and Chief Justice Lemuel Shaw would follow his example in nineteenth-century Massachusetts. Lord Mansfield instead focused specifically on the writ of habeas corpus at hand and the "return of the writ," that is, the merits of Stewart's justification for detaining Somerset:

> The only question before us is, whether the cause on the return is sufficient? If it is, the negro must be remanded; if it is not, he must be discharged. Accordingly, the return states, that the slave departed and refused to serve; whereupon he was kept, to be sold abroad. So high an act of dominion must be recognized by the law of the country where it is used. The power of a master over his slave has been extremely different, in different countries. The state of slavery is of such a nature, that it is incapable of being introduced on any reasons, moral or political, but only by positive law, which preserves its force long after the reasons, occasion, and time itself from whence it was created, is erased from memory. It is so odious, that nothing can be suffered to support it, but positive law. Whatever inconveniences, therefore, may follow from the decision, I cannot say this case is allowed or approved by the law of England; and therefore the black must be discharged.[9]

After the ruling, James Somerset and other Africans present in the courtroom bowed to the judge in a show of respect and satisfaction. Like many observers, they believed that Lord Mansfield had freed all the slaves in England, and one fugitive from slavery even credited his "Uncle Somersett" as his inspiration for claiming his freedom. Shortly after his case, James Somerset disappeared from the historical record.[10]

The actual meaning of the Mansfield decision has been a matter of controversy since the very beginning. "Technically considered," as historian William Wiecek reminds us, "the judgment in *Somerset* settled only two narrow points of English law: a master could not seize a slave and remove him from the realm against the slave's will, and a slave could secure a writ of habeas corpus to prevent that removal."[11] This narrow ruling freed Somerset on these grounds, but it also made a broad assertion about slavery: Mansfield denounced slavery as "so odious" that it required positive law to exist. In other words, English common law, which was unwritten and based on custom and precedent, did not permit slavery. The practice of slavery required "positive law," that is, statutes enacted by the government. Despite Mansfield's attempts to avoid ruling on the status of slavery, in the long run, the absence of common law sanction would undermine the legitimacy of slavery.[12]

For the rest of his life, Lord Mansfield would insist that his ruling only addressed the question of wrongful detainment; nevertheless, it was popularly believed to have freed all the slaves in England. What people heard and remembered was the moral geography of the case, and they celebrated that Lord Mansfield had declared the air of England "too pure for a slave to breathe." Sue Peabody's concept of *vernacular law*—the "legal understandings shared by common people without formal training but which influence formal legal culture"—is useful here.[13] Advocate William Davy's emphatic assertion that slaves became free "the moment they put their foot on English ground," was erroneously attributed to Lord Mansfield in many accounts. This vernacular legal space created an opportunity for the antislavery cause, as historian Ruth Paley notes: "For Sharp and the abolitionists, the importance of the *Somerset* decision lay not in the decision itself, but in what abolitionist publicity and propaganda could *make* the decision mean."[14]

SOMERSET IN THE COLONIES

The *Somerset* case was closely followed in the American colonies. Colonial newspapers reprinted British press accounts, and in Boston alone readers could learn about the case in the *Massachusetts Spy*, *Boston Evening Post*, *Boston Gazette*, *Boston News-Letter*, and *Boston Post-Boy*. The case would "profoundly influence American slave law," as legal scholar Steven M. Wise explains, "Judges North and South absorbed *Somerset* into their common law and either freed slaves or didn't, depending on whether positive law creating slavery existed in their states."[15]

For enslaved people in Massachusetts, the *Somerset* decision was a golden opportunity: they sued for freedom and for compensation for their labor (*quantum meruit*) in the Massachusetts courts. In these freedom suits, the

Mansfield decision was interpreted to their advantage: it was argued that slavery violated common law and that there was no positive law allowing slavery in Massachusetts.[16]

And yet despite its influence on U.S. law, the *Somerset* case is unfamiliar to many twenty-first-century Americans. *Somerset* complicates the plot of British tyranny and American liberty at the heart of the national creation story. Perhaps *Somerset* disappears from the American historical consciousness precisely because, as historian Van Gosse posits, "it reverses the image of a repressive metropole and liberating, democratizing colonies" so central to myth of the American Revolution.[17] For antislavery activists in 1836, however, *Somerset* was *the* significant event in the historical narrative. It offered the perfect legal and historical precedent, and while immediate abolition seemed a distant dream in the United States, it was impossible to overlook that British antislavery had succeeded with the 1833 Emancipation Act, which abolished slavery in the British Empire.

Somerset's Case (1772) would loom large in *Commonwealth v. Aves*, and the precedent's relevance would be the central question for the court. Med's advocates portrayed her as the "American Somerset" and echoed the appeal to the values of free soil and the moral geography of the region. This rhetorical move was somewhat different in the New England context: the belief that slavery could not exist on the free soil of Massachusetts was an extension of the English free soil tradition, but it was also intertwined with the region's identity as the cradle of liberty. "For nineteenth-century Bay Staters," explains historian Margot Minardi, "no slavery could take root in the soil that had nurtured the Liberty Tree and its gardeners."[18]

THE "WHEATLEYAN MOMENT"

Phillis Wheatley must have had *Somerset* in mind when she sailed to London with her enslavers' son Nathaniel Wheatley in June 1773, just before the one-year anniversary of the Mansfield ruling. The Wheatleys sent her to improve her health and to seek a publisher for her book that had failed to find a publisher in Boston. Despite the repeated characterization of Wheatley as "young," she was about twenty years old at the time. The publication of *Poems on Various Subjects, Religious and Moral*, the first book by an African American and the second by a woman in North America, made her famous. The trip also led to her manumission.

James Somerset had set events in motion when he escaped from Charles Stewart and sought legal help from Granville Sharp. Wheatley then seized the opportunity in what historian David Waldstreicher calls the "Somerset/Wheatleyan moment" to secure her own freedom. There is strong circumstantial evidence that Wheatley understood that she had two paths to freedom: self-emancipation in England under the *Somerset* ruling or negotiated manumission by the Wheatleys if she agreed to return to Boston. Because the *Somerset* case had been widely reported, it is likely that she would have read about it before leaving Boston. The suggestive possibilities of Wheatley's position become clearer when we consider that Granville Sharp himself was her main London tour guide: no doubt they would have discussed his legal triumph from the previous year and its implications for Wheatley's life.[19]

Her poem, "A Farewel to America. To Mrs. S.W." (Boston, May 7, 1773), published in local newspapers on the eve of her departure for London, reads differently through a post-*Somerset* lens, particularly in stanzas XI–XII:

> XI.
> For thee, *Britannia,* I resign
> *New-England's* smiling fields;
> To view again her charms divine,
> What joy the prospect yields!
>
> XII.
> But thou! Temptation hence away,
> With all thy fatal train
> Nor once seduce my soul away,
> By thine enchanting strain.[20]

Here Wheatley looks forward to returning home to New England, but also notes the "temptation" to remain in England. In biographer Vincent Carretta's reading, "The health that Wheatley locates in England in 'A Farewel to America' is not only physical. It is also social and political because in England she will face the opportunity to resurrect herself from the social death of slavery." But the poem features Wheatley's trademark ambiguity: Was post-*Somerset* England the temptation to be resisted? Or was returning to America without seizing her freedom the temptation to be resisted?[21]

In the end, Wheatley chose the path that granted her the most geographic mobility. Self-emancipation in London would mean that she had to remain in England permanently: returning to Boston would mean risking re-enslavement. Instead, she negotiated an agreement with Nathaniel Wheatley: he promised to manumit her if she returned to Boston to care for the sick Susannah Wheatley, Nathaniel's mother. Wheatley made sure her friends in England heard this promise, and she sent a copy of her manumission papers to a lawyer in London, making sure her property and person were secure.[22]

Her trip was a triumph in many ways: in addition to her manumission, her book *Poems on Various Subjects* was published in London in September 1773, and copies arrived in Boston for sale in December. While she had almost reached her majority by this time, the marketing of her public image continued to depend on her youth; she was often described as the "young negro poetess" and "Negro girl."[23] And the disappointments of her new life in freedom were not yet apparent.

Following her manumission, Wheatley's voice reflects a growing confidence and willingness to speak directly about slavery. She explains in a published letter to Samson Occom, member of the Mohegan tribe, Presbyterian minister, and advocate for Indian rights, that the desire for freedom is universal: "In every human Breast, God has implanted a Principle, which we call Love of Freedom; it is impatient of Oppression, and pants for Deliverance." She goes on to compare the Americans with the slaveholders in Egypt: "By the Leave of our Modern Egyptians I will assert, that the same Principle lives in us." Here Wheatley presents her own moral geography through simile, in this case what literary scholar Philip Gould describes as a "blending of biblical geography (Israel/Egypt), Revolutionary geography (America/Britain), and the geography of the slave trade (Africa/America)." Through Wheatley's multi-layered typology, readers are forced to consider that enslaved Africans rather than American patriots might be God's chosen people.[24]

In her letter to Occom, Wheatley goes on to note the hypocrisy of the patriot cause: "How well the Cry for Liberty, and the reverse Disposition for the Exercise of oppressive Power over others agree,—I humbly think it does not require the Penetration of a Philosopher to determine."[25] She continues this assertion in her 1778 poem "On the Death of General Wooster." This time, she speaks in the dying general's voice, asking God to support the patriot cause and noting the hypocrisy of slavery. She boldly borrows General Wooster's authority to call for victory and freedom for the enslaved:

> But how, presumptuous shall we hope to find
> Divine acceptance with th' Almighty mind—
> While yet (O deed Ungenerous!) they disgrace

> And hold in bondage Afric's blameless race?
> Let Virtue reign—And thou accord our prayers
> Be victory our's, and generous freedom theirs.[26]

The war years were difficult for Wheatley: freedom also meant abandonment by her former patrons. Her former enslaver John Wheatley died in March 1778, and despite all the language of "family," he left her nothing in his will. She married John Peters later in 1778, and some sources claim that they buried three children, although no birth, baptismal, or burial records have been found. Wheatley was never able to find a publisher for her proposed second book, as literary scholar Joanna Brooks describes: "The set of white women that had once hosted performances, commissioned poems, hand-copied and circulated manuscripts, and sold her first book withdrew its support.... The story of Wheatley and her white female patrons in Boston makes plain the evasions, irresponsibilities, and betrayals at the heart of white sentimentalism." Ignatius Sancho, the famous African man of letters in London, condemned the fickle nature of Wheatley's white supporters: "These good great folks—all know—and perhaps admired—nay, praised Genius in bondage—and then, like the Priests and the Levites in sacred writ, passed by—not one good Samaritan amongst them."[27]

Wheatley died at the age of thirty-one on December 5, 1784. While she died in poverty, it is important to note that she did not die in obscurity. Notices of her death appeared in Boston newspapers, and her book went through nine editions before 1820.[28] There is a sad parallel to Med's experience here: she also would be betrayed by the white women of Boston who abandoned their responsibility to her once she was freed. Both Med and Phillis were never truly "one of the family."

COWPER'S FREE SOIL

Wheatley's rhetoric had a significant influence on the transatlantic evangelical community so essential to the abolition of the slave trade. English poet William Cowper would also note the hypocrisy of slavery alongside claims of freedom, and his philosophy and imagery may well have been shaped by his reading of Wheatley's poetry. Writing after the Revolution, Cowper also highlighted the incompatibility of slavery with British values. His brand of patriotism differed from Wheatley's, however: he blamed the colonists for the war, but interpreted the war as God's punishment for British sins and expressed misgivings about British imperialism.[29]

In October 1783, Cowper began writing his masterpiece, *The Task*, a nearly forty-thousand-word book-length poem that made Cowper a household name for decades. *The Task* also includes the most notable literary interpretation of English free soil and of *Somerset's Case*, the case that would free Med and give Wheatley the leverage to negotiate her own freedom. While eleven years had passed since the *Somerset* ruling, the year 1783 featured many landmark events influencing the British Empire and the slave trade, including the infamous *Zong* lawsuit, the first Quaker petition against the slave trade, and the Treaty of Paris recognizing American independence.[30] Through his critique of British imperialism, Cowper tries to temper what literary scholar Suvir Kaul describes as "the aggressive nationalism of James Thomson's ode 'Rule, Britannia!'" (1740). Thomson's refrain ("Rule, Britannia, rule the waves; / Britons never will be slaves.") shows that slavery and the slave trade were the key to Britain's overseas power and to the enjoyment of free soil at home.[31]

In Book II of *The Task*, Cowper contrasts life in the country with a world outside disrupted by war and slavery. This former barrister had left the law behind, but in his poetry he articulates an influential vernacular legal argument in favor of English free soil:

> Slaves cannot breathe in England; if their lungs
> Receive our air, that moment they are free;
> They touch our country, and their shackles fall.[32]

Having established that there are no slaves in England, Cowper goes on to argue for a transformed legal relationship between the metropole and the colonies. He begins by establishing the inhumanity of slavery, explicating Lord Mansfield's definition of the "odious" nature of slavery:

> My soul is sick, with every day's report
> Of wrong and outrage with which earth is fill'd . . .
> He finds his fellow guilty of a skin
> Not colour'd like his own; and, having power
> To enforce the wrong, for such a worthy cause
> Dooms and devotes him as his lawful prey . . .
> Thus man devotes his brother, and destroys;

> And, worse than all, and most to be deplored,
> As human nature's broadest, foulest blot,
> Chains him, and tasks him, and exacts his sweat
> With stripes, that Mercy, with a bleeding heart,
> Weeps when she sees inflicted on a beast.
> Then what is man? And what man, seeing this,
> And having human feelings, does not blush,
> And hang his head, to think himself a man?[33]

Having affirmed the "odious" horror of slavery through a rhetoric of sensibility, which emphasizes the depiction of a suffering victim in order to inspire action, Cowper then tackles the anomaly of enslaved people moving between colonial societies where slavery was legal and the metropole where slavery was illegal.[34] He wonders why English liberty is only available in England rather than in all the royal territories. Cowper concludes that slavery cannot stand up to the free soil and free air of England, the values of which should extend across the Empire:

> We have no slaves at home:—then why abroad?
> And they themselves, once ferried o'er the wave
> That parts us, are emancipate and loosed ...
> That's noble, and bespeaks a nation proud
> And jealous of the blessing. Spread it then,
> And let it circulate through every vein
> Of all your empire; that where Britain's power
> Is felt, mankind may feel her mercy too.[35]

Here Cowper establishes the moral geography of Empire, one ruled by power in the service of mercy, and affirms the nobility of the national character. Such affirmation is sorely needed for a nation that had just lost the American colonies. In the aftermath of this defeat, Christopher Brown notes, "moral capital might be accrued by framing antislavery initiatives as an emblem of the national character."[36]

Cowper, the central poet of the eighteenth-century campaign against slavery and the slave trade, would go on to write antislavery poems such as "Pity for Poor Africans" and "The Negro's Complaint." But to the best of my knowledge, it is only in *The Task* that Cowper articulates the free soil principle in such detail.[37] The poem remained relevant into the next century, and

Cowper's well-known verses served as cultural shorthand for the values of Anglo-American free soil.

"Slaves cannot breathe in England" also had resonance for antebellum Bostonians, as the Reverend William Ellery Channing recalled: "I learned this line when I was a boy, and in imagination I took flight to the soil which could never be tainted by slaves. Through the spirit which spoke in that line, England has decreed that slaves cannot breathe in her islands."[38] It is no wonder that Med's attorney Ellis Gray Loring would conclude his arguments for Med's freedom with Cowper's famous lines:

> The generous boast of the English poet haunts the memory of every lover of liberty:
> Slaves cannot breathe in England:—if their lungs
> Receive our air, that moment they are free.
> They touch our country, and their shackles fall—
> That's noble, and bespeaks a nation proud
> And jealous of the blessing.—[39]

But while Loring noted that the English might well be "proud" of this legacy, he also cautioned Massachusetts residents that "this exalted pride cannot be fully ours" given the inclusion of the fugitive slave clause in the Constitution. "Lovers of liberty," noted Loring, are "haunt[ed]" by the moral compromises of the revolutionary generation and the concessions to the slave power.[40]

PENNSYLVANIA'S FREE SOIL BORDERLAND

The first "American Somerset" cases, freedom suits based on residence in a free jurisdiction, would take place in Pennsylvania, the inaugural free soil territory in the new United States. Med's case, hence, originates not only in London but also in Pennsylvania's free soil borderland, which historian Richard S. Newman defines as "a contested space where competing notions of ideology, legal culture, and territorial use battled one another." Following the state's Gradual Abolition Act of 1780, which freed the children of slaves born after that year, African Americans saw Pennsylvania as a "haven from slaveholders' national power," as Newman explains, even viewing "Pennsylvania's geography in moral terms."[41]

Enslaved people found staunch legal advocates in the Pennsylvania Abolition Society (PAS). During the late eighteenth and early nineteenth centuries, PAS was the world's most well-known and influential antislavery group. Originally named "The Society for the Protection of Free Blacks," PAS provided legal aid to protect free blacks from kidnapping, to assist fugitives from slavery, and to emancipate enslaved people brought by their enslavers to Pennsylvania who remained beyond the six months' sojourn permitted by law. Unlike the New England organizations, PAS never sought "test cases," but used "loopholes, technicalities, and narrow legal opinions to liberate African Americans on a case-by-case basis."[42]

Decades before the Med case, PAS was pursuing freedom suits based on residence in a free jurisdiction, and several of these cases would be cited in the Med proceedings. Despite the fact that PAS did not seek test cases, the cases in Pennsylvania had significant impact beyond the individuals they helped. Three Pennsylvania cases were referenced by Med's lawyer Ellis Gray Loring and Justice Shaw in support of Med's emancipation. In *Butler v. Hopper* (1806), Senator Pierce Butler claimed that he was still a resident of South Carolina and thus entitled to claim a person as property, but both the state and federal courts disagreed and freed the enslaved man Ben based on his eight months' consecutive residence in Philadelphia. In *Commonwealth v. Holloway* (1816), the state court ruled that the child of a fugitive from slavery, born in Pennsylvania, was free and could not be removed from the state. In *Ex parte Simmons* (1823), the federal court ruled that an enslaver could not remove the person he claimed as a slave after eleven months' residence in Pennsylvania: the fugitive slave law of 1793 did not apply to enslaved people brought by their enslavers to a free jurisdiction. These cases were significant to the Med case for two reasons: 1) because federal courts showed some willingness to emancipate enslaved people in transit, and, 2) because the courts drew a sharp distinction between fugitives from slavery and enslaved people transported by their enslavers.[43] Thus, the state and federal courts in early national Pennsylvania served as an important temporal and geographic link between the free soil rulings in Mansfield's London and Shaw's Boston.

MED'S ARRIVAL AND WHEATLEY'S REVIVAL

Back in 1830s Boston, as Med's case and other freedom suits proceeded, Wheatley's poetry underwent a revival. We might even say that Wheatley's body of work served the same purpose as Med's physical body: both bodies served as test cases and exemplars for the antislavery cause. It is important to recognize that Wheatley was not commonly perceived as an antislavery poet until abolitionists in Boston and elsewhere began reprinting her poems with that interpretive framework. As literary scholar Karen Weyler explains, "Wheatley's poetry went on to become a mainstay of antislavery periodicals ... presented as evidence of the past greatness of Wheatley as an individual and the future potential of African Americans as a race." William Lloyd Garrison's *Liberator* published poems from her book on a weekly basis from February 11 until December 22, 1832, sometimes without attribution and sometimes with the byline "Phillis Wheatley, An African Slave." Lydia Maria Child's landmark antislavery textbook *An Appeal in Favor of that Class of Americans Called Africans* (1833) also included a brief biographical sketch of Wheatley in her chapter on the "Intellect of Negroes."[44]

The following year, Margaretta Matilda Odell, a distant descendant of Susannah Wheatley, published her *Memoir and Poems of Phillis Wheatley*, the book that has shaped Wheatley scholarship despite its many unverifiable or incorrect claims. The introduction frames the book as an antislavery endeavor: "We introduce to the reader the subject of the following Memoir, whom we find in the lowest condition of humanity; for she was sold and bought like a beast in the market! and that in the same land where, shortly after, the people rose in their indignation against oppression, and asserted, in the face of a frowning world, that 'All men are born free and equal.' But the stain of slavery has long been erased from the annals of New England." The book also participates in the historical amnesia regarding the local experience of slavery. In Odell's account, slavery in New England was unfortunate but benevolent; the Wheatleys were rescuers rather than enslavers; Wheatley herself was modest and respectable; and her husband John Peters was the villain who led to her ruin. In 1838, the year of Med's death, abolitionist William Lloyd Garrison's former partner Issac Knapp published a new edition of Wheatley's poems and the Odell memoir that also included a reprint of a book by the enslaved poet George Moses Horton from North Carolina.[45] In the absence of archival alternatives, Odell's text continues to shape our understanding of Wheatley's life.

LOOKING FOR PHILLIS AND MED

Since the very beginning, Phillis Wheatley has served as a blank slate for a range of purposes. Critics dismiss her as a parrot or celebrate her as a prodigy; they condemn her as a sellout or praise her as a subversive genius. Despite her controversial reputation, her status as "the first" African American poet has secured her place in literary history. In the twenty-first century, there are dozens of children's books about her, many of which follow the "big test narrative" in which Wheatley has to prove her authorship in a kind of oral examination (a scenario now disputed by many scholars), or the "rescue narrative," which praises the enslaving Wheatleys for educating her. Other books aimed at older readers tackle slavery more directly. Perhaps the most innovative of these books is Afua Cooper's young adult novel *My Name is Phillis Wheatley: A Story of Slavery and Freedom*, which includes the horrors of the Middle Passage and fully imagines her African background and life before her kidnapping.[46]

There are no books about Med's case, for readers of any age. Her erasure from history was complete, and, in any case, authors would not be able to write the inspirational narrative that drives books about Wheatley. We have only a child failed by the adults around her. Historians have been foiled by the total archival absence beyond the legal records and the strategic silence of the adult participants. This means that in looking for Med, we need to be responsibly creative. As historian Kidada E. Williams recommends, in such circumstances, we need "to 'think past' the first or last archival trace. Combining literary and historical analysis can help us imagine and represent the facts of life we encounter in fragmentary form in our research."[47] In Med's case, Williams's method suggests that we might use the texts by other formerly enslaved people, like Wheatley, to imagine Med's interiority.

Six decades after Somerset and Wheatley claimed their own freedom, Boston's antislavery community used Wheatley's poetry to demonstrate African equality. At the same time, the Boston Female Anti-Slavery Society and its legal team used the *Somerset* precedent to claim freedom on Med's behalf.

CHAPTER 2

Slaves Cannot Breathe in Boston

Med's case was heard in the new Suffolk County Courthouse at 26 Court Street, about a half mile away from the Aves residence on Pinckney Street. Designed by the architect Solomon Willard, best remembered for his work on the Bunker Hill Monument, the courthouse was a simple Greek revival building made of Quincy granite (figure 6). Its three stories housed every level of the judiciary: the Police Court, the Municipal Court, the Court of Common Pleas, the Supreme Judicial Court, and the federal court. The new spacious courtrooms measured fifty feet by forty feet and were comfortably furnished. The new building was not without its critics, however. "Noted mostly for its severity," architectural historian John McConnell reports, "it was described ... as 'a granite barn with a porch at either end.' It nevertheless made an unambiguous statement about the directness and monumentality of justice in Suffolk County." This monument to justice would also become a site for abolitionist activism. An 1897 article "Anti-Slavery Landmarks in Boston" recalls that Court Street was "associated [with] some of the most exciting episodes of the anti-slavery conflict," including the Med case and the trials of fugitives George Latimer, William and Ellen Craft, Shadrach Wilkins, Thomas Sims, and Anthony Burns.[1]

BOSTON CONTEXTS

Boston in the 1830s is often remembered for the rise of Garrisonian immediatism—William Lloyd Garrison's call for the immediate abolition of slavery—and the responding anti-abolitionist violence. It is important to

FIGURE 6. *View of the new court house, Court Street, Boston.* Boston Pictorial Archive, Boston Public Library, digitalcommonwealth.org. This work is licensed for use under a Creative Commons Attribution Non-Commerical No Derivatives License (CC BY-NC-ND).

remember, however, that decades of black activism had preceded Garrison, "from Richard Allen and Prince Hall in the 1790s to David Walker and Maria Stewart in the late 1820s." Inspired by slave rebellions and the colonization debates, historian Richard Newman notes, "Walker urged his fellow Bostonians to stand up as never before against racial injustice." Garrison was in turn inspired by Walker's rhetoric; he also followed in the footsteps of other black Bostonians such as Robert Roberts, Primus Hall, John Hilton, Susan Paul, Nancy Prince, and James Barbadoes. This was also a time of extensive organization. In the period historian Manisha Sinha describes as "abolition emergent," Garrison convened the New England Anti-Slavery Society (NEASS) in 1832, the world's first racially integrated abolitionist society, in a church basement on Beacon Hill. Black abolitionists had already organized the General Colored Association in 1826, and several members also joined NEASS. The national American Anti-Slavery Society (AASS) was established in 1833, and soon after, NEASS would reorganize as the Massachusetts Anti-Slavery Society, a state affiliate of AASS.[2]

While Garrison would loom large over the Boston antislavery community in the 1830s, he was living in Connecticut during the Med proceedings and had no involvement with them. Developments in Boston for several years prior to Med's journey would set the local stage for her case. An 1832 slave transit case created the legal space for action on Med's behalf, while the "mob year" of 1835 and the *Chickasaw* courtroom rescue in August 1836 empowered members of the Boston Female Anti-Slavery Society (BFASS) and tested their commitment to practical action.

In re Francisco

The Med case was not the first time that the Curtises and Samuel Sewall had met in Chief Justice Lemuel Shaw's court over issues of slavery and freedom. In December 1832, Chief Justice Shaw heard them argue the slave transit case, *In re Francisco*. A writ of habeas corpus was brought against Mrs. Howard, a woman who had lived in Cuba, asking her to produce the body of a twelve- or fourteen-year-old boy, Francisco, whom she was planning to re-enslave back in Cuba. In the return of the writ, Mrs. Howard responded that Francisco was her servant, not her slave, and that he was free to make his own choice. Her attorney, Charles P. Curtis, argued that there were ties of affection between them and that the court should let Francisco decide. The NEASS report stated that Samuel Sewall "urged that Francisco, on being brought into Massachusetts, became free; that it was evidently Mrs. Howard's intention to make him a slave again, when she arrived at Havana; that he was entitled to the same protection of the court as any other free person in Massachusetts; and that the court ought to interfere to preserve him from slavery." Sewall also argued that the court should appoint a guardian since he was too young to make this decision. The key point was that all parties agreed that Francisco was free. The debate centered around what should happen next: Should he return to Cuba with the defendant? Or should he be remanded to a court-appointed guardian?[3]

A central question here was whether Francisco was able to exercise consent. Justice Shaw deemed him old enough as a young teenager to be able to express his preference. As legal scholar Barbara Woodhouse puts it, for Shaw, the determining factor was capacity—"a person's ability to reason and understand"—and throughout various freedom suits he would seem to assign different capacities to different aged children. To some extent, this seems like common sense: any parent would give different privileges and responsibilities to a twelve-year-old than to a six-year-old. Young adulthood for Justice Shaw suggested a kind of threshold for partial will and consent. But as American studies scholar Anna Mae Duane cautions us, consent has high stakes and no such intermediate state: "In the circuitry of the law, consent is a master switch, determining who counts as a child and who counts as a citizen, whether that person is innocent or culpable, and whether he or she is enslaved or free."[4]

Justice Shaw spoke privately with Francisco, learned that he wished to remain with Mrs. Howard, and then ruled that Francisco's choice should be respected given Mrs. Howard's public statements. He stated, "The boy, by the law of Massachusetts, is in fact free; and Mrs. Howard having, by her return to the writ, disclaimed to hold him as a slave, has made a record of his freedom, and cannot make him a slave again in the Island of Cuba." Most significant for Med's future was the fact that Shaw agreed with Sewall that Francisco was indeed free by the laws of Massachusetts: the headline in an 1833 article read, "A slave of a foreign country coming to Massachusetts is entitled to his liberty."[5]

But Shaw disagreed with the NEASS lawyers over the relevance of Mrs. Howard's intent: he said her statement not to claim him as her property anymore made the slavery question a moot point. Nevertheless, this case would change everything for Med, as historian Leonard Levy explains: "The importance of the case lies in its doctrine, based on the illegality of slavery in Massachusetts, that a slave, brought to that state by his master, might have his status transformed from one of bondage to one of freedom. By this opinion, Shaw cast from an old rule a new mold for the law of freedom in Massachusetts."[6] This was a one-size-fits-all doctrine: that enslaved people of all ages gained their freedom by being brought to Massachusetts. The question of minor status, with all its complications, was not addressed once Shaw determined Francisco was capable of making his own decisions.

Francisco's case would make Med's case possible. While Shaw would later explicitly reject arguments about the free soil or pure air of Massachusetts, he did here affirm the idea that arrival in Massachusetts might transform slave status. The Boston antislavery advocates took notice and waited for the appropriate test case. Med's age seemed perfect: she was clearly too young to be interviewed by Shaw. Her attorney Ellis Gray Loring would remind Shaw of his ruling in the Francisco case and argued that if Francisco, brought to Massachusetts from Havana by his enslaver, was declared free, then it followed that Med, brought to Massachusetts from New Orleans by her enslaver, would be free as well.[7]

BFASS and the "Mob Year" of 1835

Med found her strongest advocates in the Boston Female Anti-Slavery Society (BFASS), which was founded in 1833, initially serving as a women's auxiliary to the Massachusetts Anti-Slavery Society but quickly becoming a model and leader in grassroots activism. It became one of the most famous women's organizations in the country and grew from twelve to two hundred fifty members, mostly white but including twenty-five African American members as well, after a problematic, incomplete integration process. The society gave an honorary membership to Hope Savage Shaw, the wife of Chief Justice Lemuel Shaw, who would rule on so many important slavery cases. While the organization would splinter over political differences by 1840, its accomplishments would be significant: "It orchestrated three national women's conventions, organized a multistate petition campaign, sued southerners who brought slaves into Boston, and sponsored elaborate, profitable fundraisers that kept male abolition organizations solvent."[8]

Key members of BFASS included the six Weston sisters, who comprised the most well-known abolitionist family in Massachusetts. Historian Lee Chambers describes their influential leadership: "Together, the four elder Weston sisters led three female antislavery societies and a national women's antislavery organization. Maria and Anne served on the governing boards of the Boston, Massachusetts, New England, and American Anti-Slavery Societies, while Caroline and Debora served actively in three local associations in Boston, Weymouth, and New Bedford." All six sisters were essential fundraisers for the cause, mostly through the Boston fair they organized and administered from 1834 to 1858. Maria Weston Chapman also wrote the BFASS annual reports and edited the gift annual *The Liberty Bell* most years between 1839 to 1858.[9]

Lydia Maria Child called Chapman "one of the most remarkable women of the age," which was high praise indeed from the writer Garrison dubbed "the first woman in the republic." Child had been one of the leading women writers in the United States, until she forfeited her popular reputation by publishing *An Appeal in Favor of That Class of Americans Called Africans* in 1833, a comprehensive study of the slavery question that called for the immediate abolition of slavery and all discriminatory laws. Now excluded from the literary circles that had launched her career, she was welcomed by the antislavery activists in Boston. Although she had reservations about separate female organizations, she played an active role in BFASS and worked closely with the Weston sisters.[10]

The BFASS commitment to the antislavery cause was tested and radicalized by what they would call the "mob year" of 1835. "Besieged by escalating violence against abolitionists," American studies scholar Carolyn Karcher explains, "women attending antislavery meetings sometimes found themselves in the unprecedented position of defending male abolitionists from mobs that did not dare to assault white 'ladies.'"[11] These situations made questions about women's proper sphere seem irrelevant: after this trial by fire, BFASS was empowered to take independent action.

Lydia Maria Child and her BFASS colleagues were first tested during an August 1, 1835, meeting to celebrate the first anniversary of emancipation in the British West Indies. George Thompson, one of the most prominent British antislavery activists and orators, was the target of an antiabolitionist mob, and the BFASS women surrounded him and escorted him to a secret back exit. Thompson eventually made his way to New York, where Child and her husband David Lee Child helped hide him from antiabolitionist forces. As she wrote to Louisa Loring, "Very large sums are offered for anyone who will convey Mr. Thompson into the slave states. I tremble for him, and love him in proportion to my fears."[12]

The most famous incident of antiabolitionist violence in Boston was a direct attack on the BFASS annual meeting in October 1835. The mob disrupted the proceedings, based on the rumor that Thompson would appear, and the mayor of Boston said he could not guarantee the women's safety. After the meeting broke up, the mob nearly lynched William Lloyd Garrison, who was then housed in the city jail for his own protection.[13]

BFASS member Anne Warren Weston wrote a series of letters to her Aunt Mary Weston, reporting on the mob scene in Boston. Her first letter was meant to reassure her family: "We are all safe and sound. Garrison is in the city gaol for safety. Mr. Thompson is not in town. . . . There have been very thrilling scenes going on here. . . . In the midst of all, Garrison behaved like an angel. . . . Do not any of you be alarmed. Tell my mother to be of good cheer." Weston paints a picture of invigorated, brave women held back by their nervous male counterparts. Her letters also reveal the sense of chaos and confusion: "There is great fear among the brethren and all the leaders are gone." She is outraged in the aftermath of the mob: "I must say I feel like a slave when I have the knowledge that an Anti S. meeting cannot be holden

[sic] in this city, and that is certainly the case at present." This statement seems overblown: surely limits to the freedom of assembly are not really akin to slavery. But she does not overstate the danger: "The truth is, that the Abolitionists in Boston are not now under the protection of the laws. . . . Thompson and Garrison are not safe in Boston."[14] Consequently, Garrison and his family moved to Brooklyn, Connecticut, for their safety, where they remained until the end of September 1836, effectively missing the Med case.

The mob year forced BFASS members to recognize how the slave power limited their own freedoms: "It was not for the slave and his master only that we did it;—the right of association, the right of freely speaking, the right of occupying our own buildings and walking our own streets,—was denied to ourselves." Harriet Martineau, commenting from Great Britain also explained these risks in her book *The Martyr Age in the United States*. Drawing on her experiences from her 1834–1836 tour of the United States, she asserted that it was much more difficult to be an abolitionist in a place where slavery actually existed than to be an abolitionist in Europe protesting slavery far away in the colonies.[15]

Freedom Summer

The summer of 1836 was one of the coldest on record: repeated hard frosts meant that the Indian corn never ripened in Massachusetts.[16] For BFASS, the unseasonable summer of 1836 featured increased political activism on a national and local scale. While women could not vote, they could exercise their First Amendment right "to petition the government for a redress of grievances." In concert with abolitionists from around the country, BFASS and the Weston sisters had organized a massive campaign petitioning the federal government to end slavery. These campaigns were so successful that by May 1836, the House of Representatives had passed the "gag rule" to automatically table (postpone action on) these petitions. In defiance of the gag rule, at the BFASS quarterly meeting on July 14, 1836, BFASS decided to petition Congress "immediately to abolish Slavery in the District of Columbia, and to declare every human being free, who sets foot upon its soil"; they also pledged to continue this petition annually until this goal was achieved.[17]

In addition to defending their First Amendment rights on a national level, the battle-tested BFASS members also took immediate direct action in support of the enslaved people who accompanied the "summer sojourners from the south." They were frustrated by the presence of slavery in their supposedly free state: "Year after year they have visited New-England, and found preachers and editors becoming more and more obsequious, ... and the northern conscience becoming familiarized with the crime of slaveholding.... We resolved in our feeble measure, to make a direct application of the first principles of Christianity, to the cases of such slaves as were brought within the sphere of our observation by their masters."[18] In other words, BFASS claimed that it was their Christian duty to assist enslaved people brought to Massachusetts by their enslavers.

BFASS helped several enslaved people in this situation and published an interview with "L. T.," one of "those who have received our aid." L. T. described her life in slavery and how she had been brought to Massachusetts by her enslaver and then claimed her freedom. But her owner did not give up easily: "A reward was offered, and a vigorous search kept up for many days.... A search was threatened in Belknap-street; and ... the alarm and indignation of the inhabitants of that part of the town were extreme; as the ruffians who conducted it declared that they would seize and carry off any colored woman they could find."[19] Belknap Street, now Joy Street, crossed Pinckney Street where the Aves house was located.

This search on Beacon Hill was another turning point for BFASS, one that would inspire their legal strategy and motivate the Med case: "It was at that moment, while penetrated with sympathy for the sufferers, and with grief and shame at the supineness of the community generally in view of such occurrences, that we resolved to disinter the law of Massachusetts. How painfully we felt at that moment, that it was buried in oblivion, notwithstanding the public thanksgiving of the year, that 'our soil is unpressed by the footsteps of a slave.'"[20] Here Chapman argued that they were not making new law but rather digging up and restoring the existing law of freedom. It was a strange metaphor—that the free soil principle needed to be unearthed—but Chapman explained that because this law was buried and forgotten, it needed to be disinterred and resurrected.

There are interesting hints in the historical record about BFASS's clandestine involvement with fugitive and slave transit cases. The BFASS annual report does not reveal L. T.'s fate, but letters among the Weston sisters show that they played a key role in her escape from Boston: "How is Lucilla Tucker? We (the Boston Female Anti-Slavery Society) have paid 14 dollars on her account to Jos. [?] Easton of N. Bridgewater who carried her from Boston to Bridg'er, kept her there for some time I forget how long, gave her medical attention and finally carried her to N. Bedford." BFASS had also hidden other formerly enslaved people in New Bedford, such as the "Thacher girl." As Anne Warren Weston wrote to Chapman: "The Thacher [Thacker?] girl is here in town and is known as 'Mrs. Chapman's protege.' Nothing can happen but you contrive to get the credit." Debora Weston also wrote to her sister: "Have you done anything in particular since I left town for the Thacher girl. She is here now carefully tended in N. Bedford poor house."[21] The Thacher girl's situation demonstrated how the abolitionists cared for emancipated children by using existing social welfare structures.

The *Chickasaw* Rescue

Just weeks before the Med case, Boston was rocked by a slave rescue (or "abolition riot," as described by the proslavery press). On July 30, 1836, the Baltimore ship *Chickasaw* had sailed into Boston Harbor with two African American women, Eliza Small and Polly Ann Bates, on board. They were claimed by Matthew Turner, an agent of John B. Morris, as fugitives from slavery, but some witnesses suggested that they were legally free. According to the BFASS account, written by Maria Weston Chapman, "some men of color" noticed the ship pull away from the wharf in a suspicious manner, so they "took a boat with the intention of going on board. They were ordered off but on rowing round the vessel, they discovered it to be the Chickasaw, in the Baltimore trade, and on further examination, perceived two women making signals of distress to them from the cabin windows."[22]

The men then returned to shore and appealed to antislavery attorney Samuel Sewall for assistance, who filed a writ of habeas corpus and secured a court appearance before Justice Shaw. The courtroom was packed with antislavery supporters, including a large African American group and a BFASS delegation. "We felt great sympathy with these women," Chapman reported, "and determined to give them at the trial, whatever comfort our presence might afford."[23] They were there for more than moral support: they knew that even if the judge released the women, enslavers and their agents often used trumped up criminal charges to have their targets rearrested.

As the arguments began, the claimant argued that the women were the property of Morris and must be returned to him under the fugitive slave provisions of 1793. Sewall countered that all people were born free, as laid down in the Bill of Rights, and had a natural right to their liberty. Justice Shaw saw neither argument as relevant: Chapman observed that the question at hand was simply, "Has the Captain of the brig Chickasaw a right to convert his vessel into a prison?"[24]

Chapman reported total silence in the courtroom as the crowd awaited Shaw's answer: "All parties listened breathlessly for the decision," and after a lengthy speech, Justice Shaw concluded that the women had been unlawfully detained and that "the prisoners must be discharged."[25] Chapman then described an exciting, chaotic courtroom scene:

> All rose at the word.... The agent extended his hand to seize them. A spell seemed to hold them in the same position, one deeply exciting instant. The next, and the room was empty. A single voice among the crowd said, Go! Go! There was no other noise, but the sound of feet, and a slight shriek from one of the women who fainted in the lobby, and was carried down stairs.[26]

Sewall was glad to learn that the women made it safely to Halifax, although he regretted the "disorderly proceedings of the colored people."[27]

The proslavery press reacted harshly to this turn of events. The *Centinel and Gazette* denounced BFASS as a "parcel of silly women, whose fondness for notoriety has repeatedly led them into scenes of commotion and riot" and called on their husbands and guardians to control them and teach obedience to the laws. The *Boston Transcript* condemned the "indecency" of their conduct.[28] The BFASS women felt compelled to defend themselves against these charges of "unwomanly interference" in letters to other female antislavery societies:

> The discharge of the two women, claimed as runaways from Baltimore, having been attended with some little confusion, and the absence of a few legal technicalities, has been made the basis of great bitterness against our Society and of the most unmeasured personal vituperation against some of our members, who, during the scenes of their illegal imprisonment and subsequent trial dared to express the heartfelt compassion and sympathy by which they were inspired. But none of these things move us, and we only pray that more extended opportunities of affording relief to the oppressed may be granted us and may our hearts be more eager to improve them.[29]

Samuel Sewall, despite his surprise at the turn of events, was generally blamed for the "abolition riot." He received a threatening letter from "a member of the Baltimore Bar": "Should you, however, put your countenaunce inside the limits of the City of Baltimore I trust you will be received with that hospitality for which our city is proverbial; and that your distinguished efforts in the cause of abolition, as displayed on Monday last, be properly appreciated.... N.B. In Maryland your name would have been stricken from the rolls of the court as an unworthy member of an honorable profession, in consequence of your indignity to the Court." Another angry correspondent warned Sewall to stay out of slave states: "This conduct was extremely reprehensible in you. Your name is held up to the public as aiding the two above negroes to escape from their lawful master, and sir, I beg leave to inform you that if you are ever discovered within the limits of this or any other slave state, your neck will be apt to pay for your temerity."[30]

Sewall also had his champions. The New York *Emancipator*, published by the American Anti-Slavery Society, argued that there was no "rescue" because the women had been discharged under the Habeas Corpus act and that the fake outrage of the press shows "subserviency to the South in this matter of slavery." The paper conceded that there was "indecorum," but that there was no violation of law because the women had been discharged.[31]

Soon after the excitement of the *Chickasaw* case, the Boston *Daily Advertiser* published an advertisement for the return of a fugitive from slavery, which reminded BFASS that, in addition to their advocacy for individual enslaved people in Boston, they also needed to focus on broader legal principles regarding enslaved people in transit:

> We were forcibly reminded by it, of our former resolve to seize the first opportunity to test the validity of the BILL OF RIGHTS. It has always been our impression that the laws of Massachusetts would shelter the slave brought within the local limits by his master; but we found a different idea the prevailing one in the surrounding community, and the popular voice was confirmed to us, by nine members of the Boston bar. In Hilliard's "Elements of Law, a summary of American Civil Jurisprudence, for the use of Students, men of business and general readers," we found it laid down, that "a slave, bought in one state, *acquires* NO RIGHTS *as a freeman by being brought into another;*" and our minds were more deeply than ever convinced of the necessity of immediately trying to counteract this general idea so dishonorable to Massachusetts.[32]

Francis Hilliard did indeed offer this reading of the law and made a connection to fugitives: "Still, however, a slave bought in one State, acquires no rights as a freeman by being brought into another. No contract made with him would be binding on the master. Upon the same principle, if a slave escape into one state from another, the master may seize and remove him without any warrant for the purpose." He seemed to do so with some reluctance: "The history, justice, expediency, and prospects of slavery, though topics of deep interest and importance, are foreign from the objects of the present work."[33] In other words, Hilliard's book and local Boston attorneys denied the free soil principle underlying slave transit suits, and BFASS wished to counter this legal interpretation.

The events leading up to the Med case involved both adults and children, but the decision to use a child for the big test case changed everything. Med was too young to express her own will, and her tender years made her the perfect poster child for BFASS: sweet, vulnerable, and silent. If enslaved people had no place in Massachusetts, if they were an anomaly in violation of the state's moral geography, then enslaved people who entered Massachusetts could claim a new life in freedom. The free soil model seemed to work for adults, but antislavery activists did not fully consider what it would mean for children, given that childhood was posited as the opposite of full citizenship.[34] And they did not consider what it would mean to be the free child of an enslaved mother.

COMMONWEALTH V. AVES

The BFASS members were ready to defend the free soil of Massachusetts and deny the right of enslavers to travel with the people they claimed as property. And Med's presence in Boston would provide the perfect opportunity for legal action: "It was at a meeting of the Board, held August 11th, that we were informed by the Vice President of our Society, that a family in the city, recently from the south, had a child in their keeping, presumed to be a slave.... Our unanimous opinion was, that it was the duty of those who had come to the knowledge of these facts, to prevent, if possible, such a violation of the rights of the child."[35] With this decision, little Med entered history, and her life was changed forever.

Med's circumstances paralleled those of the teenager Francisco, whom everyone agreed was free, but at the age of six Med was clearly too young to make her own legal decisions. The other key difference between the Francisco and Med cases, however, was that while Mrs. Howard had claimed that Francisco was now just her servant, Child noted that in Med's case, "the pro-slavery lawyers did not pretend to deny that the intent was to carry the child back into slavery.... They took the new and extraordinary ground that Southern masters had a legal right to hold human beings as slaves while they were visiting here in New England."[36]

Med's case was complicated by the fact that her mother, whose name we never learn, was expecting her return: "We learned that the mother was alive, in New Orleans, and this circumstance admonished us to do nothing which should interfere with the paramount claims of maternal love. We are mothers, and felt their sacredness." But the BFASS women contended that these sacred claims of motherhood were desecrated by enslavers such as Samuel Slater: "He asserts that the child is *his*, and not the mother's; and sets up a claim of absolute ownership.... He contends for the right to sell the child away from the mother, whenever or wherever it shall please him to do so." Here BFASS anticipated the biggest objection to their case: that a ruling in their favor would separate a mother and child. They countered that it was *Slater* rather than the abolitionists who were separating the pair. In fact, BFASS contended that if Slater were so concerned about the separation, he should free Med's mother as well: "He can at any time unite the mother and child, by sending the mother to Massachusetts."[37] Literary scholar Edlie Wong cautions that the "mother love" underlying BFASS's social activism also had its troubling elements: "The tacit understanding was that slave women with little individual control over children were incapable of being good mothers, as BFASS assumed responsibility for Med's well-being in her mother's symbolic and physical absence."[38]

Med's own desires were not even considered because of her young age, but for BFASS, she provided the perfect test case with seemingly little downside: "If we should fail, the condition of the child would remain but where it was; while if we should succeed, a decision would be obtained of greater importance than any within the last half century." In other words, according to BFASS, Med had nothing to lose, and the cause had everything to gain by pursuing the case. BFASS did not consider that, for Med, the stakes were more complicated: winning freedom would also mean losing her family. And freedom for a child really meant being under the control of different adults. There were some vague assurances about her future welfare, as the *New Bedford Mercury* reported in an article about the initial hearing: "Mr. Sewall intimated that if the child should be discharged, it would be provided for here."[39]

Glossing over these complications, BFASS then moved swiftly: "We decided to claim for her the protection of the laws of Massachusetts, and applied to Ellis Gray Loring, Esq., for his professional aid, Levin Harris acting as promoter of the suit. The plea for the Commonwealth, was conducted at the first hearing, by Messrs. Loring and Sewall, and at the second, by Messrs. Loring and Choate. For their admirable arguments, we refer to 'the case of the slave child Med,' a pamphlet containing the proceedings on both sides, and the decision of the court."[40]

The oral arguments were heard on August 26, 1836, and reportedly ran from 9:00 a.m. until 7:00 p.m., with a recess for dinner. *Commonwealth v. Aves* featured attorneys, activists, and judges who had appeared together in court many times before to argue slave transit suits and fugitive cases and who would do so again in the future. The parties were represented by some of the greatest legal minds of the day. Benjamin Robbins Curtis and his distant cousin C. P. Curtis appeared for the respondent, Thomas Aves, while Ellis Gray Loring and Rufus Choate represented the petitioner. BFASS had wanted to hire Senator Daniel Webster, but when he was not immediately available, they were able to enlist Choate, regarded as one of Boston's finest trial attorneys and a politician who had served in the U.S. House of Representatives (1830–1834). He would later serve in the U.S. Senate (1841–1845).[41]

While all four lawyers presented oral arguments, the case was really a contest between Curtis and Loring, young attorneys who would go on to achieve national prominence: Curtis would later be appointed to the U.S. Supreme Court, while Loring is best remembered for his role in the *Amistad* slave mutiny case. In a letter to Loring, Supreme Court Justice Joseph Story praised the high caliber of the debate: "I have rarely seen so thorough and exact arguments, as those made by Mr. B. Curtis and yourself. They exhibit learning and research and ability of which any man may be proud." Justice Shaw agreed that the case was "fully and very ably argued."[42]

While *The Case of the Slave-Child, Med* pamphlet provides a detailed account of the arguments and the ruling, there is very little documentation of the courtroom atmosphere. Child's letters are one exception, but she cuts off her description with a dismissive "I will not fill this sheet with particulars," an omission keenly felt by contemporary historians. We do not know for sure whether Med was present in the courtroom, and, indeed, it is hard to find any trace of her in the proceedings. While "the said Med" appears in the writ and the return to the writ, her name does not appear in the legal arguments. Curtis only mentioned her twice as "this child" in his opening. Loring opened with a consideration of "mother and child" and in his conclusion discussed "the child" as the embodiment of the legal consequences at work: "The greatest cruelty of all is contemplated here, namely, the removal of the child to a place where slavery, with its usual features, will again attach upon her."[43]

Loring's opening arguments revealed that the mother-child relationship would remain central to the case. Before turning to the legal questions, he emphasized, like BFASS, that the Slaters were to blame for breaking up Med's family: "It is slavery and not freedom that is separating mother and child."[44] He even offered that if the respondent were to manumit Med, they would send her back to New Orleans to be reunited with her mother. He also claimed the right to speak for Med and her mother, who, he explained, would certainly choose Med's freedom if they had the proper and complete knowledge of the circumstances:

> But is there really any inhumanity in making this child a free citizen of Massachusetts? Is it unkindness to the child? Surely not. If she were able to form an intelligent wish, we are bound to presume she would prefer freedom to slavery.... Is it unkindness to the mother? Not if she desires the true good of her child. No doubt she felt anxious that her daughter should be returned to her. But her apprehension was of a very different event from that we seek to bring about. The poor ignorant slave did not contemplate the possibility of her child's emancipation. Her dread was lest it might be sold on the way.[45]

According to Loring, Med cannot choose because she is too young to consent, that is, not yet able "to form an intelligent wish." But Med's mother, an adult, cannot choose for her either because she is a "poor ignorant slave"; in addition, she cannot make an informed choice because she does not have all the facts. Emancipation, Loring concluded, would be the best possible outcome for Med: "This child, if freed, will be educated for usefulness and respectability. She will never want a friend, nor the means of improvement and happiness."[46]

Med's circumstances, the story of an enslaved child 1,500 miles from her mother, then became framed as a precise legal question: "Can a slave, brought into Massachusetts by a citizen of a slave-holding state on a temporary visit, be restrained of [her] liberty while in Massachusetts and be taken out of the state against [her] consent?"[47] In other words, what was the status of visiting enslaved people in the free state of Massachusetts? Could the summer sojourners bring enslaved personal attendants with them as they sought refuge from the southern heat? Could the sojourn versus domicile distinction that had been the basis of regional accommodations on this issue still hold?

Justice Shaw was surprised that the question had not been settled previously. He noted in his ruling that the law was clear and that the impact would be significant: "The case presents an extremely interesting question, not so much on account of any doubt or difficulty attending it, as on account of its important consequences to those who may be affected by it, either as masters or slaves."[48] The lead attorneys took different rhetorical approaches to their arguments: Curtis addressed the legal question as narrowly as possible, while Loring's arguments were wide-ranging. In addition to his skilled references to the law, Loring would also draw from the Bible, poetry, and philosophy. For Loring and BFASS, the case was not only about Med but also about the nature of freedom, the values of Massachusetts, and the free soil of New England.

The legal arguments were detailed and complex, but three major questions dominated the case:

1. Was the *Somerset* ruling a relevant precedent?
2. Was comity applicable in this conflict-of-laws case? In other words, should Massachusetts respect the rights of visiting enslavers?
3. What did the Constitution say about all these matters?

The relevance of the *Somerset* ruling—that an enslaver could not detain and remove an enslaved person from England and that slavery required local law—was a central contested point in the Med case, one that would be addressed by all four attorneys: the Curtises contended that the case simply did not apply, while Loring and Choate relied heavily on both the legal precedent and the popular interpretations that followed.

The respondents argued that while *Somerset* was clearly the law of England, Somerset's case had significant differences which limited its relevance: "Sommersett's case was decided by an English court, on considerations proper to that country; that this case is to be decided by a Massachusetts court, upon reasons proper to ourselves." In fact, Curtis noted, much instruction could be found in the more recent *Slave, Grace* ruling, which would "probably prevent us from being misled, by the highly figurative and declamatory language, which was indulged by some of the eminent men concerned in that cause."[49] In 1822, Grace had been brought by her enslaver from Antigua to England. After a year, they returned to Antigua, and in 1826, Grace sued for her freedom claiming that her residence in England had freed her. Lord Stowell ruled that Grace had reassumed her enslaved status upon returning to Antigua, that English soil only gave her a kind of limited, temporary liberty that, as legal scholar William Wiecek describes, "evaporated upon her return to a slave jurisdiction."[50] Stowell explained "that although the rights of the mistress over the slave were suspended, while in England, because the English Common Law provided no means of enforcing those rights, yet they existed, and might be exercised and enforced, on the return of the slave to Antigua." The *Slave, Grace* case highlighted competing legal visions of enslaved status—"once free, forever free" versus "reattachment"— and reflected even more fundamentally different beliefs about the transformative power of free soil. But for Curtis, the argument was clear: that the *Slave, Grace* decision was an important corrective to the *Somerset* case and was the more relevant precedent. Curtis was going against the grain of American legal precedent here: in many early cases, enslaved people who had lived in free states were set free for this reason by courts in slave states.[51]

Loring's endorsement of *Somerset* was the more mainstream position. Two points were essential: that "the case of Sommersett, decided in 1772, was mainly argued and determined on the ground of slavery's being corrupt and immoral"; and that slavery was a local institution, one that has to be supported by positive law. Following Loring's broader argument, Choate went on to emphasize the applicability of *Somerset* to Med's circumstances. In fact, as Choate argued, *Somerset* had always been part of the legal culture in Massachusetts: "The case of Sommersett was re-printed and circulated here—it was cited in the courts. Negroes were encouraged by it to sue for their liberty—and the Courts of Justice, long before the State Constitution . . . universally sustained their claim." He claimed that *Somerset* was "not merely of the common law of England" but "part of the universal jurisprudence of all civilization." Charles P. Curtis questioned these expansive claims: "If so, why did it not also become law in all the other colonies—in New York, New Jersey, Pennsylvania, Connecticut, Rhode Island? Yet all these States have had slaves long since Sommersett's case, and without regard to Lord Mansfield's decision."[52]

The conflict of laws was a second major point of contention in Med's case. The presence of enslaved people in a free jurisdiction created a significant legal problem for judges in free states: in this case, the laws of Louisiana and

Massachusetts were in conflict, and Justice Shaw needed to decide which law to apply. The legal theory of comity, the "courtesy or consideration that one jurisdiction gives by enforcing the laws of another, granted out of respect and deference, rather than obligation," was one source of legal authority. There were many practical reasons for this courtesy, as legal historian Paul Finkelman explains: "A free state might recognize the slave status of a slave within its jurisdiction because the free state viewed harmony within the Union and respect for other states as a higher value than its own ideology of freedom."[53] Comity was not automatic, however: there were long-established exceptions to comity, such as when comity would cause injury to the state and its citizens or when the law itself was immoral.

Curtis's challenge was to explain why a free state should recognize the laws of a slave state and to explain how it might do so without injury to the Commonwealth; he also needed to explain why the exceptions did not apply in this case. According to Curtis, comity meant that the law of Massachusetts respected the rights of visiting slaveholders to this limited degree: "The Law of Massachusetts will so far recognize and give effect to the Law of Louisiana, as to allow the master to exercise the qualified and limited right over his slave, which is claimed in this case." Curtis argued that it would create "no practical difficulty" for Massachusetts to give "qualified effect to the Law of Louisiana" and that there would be no slippery slope into slavery that antislavery activists feared. For example, Curtis observed, the fugitive slave clause of the Constitution had not led to the establishment of slavery in the free states and while the fugitive clause was not directly relevant to this case, it did suggest that free states could extend qualified and limited rights to slaveholders within their borders.[54] According to Curtis, allowing Aves this limited right to keep Med as a slave violated no law of Massachusetts and had no impact on Massachusetts residents; therefore comity still applied.

Loring disagreed passionately with this vision of "limited slavery" within the free state of Massachusetts and argued that the introduction of the Louisiana slave system in Massachusetts would both contravene state policy and violate public law. The Declaration of Independence and the Massachusetts Declaration of Rights (1780) could not be clearer in their endorsements of human freedom. Furthermore, slavery would violate the public law against slavery, which had been settled by the *Somerset* decision before the revolution—"that the common law abhors, and will not endure the existence of slavery on English soil"—and later affirmed by the Declaration of Rights and a series of judicial decisions. Finally, to permit the operation of slavery in Massachusetts would be to set a "pernicious and detestable example." There was no such thing as "limited slavery," Loring concluded: any recognition of ownership in human beings would disrupt the moral and legal landscape of the state.[55]

The immorality of a law was an established exception to comity, which put Curtis in a difficult rhetorical position. Without making a proslavery argument, Curtis would "attempt to prove that slavery is not immoral, and that to allow the master to exercise this right will not exhibit to our citizens as an example pernicious and detestable." This argument required Curtis to walk a rhetorical tightrope, arguing that "natural morality" and "legal morality" were different things. Curtis conceded that slavery was indeed a "violation of the law of nature," but that the question at hand was whether slavery was immoral *according to the law*. His conclusion was that the Constitution had settled the question of legal morality by its recognition of slavery: by this logic, Massachusetts judges could not enforce the fugitive slave clause and, at the same time, deny Slater his property rights on the basis of slavery's immorality. "By the law of the commonwealth," therefore, slavery is not immoral."[56]

But Loring would not accept such distinctions and insisted that the immorality of slavery was indeed relevant to the case at hand, for it established the impossibility of comity. Loring argued that Massachusetts did not have to accept the *lex loci* of Louisiana over slaves in transit because slavery was offensive to morals. He realized he was on shaky legal ground here, in arguing a moral standard rather than a legal one, but he asked the court's indulgence in his attempt to prove the immorality of slavery. He cited a range of authorities from ethics and natural law, and then explored how these principles had been applied by legal authorities. As Loring contended, "The case of Sommersett, decided in 1772, was mainly argued and determined on the ground of slavery's being corrupt and immoral. The air of England was declared to be too pure for slaves to breathe in." This, of course, was not what Mansfield said in his ruling (and Justice Shaw would correct Loring in his opinion), and Curtis had already warned the court not be "misled, by the highly figurative and declamatory language" of Somerset's advocates. Nevertheless, this powerful popular antislavery interpretation remained central to Med's case.[57]

Loring went on to establish the immorality of slavery in the United States by citing several slave codes and noting proudly that the Massachusetts Declaration of Rights proclaimed, "All men are born free and equal."

Furthermore, Loring noted that "Slavery was abolished in Massachusetts, from a conviction of its immoral nature" and quoted from the opinion of Judge Sedgwick in *Greenwood v. Curtis:* "So strong and so natural is the abhorrence of slavery, in the heart of a man unpolluted by its practice; so opposed to the just principles on which our revolution was founded; and so contrary to the mild, merciful, and benignant dictates of the religion we profess; that a labored discussion of the question is deemed to be superfluous."[58]

Finally, he argued that the Bible did not sanction slavery and that true Christians knew that slavery was wrong, even if there was no explicit denunciation in the scriptures. Christians who used scriptural authority to justify slavery were missing the point: "Christianity does not so much claim to be a body of ordinances, as a quickening spirit.... [It] prostrates human selfishness, in enjoining us to do to others as we would have them do to us; and subverts political and personal slavery by teaching the brotherhood of men."[59]

Having established the immorality of slavery, Loring then went on to address the relevance of the Constitution to this matter. Curtis had claimed that one could not denounce slavery as immoral when the Constitution had established slavery as moral in a legal sense. Loring explained that the limited compromise over slavery in the Constitution could not be expanded, and that the Constitution only regulated the case of fugitives, which was not relevant here. Loring was strongly critical of that "barter of conscience," which violated the *express law of God* as stated in Deuteronomy: "Thou shalt not deliver unto his master, the servant which is escaped from his master unto thee." He contended that this compromise did not mean that Massachusetts would abandon its views about slavery or "her policy of excluding it from her soil." And yet Loring conceded that it was the law of the land, and he would abide by it.[60]

Loring concluded his arguments with lines from the poet William Cowper, worth repeating here:

> Slaves cannot breathe in England: if their lungs
> Receive our air, that moment they are free.
> They touch our country, and their shackles fall—
> That's noble, and bespeaks a nation proud
> And jealous of the blessing.—[61]

But Loring warned the court that Massachusetts cannot share England's pride because of its obligation to enforce the fugitive slave clause of the

Constitution, and he urged the court to stop appeasing the slave power: "Let us stop there. Let not the accursed system thrive among us."[62]

Loring's close friend Child wrote this brief eyewitness account of the oral arguments:

> The opposite counsel were full of sophistry and eloquence. One of them really wiped his own eyes at the thought that the poor little slave might be separated from its slave mother by mistaken benevolence. His pathos was a little marred by my friend E. G. Loring, who arose and stated that it was distinctly understood that little Med was to be sold on her way back to New Orleans, to pay the expenses of the mistress's journey to the North. The judges decided unanimously in favor of Med and liberty![63]

And indeed they did: on August 27, Chief Justice Lemuel Shaw of the Massachusetts Supreme Judicial Court ruled that slaves brought to Massachusetts by their owners could not be held against their will. He was careful to note that this opinion did not apply to fugitives and defined the legal issue quite narrowly: "The precise question presented by the claim of the respondent is, whether a citizen of any one of the United States, where negro slavery is established by law, coming into this State, for any temporary purpose of business or pleasure, staying some time, but not acquiring a domicil here, who brings a slave with him as a personal attendant, may restrain such slave of his liberty during his continuance here, and convey him out of this State on his return, against his consent."[64] He indicated that he rejected the popular antislavery interpretations about free air and free soil and began with a narrower interpretation of the law:

> It is believed to have been a prevalent opinion among lawyers, that if a slave is brought voluntarily and unnecessarily within the limits of this state, he becomes free, if he chooses to avail himself of the provisions of our laws; not so much because his coming within our territorial limits, breathing our air, or treading on our soil, works any alteration in his status or condition, as settled by the law of his domicil, as because by the operation of our laws, there is no authority on the part of the master, either to restrain the slave of his liberty whilst here, or forcibly to take him into custody in order to [prevent] his removal.[65]

While Shaw rejected the vernacular interpretation of free soil from the antislavery side, his ruling accepted the relevance of *Somerset* and rejected comity.

Shaw concluded that there was no slavery in Massachusetts and that slave property could not be recognized in the state; because slavery was contrary to natural right, it depended on local law for its existence and enforcement. The local laws of Massachusetts applied to all people who crossed its borders: "That ... all persons coming within the limits of a State, become subject to all its municipal laws, civil and criminal, and entitled to the privileges, which those laws confer; that this rule applies as well to blacks as whites ... ; that if such persons have been slaves, they become free, not so much because any alteration is made in their *status*, or condition, as because there is no law, which will warrant, but there are laws, if they choose to avail themselves of them, which prohibit their forcible detention or forcible removal." In other words, slaves brought to Massachusetts were not automatically free: they needed to take advantage of their legal opportunity. Finally, Shaw contended that comity did not apply and rejected the moveable personal property argument: "Then the law of slavery must extend to every place where such slaves may be carried."[66] For all these reasons, Med's custody was ruled unlawful, and she was ordered into temporary custody to await the appointment of a probate guardian.[67] While the ruling did not specifically address the status of children, this action did acknowledge her minor status.

The exact wording of the order reveals the complicated relationship among will, consent, and power: "The child who is the subject of this *habeas corpus*, being of too tender years to have any will or give any consent to be removed, and her mother, being a slave and having no will of her own and no power to act for her child, she is necessarily left in the custody of the law."[68] Shaw here asserted that Med was too young to have will or to give consent to return to New Orleans; her adult mother was enslaved and therefore had no will and no power. Loring and BFASS argued, with the agreement of the court, that the only way Med could become a free adult citizen was to be separated from her mother and remain in Massachusetts. They would consent for her because victimhood in a state of slavery without will or power was her fate should she return to Louisiana.

While both Justice Shaw and Loring made arguments in favor of local law, Loring made an additional argument for moral geography. A slave in Massachusetts was out of place and noncompliant with the atmosphere of personal liberty; as Loring explained, a "Louisiana slave, held as such in Massachusetts, is anomalous."[69] The average citizen could read in newspapers across the country about the complicated legal questions of comity, domicile, moveable property, and constitutionality at the heart of this case, and they could also be inspired by the concept of Anglo-American free soil and free air proclaimed by Loring. The winning side claimed this moral high ground, as a protector of children and the free soil of Massachusetts. The respondent had the trickier job of arguing that freedom would separate mother and child (even though an enslaved parent did not have any of the rights of a free parent) and that slavery might indeed be immoral, but that it was not immoral in eyes of the law.

As Chapman had predicted, the case had a significant and lasting impact: Shaw's decision became incorporated into the law of almost every free state and a wave of freedom suits followed. In a thank you letter to Ellis Gray Loring, the BFASS women praised his efforts: "The Boston Female Anti-Slavery Society may be excused for rejoicing at this event. They rejoice for the poor child, for their colored brethren and sisters, for Massachusetts, for themselves, and last but not least, for you Sir, who have won this victory for them.... Fearing God and fearing him only, you have gone forward bold and strong in the right."[70]

Loring acknowledged his part but also expressed his gratitude for the team effort: "I have certainly done what I could for the good of the little girl and the advancement of our inspiring cause." He went on to praise BFASS's fieldwork and the "moral strength" of female agency.[71] The Massachusetts Anti-Slavery Society also praised the role of the BFASS women and their legal advocates:

> This suit was prosecuted by that watchful, heroic, unfaltering band, the BOSTON FEMALE ANTI-SLAVERY SOCIETY. It is to WOMAN, therefore, that Humanity owes this great decision. Those indefatigable friends of human liberty, Samuel E. Sewall and Ellis Gray Loring, Esqrs. assisted by Rufus Choate, Esq. conducted the plea for the Commonwealth. The Argument of Mr. Loring was a masterly effort, and has obtained for him no small amount of honorable and enduring renown.[72]

The *Liberator* published articles about the Med case for months, reprinting every step of the proceedings, from the writ to the arguments to the ruling. It also published a roundup of enthusiastic press coverage. The *Boston Centinel* reported that "The last decision of the Supreme Court of Massachusetts, in relation to a female slave, is, without doubt, though correct, the MOST IMPORTANT one that has ever been made in any of the free

States." The *Hallowell Free Press* weighed in from Ontario that the ruling "will be universally recognized as constitutional, just and equitable." "A Yankee" in the *Boston Courier* critiqued the Southern press for its alarmist inaccuracies and misrepresentation of the law: "The only question, then, for our Court to determine, was, whether the colored child in question was free, *by the laws of Massachusetts*; and on this point no Massachusetts Court, since the Revolution, could entertain a doubt." And the *Haverhill Gazette* could only celebrate: "We hail it as a new evidence of the approaching triumph of Emancipation, and the ascendancy of liberal feeling and enlarged philanthropy. Hereafter, with the single but painful exception of the runaway slave, the soil of Massachusetts can be trodden only by free men."[73]

Other newspaper coverage was negative but measured. The *Richmond Enquirer* reprinted an article from the *New York Express* suggesting that it was state legislatures that needed to clear up questions about slaves in transit, not the courts. It also reprinted an article from the *Boston Advertiser* that asserted that whether "other non-slave-holding States will consider themselves bound by this adjudication, is doubtful; but the high rank held by the Supreme Court of Massachusetts, gives great weight to its decision on this, as on other points." The *Louisville Advertiser* urged caution: "As we understand this case, we see nothing to irritate or alarm the South." Enslavers just had to leave the people they claimed as property at home when traveling to a free state.[74]

But the decision also met with harsh criticism. The *Baltimore Chronicle* raged, "Every Southerner will hear of this decision with feelings of indignation and surprise." The *Boston Transcript* denounced the decision as a sin rooted in fanaticism: "Who will answer for the 'deep damnation' of the sin which separated—nay stole, a child, . . . from its mother in the South, that she might be called free in the North? . . . Separate mother and child in the name of *Freedom*? What fanaticism is this?" The *New York Courier and Enquirer* agreed with this assessment: "The wanton cruelty in the case of the little slave child, recently wrested from the protection of its mistress in Boston, is enough to curdle colder blood than ours towards those miserable . . . fanatics. We have only to hope most fervently that the Supreme Court of the United States will yet take this child from the fangs of the rabid fanaticism that has clutched it."[75]

The question of Med's custody concerned the court from the very beginning of the proceedings. In his oral arguments, before launching into his considerations of comity and the Constitution, Loring suggested that Med could be taken into custody by the petitioner, Levin Harris, or that she could be committed to the Overseers of the Poor while the probate court issued letters of guardianship. But his best solution was the Samaritan Asylum, "a well administered charity . . . incorporated by the State for the relief of colored orphans, [which] stands ready on her liberation, to receive the child from the proper hands, and to give her suitable support and a good education." Like other emancipated children at the time, Med would be pulled into existing social welfare structures.[76] Boston's abolitionists now had to determine the meaning of free soil for children, and Med would never see New Orleans again.

CHAPTER 3

All Girls Are Bound to Someone

Chief Justice Lemuel Shaw had set Med free, but no one knew what would happen next. Like so many freedom narratives, the Med pamphlets end with a "mission accomplished" tone, but they do not address the complicated process of emancipation. The ruling's impact on Med and future litigants led to a complex series of additional questions: What did "freedom" mean for a child? What did it mean to be the emancipated child of an enslaved mother? Could children consent to slavery or freedom? At what age might they have this capacity? What if they "chose" slavery? And if they chose freedom, who would be responsible for their upbringing?

SHOWDOWN

Despite Justice Shaw's order, private correspondence suggests that the Aves/Slater family did not surrender Med without a fight. A somewhat illegible, undated letter from abolitionist Caroline Weston to her sister Debora Weston described a dramatic scene in which antislavery activists urged Thomas Aves to comply with the court ruling:

> In the evening Misses Sargent & Sullivan called at Maria's and said the Coloured people were much aggravated that the child remained at Avis's & said they would go and take her away—Mrs. Prince in particular was very warlike—it was near 9—Maria & Henry went to Ellis G.'s and found him at home made a statement of the case, and Ellis took a carriage to Francis Jackson took him with him & went to Mr. Avis's. Mr. Slater was <u>there</u>. Mr. Loring stated the case said that the colored people would be transgressing no law if they took her

as threatened—& it would be a very unpleasant circumstance for Mr. Avis. He had better place her in Mr. Loring's custody for the asylum. Mr. A. blustered much about being "ruled by niggers." Mr. Slater talked they said like a slave holder, but the young ladies fired off well—& begged their father not to let her go "Hold on to her father." Should like to see a mob [——-?] "Don't feel afraid of a mob." . . . It was later when the conference concluded & Mr. Avis went upstairs & brought <u>Med</u> down & delivered her to Mr. Loring. Who got to Miss Sargent's with her about 12 at night. Next morning she was taken to the Asylum. Maria saw her there a [?] child & seemed very happy. She is to be called <u>Maria Somerset</u>. Mrs. Child has written a letter addressed to Mrs. Slater—an attempt at conversion.[1]

This tense, emotional scene involved many leading Garrisonian abolitionists and revealed the stakes of the ruling for African American Beacon Hill residents, referred to here only as "the Coloured people," with the exception of the "warlike" Mrs. Prince. Nancy Prince, one of the African American members of the Boston Female Anti-Slavery Society (BFASS), was renowned for chasing slavecatchers out of Beacon Hill and is best known today for her *Narrative of the Life and Travels of Mrs. Nancy Prince*. Several other important local activists appeared in this scene: Henrietta Sargent and Catherine Sullivan were BFASS members; "Maria and Henry" were Maria Weston Chapman and her husband; "Ellis G." was Med's lawyer, Ellis Gray Loring; Francis Jackson was an antislavery radical who would later serve as treasurer of the Boston Vigilance Committee. Caroline Weston's report that "Mr. Slater was <u>there</u>," was a surprising turn of events, because he was not in town for the court case, leaving his father-in-law Thomas Aves to represent his interests.[2]

Once the Slater/Aves family was persuaded to comply with the court's ruling, Med was brought to the Samaritan Asylum for Indigent Children until the probate court could determine her custody, as suggested by the court in the official ruling. This is the only extant account of what happened that night; apparently the antislavery activists were trying to avert vigilante mob action without involving the police or the courts.

SAMARITAN ASYLUM

The Samaritan Asylum for Indigent Children (sometimes referred to as the Samaritan Asylum for Colored Orphans) was founded because local institutions for impoverished or orphaned children would not receive African

Americans. As the organization's founding constitution explains, "Believing that our colored population have been greatly neglected by the charitable institutions of the day, and that consequently an Asylum for children, designed *especially* for that class of people is much needed, we do hereby agree to support an institution, which shall have for its object, the mental and moral elevation of our colored citizens, and which shall seek the accomplishment of this object by adopting the children of indigent and vicious parents, and giving them such an education as shall enable them to procure a respectable maintenance."[3]

The asylum was organized in April 1834 and officially incorporated in March 1835: "Be it enacted ... That Mary S. Parker, Abigail Pico, Hephzibah Sullivan, Susan Paul, with their associates and successors, are hereby incorporated by the name of the Samaritan Asylum for indigent children, for the purpose of providing for the support and education of indigent children, especially among the colored population."[4] Many of the officers and managers were also BFASS members, and BFASS offered some financial support at times, which was a matter of some controversy within the group.[5] It was located nearby in the West End at No. 29, Poplar Street, about eight blocks away from the Aves house on Pinckney Street, and just a block away from the Massachusetts General Hospital, which had opened its doors in 1821, the first hospital in New England to treat members of the general public.

The Samaritan Asylum was always a small-scale, cash-strapped enterprise; it was more of a group home than a large institution. A fundraising letter in the *Liberator* reported caring for seven or nine children and described plans "to rent a house, engage a governess and commence house-keeping. We hope and feel that christian benevolence will sustain us in 'lengthening our cords, and strengthening our stakes.' Feeling it a duty to our long neglected colored race, we shall present their claims to the public." Here the officers referenced the biblical Isaiah's call to "enlarge the place of your tent," that is, to create a dwelling place for all. The managers continued the metaphor here, noting that an expanded "tent" required longer cords and stronger stakes to support the increased weight of inclusion.[6]

Around the time of the confrontation at the Aves residence, on September 12, 1836, William Lloyd Garrison's publishing partner Issac Knapp petitioned for guardianship of Med in Massachusetts Probate Court; it is not clear if Garrison's partner ever officially took custody of Med or if said guardianship was short-lived.[7] It is also unclear why she was not taken in by a family in the neighborhood.

For twenty-first-century observers, it is very difficult to understand this turn of events: how could the abolitionists have left Med at the asylum? Despite her celebrity, Med was not treated any differently than other poor children, whether orphans or with parents deemed unable to support them. At this time, poor laws would "authorize local authorities to remove any child lacking support." Legal scholar Barbara Woodhouse's discussion of Frederick Douglass is instructive here:

> As Fred Bailey realized long before he became Frederick Douglass, the lines between freedom and bondage, and between persons and property, were patrolled and reinforced by concepts of minority and dependency, as well as by concepts of race and color. Douglass' autobiography provides a vivid flash of insight. At one point, Douglass is gazing longingly at ships sailing north to freedom. He comforts himself by reflecting that it is not race alone that defines his bondage: "I am but a boy, and all boys are bound to some one." It was simply a fact of economic and social life that all children were indeed "bound" to somebody—legally under some adult's custody and control.[8]

Douglass tells his story from the point of view of an adult fugitive from slavery; we might consider how Douglass's life would have changed if he had been a minor in freedom, facing the challenges of all poor children.

These challenges were also demonstrated by the gradual emancipation laws passed by Pennsylvania, Connecticut, Rhode Island, New York, and New Jersey, in which children born to enslaved mothers were freed but then required to work as servants until adulthood. We might ask about the children freed by gradual emancipation statutes: "How free is a free child whose parents are still in bondage?" After all, emancipated children could not provide for their own support and education. The solution—"binding poor children to multi-decade terms of service"—was rooted in colonial poor laws and was a "familiar legal practice."[9] In Med's case, it was not clear who would take responsibility for her support. BFASS did donate money to the asylum in 1837 and 1838, but there were no funds specifically designated for Med or any records of indenture.[10]

Why was Med embraced when she represented slavery in the South but rejected once she became an unaccompanied minor in New England? Harriet Wilson's experiences, as described in her autobiographical novel *Our Nig: Or, Sketches from the Life of a Free Black*, might help us understand this dynamic. While Wilson was never enslaved, her novel contends that "slavery's shadows fall" even in the free north.[11] Like Med, Wilson's alter-ego Frado found herself on her own at the tender age of six. Frado's mother abandoned her out of economic desperation, and she was bound out to the horrible Mrs. Bellmont, a character based on the real-life Rebecca Hutchinson Hayward, an abolitionist who had no trouble abusing and exploiting the young black girl in her charge.[12]

Wilson's story is an unspeakable one in many ways, and so she uses the "disorderly girl" figure from nineteenth-century woman's fiction "as a means to narrate... the unsanctioned story of racial abuse in the antebellum North." Her character Frado, a "truth teller" and "stand-in for the author herself," survives by her resourcefulness and charisma. Had Med lived, Frado's fate as an indentured servant and impoverished adult might have been her own. Wilson wrote her book in order to support her son George, but sadly he died at age seven at the county Poor Farm before Wilson was able to provide a home for him.[13] All three "orphans"—Med, George, and Harriet/Frado—were taken from their mothers by political and economic circumstances; these separations led to early deaths for Med and George, as well as lifelong health problems for Wilson. These outcomes are a devastating critique of a society unwilling to care for poor black children.

Before Med's death, both Samuel Slater and Lydia Maria Child wrote letters protesting the imperfect outcome of the case and addressing Med's anomalous status as the free child of an enslaved mother. Slater's letter was published widely, while Child's was sent directly to Mary Aves Slater and read aloud at a BFASS meeting.[14]

Slater's letter is the only place his voice appears in the historical record, and so it merits our extended consideration. He gave his version of events in a scathing letter to the editor, published in the *Boston Commercial Gazette* and reprinted in the *Liberator* under the Refuge of Oppression column.[15] Angry and frustrated, he wished to set the record straight regarding the "vile and disgraceful proceedings in this case." He claimed that Knapp's guardianship was really just an attempt to claim Med's labor and that he was the rightful guardian of the newly freed Med:

> As soon as I understood the child was to be bound out, I demanded the privilege of guardianship, but under all the responsibilities of the laws, this was denied me, on the plea that as soon as the child returned to New Orleans, it would return to its former state, that is a slave. Once free, I should suppose it would be always free, but whether so or not, the Abolition Lawyer had the child bound out to his friend Knapp, and so the business was finally disposed

of. Now I should like to know if this Knapp has given any security that he will not remove to a slave State until this child is of age; if he has not, what is the objection urged against my taking it worth, for the child would have been bound out a free child as much in one case as in the other. The fact that they objected to my proposal, and have bound her out to themselves, is sufficient to prove that it was the services, and not the freedom of the child they wanted.[16]

In other words, Slater felt that he should be the one to take charge of Med's indenture, that there would be no difference between him and Knapp, because under the "once free, forever free" principle Med could not be re-enslaved, and that the results proved that there was an economic motivation behind their freedom suit.

Slater went on to denounce the abolitionists for separating a mother and child: "These fellows have robbed the mother of her child, and to cap all they call it freedom—is it not freedom with a vengeance? A mother bond or free should be the representative of her own child, and surely it ought to be so in this land of liberty." He did not seem to consider that for Med's mother, who as a slave had no legal claims to her daughter, this was not a "land of liberty." He concluded by denouncing the abolitionists as "fanatics" and "disunionists."[17]

Both sides in the case agreed that separating Med's family was wrong, but they disagreed over the responsibility for the separation and the proper remedy. Slater, of course, blamed the abolitionists: "Now upon the principle of humanity, these fellows ought to have given me the child, or to purchase the balance of the family, a mother and two children, and bring them here."[18] The abolitionists, in turn, called for the Slaters to manumit Med's mother and siblings. Both sides recognized that Med's unusual status raised all kinds of difficulties, but they found themselves in a standoff: Slater would not accept further economic losses, and Garrisonian immediatists would never agree to compensation for slaves.

FREE SOIL AND GOSPEL GROUND

Samuel Slater's mind was made up, but BFASS also reached out to his wife Mary Aves Slater to see if she might be persuaded to free Med's mother and siblings. Child, writing on behalf of the organization, sent a letter to Mary Aves Slater, the "attempt at conversion" referenced by Caroline Weston in her account of the showdown at the Aves house. This extraordinary letter, dated

September 5, 1836, asked Slater to transcend the geopolitical borders that divided them: "Let us try to meet together on Gospel ground. We beseech you, to ask your own heart, in simple sincerity, whether in being a slaveholder you are *doing unto others as you would they should do unto you.* Can it be that you <u>think</u> you are doing right to buy and sell human beings?"[19]

The letter established the golden rule from the biblical Sermon on the Mount, "Do unto others as you would have them do unto you," as the standard for moral judgment.[20] Loring had briefly mentioned this biblical verse during his courtroom arguments, while Child made this central ethical teaching of Jesus ("Do as you would be done by") the center of her case for freeing Med's family. The letter first appealed to Slater's own feelings as a mother:

> Look at your own sleeping babe! Think of him captured by the Algerines, and sold into slavery.... Could you be willing that another should do this unto you? Would any custom, any laws, any standard of public opinion, ever lead you to believe in the righteousness of such proceedings? Oh, no! With the wild earnestness of a mother's love, you would claim your own lost child. With all the energy of faith, you would urge that God had made him free![21]

The letter went on to debunk the typical proslavery arguments using the "do unto others" standard. Child contended that it was not enough to be "kind" to enslaved people: it did not fulfill Christian duty and left enslaved people at risk of being sold to a "cruel master." And she noted that Slater would not be satisfied herself if she were enslaved by a "kind" enslaver: "Under an exchange of circumstances, you would not think your employer performed the whole of Christian duty by keeping you comfortably fed and clothed, and refraining from personal abuse." Furthermore, the idea that enslaved people were "better off" in slavery was ludicrous if she put herself in the position of a slave: "Do you say that the slaves are in a better condition than the free? . . . You know what would be your own most earnest wish if you were a slave." Finally, the letter debunked the "African inferiority" argument: "Do you excuse slavery on the ground that the colored race must ever be far inferior to us? If this be true, we are doubly bound to protect them." Child reminded Slater that Jesus died for all people and that there would be a color-blind reckoning on Judgment Day: "Before His tribunal, the evidence of a slave will be admitted as freely as that of a white man. May God in his mercy grant that none may appear there to accuse you."[22]

After testing the proslavery arguments against the golden rule, Child shifted back to the matter at hand, the separation of Med from her mother:

> One circumstance, accompanying the freedom of little Med is to us a painful one. The child is separated from her mother. True it is, that this feeling would never make us blind to the plain duty of saving a human being from slavery.... We know very well that a slave is only nominally a mother. She cannot save her child from severe treatment—she cannot prevent her being sold—she cannot protect her from prostitution. We know that if Med had remained in slavery, she would, almost inevitably, have grown up in mental debasement and moral pollution. We could not unite mother and child together and place them under the regenerating influences of Christianity. But you can restore them to each other without injury to either. Give the woman and her children their freedom. As you hope for a quiet conscience, a happy death-bed, and an approving God, do as you would be done by![23]

Child here established a hierarchy of values: freedom trumps maternal love in this case because enslaved mothers have no legal rights to their children. Only Slater could reunite the family "without injury to either." God and conscience made this an imperative. Child's rhetoric anticipates the constructions of motherhood found in the *Liberty Bell*, the antislavery gift annual edited by Maria Weston Chapman and to which Child was a regular contributor. In the pages of the *Liberty Bell*, white motherhood authorized them to rescue enslaved people; enslaved mothers could only wait to be rescued and could not be true mothers until they were freed.[24]

The conclusion of the letter suggested that they were on opposite sides of this case because of an accident of political geography: "Dear madam, we have not written in a fancied spirit of superiority, but in the earnest sincerity of Christian love. You have been blinded by circumstances, which might have blinded us had we been placed under their influence." Child urged Slater to return with them to "Gospel ground," the sacred space that knows no boundaries because the "good news" is everywhere. Gospel ground might serve as a means to common ground and to right outcomes, and yet it admitted no compromise on this fundamental moral issue. For Child and her BFASS colleagues, justice could only be found in the free states and in the promise of the gospel. They called on Slater to return to her New England roots and reject the values of her adopted southern home.

We do not know if Slater ever replied to this letter, but Child's letter was read aloud at the BFASS annual meeting in October 1836. Constitutive rhetoric might help us understand the purpose of this performance: Mary Aves Slater, to whom the letter was addressed, was not there, after all, so we need to think beyond the classical rhetorical focus on persuasion. Literary theorist Kenneth Burke reminds us that "the classical notion of clear persuasive intent is not an accurate fit for describing the ways in which the members of a group promote social cohesion by acting rhetorically upon themselves and one another." In other words, "preaching to the choir" by reading this letter was an important rhetorical act for the formation of individual and group identity. The concepts of free soil and gospel ground laid out in the letter also fulfilled an important "ego-function" in that BFASS members established and affirmed their own identities at the same time as they addressed Slater.[25]

There is a clever ambiguity to Child's core concepts: it is difficult to speak *against* free soil or gospel ground, and these concepts take on a vernacular legal power of their own. Historian Sue Peabody cautions us that "mechanisms of exceptionalism (like the Free Soil principle) can paradoxically work to reinforce slavery itself by legitimating its continued existence outside the boundaries of the 'free' nation state."[26] This makes gospel ground even more revolutionary: if free soil liberated all who crossed a political border, gospel ground freed *all people everywhere* as required by the golden rule.

Free soil and gospel ground were also powerful expressions of moral geography. While Justice Shaw denied any special moral geography in his ruling—the free soil of Massachusetts had no liberatory powers—it was telling that he felt compelled to explicitly deny such powers. In their subsequent letter, Child and BFASS took things a step further with gospel ground: the ultimate moral geography. In her vision of a nation governed by the golden rule, Child brilliantly used a geographical metaphor to restore right order and remind the citizens of the Commonwealth of "what is good, right and true."[27] In this argument, jurisdictions became irrelevant: Med was born free as a child of God.

POST-MED CASES AND THE FREEDOM SUIT SCENARIO

The influential Med precedent enacted one version of what we might call the "freedom suit scenario." A familiar term from performance studies, a scenario is "'a sketch or outline of the plot of a play, giving particulars of the scenes, situations, etc., . . . The scenario predates the script and allows for many possible 'endings.'" Scenarios have influence beyond the theater world; they also function, as performance studies scholar Diana Taylor reminds us, "as meaning-making paradigms that structure social environments, behaviors, and potential outcomes."[28]

In many ways, there was nothing surprising about this iteration of the freedom suit scenario. It had taken place before in the 1832 Francisco case and would be repeated until the Civil War. Med's version featured a familiar courtroom scene, set in a classic granite courthouse, a place where New England justice would be dispensed in a battle with the southern slave power. Characters included two young lawyers at the start of their illustrious careers and a prominent, stern judge. White men debated and judged the fate of the enslaved, while white women and African Americans were relegated to the gallery. And at the center of it all was a young enslaved girl far from home, her six years placing her squarely in the category of what literary scholar Nazera Sadiq Wright calls "youthful girlhood."[29] The abolitionist lawyers wore the white hats, using legal acumen and biblical values to win freedom for their enslaved client and defeat the enslavers. All parties tried to claim the moral high ground as the protector of children, but in the end, truth and justice prevailed, order was restored, and free soil triumphed. It was a compelling narrative with a satisfying conclusion, but in reality the freedom suit scenario had a different ending for Med and the children who followed her. The freedom suit scenario did not work well for children; it did not account for their capacity for consent or for their future care.

In the subsequent cases, the freedom suit scenario was revised, inverted, and replayed in unexpected ways.[30] Despite the authority of the Med legal precedent, not a single case followed the Med scenario, to the confusion of the abolitionists and the delight of many proslavery observers. Unthinkable questions became central: Who were the real kidnappers? Who were the genuine protectors of children and family unity? Could anyone really choose slavery over freedom?

The abolitionists were doing important work, and yet their tragic flaw was their inability to see beyond the freedom suit scenario, to understand what the outcomes meant for actual children, and to revise the script in response to complicated situations. In many ways the abolitionist campaign to save enslaved children brought to Massachusetts by their owners was a disaster. Justice Shaw had ruled, quite narrowly, that enslaved people brought by their enslavers to Massachusetts could not be removed without their consent, and so the question of consent and the appropriate age for consent became central to subsequent cases. In the freedom suit scenario, the answer was clear: no people could possibly consent to their own enslavement, and young children needed abolitionist advocates to speak for them. In practice, all of the cases seemed to turn on the enslaver's intent and the child's consent, and these questions led to confusing procedures and unexpected variations. And no one really knew what freedom meant for a free child of enslaved parents.

Emma: Cheerfulness = Consent

Just two months after the Med case, the *Liberator* reported on a case with very similar circumstances: on October 15, 1836, "Asa D. Gove, of New Orleans, was brought before the Police Court . . . on the charge of having secretly confined a colored girl, named Emma, with intent to send her out of the State against her will." This setup seemed identical to Med's freedom suit scenario: like Med, Emma (sometimes called "Amy") had been brought to Boston by her enslaver from New Orleans. Things quickly went wrong, however, when Gove defied the writ and refused to produce Emma for the court. Attorney Samuel Sewall, one of Med's early advocates, argued that Gove's actions proved his illegal intentions: "If she was not his slave, would he not at once have disavowed any claim to her, and have surrendered her on the habeas corpus?" Judge James C. Merrill conceded the force of this argument, but he inexplicably argued that despite Gove's defiance, there was not sufficient evidence to prove that Emma had not consented to leave Massachusetts. It is unclear why Gove faced no consequences for defying the writ. Emma never appeared in court, but because several witnesses testified that they saw her playing happily outside, the judge concluded that she was "cheerful and contented" and dismissed the case.[31] Sewall was extremely frustrated by this decision: "This owl-like decision made me very angry,—as if a child could not laugh and play without its being proof of a wish to go as a slave to New Orleans."[32] This was an unexpected twist in the freedom suit scenario: while Med was deemed too young to consent, Emma somehow consented in absentia by playing outside, and her enslaver was rewarded for his defiance.

Elizabeth: A "Peculiar" Misunderstanding?

About a year after the Med and Emma cases, another case would turn the freedom suit scenario on its head. On September 17, 1837, a five-year-old African American girl, Elizabeth Bright, was taken outside her Cambridge home by Sophia and John Robinson, an African American couple from Beacon Hill. Her legal guardian and former enslaver Henry Bright had recently moved with his family from Alabama, and the Robinsons feared that she would be returned to slavery at a future date. But unlike Samuel Slater in the Med case, who asserted Med was his lawful slave, Henry Bright insisted that this was all a terrible misunderstanding, that Elizabeth was now free and his legal ward, that he only asserted the rights of guardianship based on a promise to her dying mother, and that his enslaving days were over.[33]

Bright had a keen understanding of the antislavery forces in Boston, and after Elizabeth's disappearance, he visited Samuel Sewall and Ellis Gray Loring to seek their assistance. Upon their advice, he wrote a public letter stating his intentions and a bond pledging to forfeit $500 if Elizabeth was sent back to slavery, but the African American community remained skeptical and declined to give up the child. Mediation by African American minister Reverend Samuel Snowden and a face-to-face appeal with the Robinsons had no impact either.

Bright went on to seek legal remedies: he got an official letter of guardianship from the Middlesex County probate judge, but the Robinsons still refused. He petitioned Chief Justice Lemuel Shaw for a writ of habeas corpus, which Shaw granted, but just like in the Emma case, the judge refused to hold the Robinsons in contempt when they denied knowing Elizabeth's whereabouts. Bright then filed a civil suit, then finally complained to the grand jury, which indicted the Robinsons on kidnapping charges on November 7. The municipal court Judge Peter Oxenbridge Thacher heard arguments on December 20, and the Robinsons were found guilty of two out of three charges of kidnapping. The Robinsons appeared back in court for sentencing on December 29, at which point they brought Elizabeth to court and surrendered her to the Brights.[34]

Behind the scenes of Bright's legal maneuvers, the abolitionists had extensive involvement. Ellis Gray Loring had quickly realized that things were going terribly wrong and worked on damage control. He wrote to John Robinson and urged him to return Elizabeth before the grand jury proceedings:

> I am informed that Mr. Charles G. Loring is going to prosecute you and Mrs. Robinson before the Grand Jury tomorrow. You recollect Judge Shaw mentioned that if you could be brought within the law of kidnapping, you and your wife would be liable to go to the State Prison for 10 years. This is a very serious matter—and I hope you will look straight at it. You know that there

may be persons on the Jury who would not feel much scruple in convicting coloured people on a charge of this kind, innocent or guilty, and a great effort will probably be made to convict you. If it is still in your power to produce the child, I do think as I have told you from the first, that you had better do it. You will pardon my urgency. I speak wholly in friendship to you, and from what I think right.[35]

Later courtroom testimony forced Loring to admit that he was speaking for his own interests as well. Under oath he conceded that the Robinsons had consulted him prior to the kidnapping and that he had given them legal clearance to take Elizabeth. BFASS President Mary Parker also had to admit prior involvement, but like Loring, she went on to distance herself from the case.

The newspapers were highly critical of Loring following these revelations: "We think the testimony of Ellis G. Loring, Esq. . . . does not reflect much to his credit as a legal man or a philanthropist. . . . It appears that Loring was consulted by Robinson and his wife, about the propriety of assisting the child, before the abduction took place. . . . Why then, in the name of common sense, did he not attempt to prevent these people from the commission of a crime . . . ?" In fact, the coverage was harder on the white abolitionists than the Robinsons: "But it seems that the colored people, having been excited and urged on by the untimely measures of a few reckless fanatics, were anxious to prevent the removal of the child to a slave state, which measure they would have seen as impracticable, had they examined the matter a little. We do not blame Mr. and Mrs. Robinson for their good wishes towards the child, but we do think that they have been grossly abused . . . by the mad policy of some over-enthusiastic persons."[36]

What did not make the papers was the fact that the Weston sisters were also part of the conspiracy: they used their connections in the abolitionist community in New Bedford, Massachusetts, to keep Elizabeth hidden. As Debora Weston wrote to her sister Anne Warren Weston, "Tell Maria that the little child of Henry Bright's which Mrs. Robinson brought here is doing very well and is nearly recovered from a very bad cold which it had. The N. B. ladies are going to do every thing they can for her. The child is contented and happy. Tell this to Mrs. Robinson."[37] Here the Weston sisters broke ranks with their usual allies Loring and Sewall. In another strange twist, Benjamin Robbins Curtis, the lawyer who had defended the rights of Med's enslavers, defended the Robinsons in this case.

This case featured a different conversation: all accepted *Commonwealth v. Aves* as the law of the land, and they all agreed that Elizabeth was free in Massachusetts. The point of contention was the character and trustworthiness of the Brights. As everyone waited for the sentencing phase of the trial, the abolitionists continued to discuss the Brights' intentions among themselves. As abolitionist Increase Smith wrote to Caroline Weston from Hingham, Massachusetts, "What is all that trouble about Mr. Bright's lost child? Can Mr. B. with his securities be trusted? Mr. Loring seems to think he may be. I sincerely hope the defendants will not be subjected to the heavy penalty to which they are exposed."[38] While the white abolitionists were coming around to believing Bright, the African Americans contended that "the slaveholders, with their smooth tongues" could not fool them.[39]

While the free soil of Massachusetts did not seem to be part of the conversation, it was interesting that Judge Thacher used this language at sentencing: "While breathing the free air of this Commonwealth, she was suddenly, forcibly, and against her will, seized and carried away from her friends, to whom she was committed by a dying mother, and who were discharging with affection and fidelity, the sacred trust. Those who committed this deed, and all those who advised, counselled and encouraged it, have incurred a most weighty responsibility."[40] The case was not just a local matter; one letter to the editor argued that the case had national importance: "The peculiar features of the case, inasmuch as they have a direct bearing on the all-absorbing question of abolition, cannot but excite a deep interest in the bosoms of all men who have at heart the permanent continuance of our union."[41]

Elizabeth's case featured a carnivalesque revision of the freedom suit scenario: this time the alleged enslaver filed the writ of habeas corpus, and the abolitionists were charged with kidnapping. The "black hat" lawyer from Med's case defended the alleged abolitionist kidnappers, and the "white hats" from Med's case confusedly switched sides mid-trial. The white lawyers lost control of the scenario; the African Americans and white women typically relegated to the gallery became the primary actors; and the case was tried, to some extent, in the court of public opinion. Were the Robinsons abolitionist heroes or misguided by fanatics? Were the Brights sincere in their intentions toward Elizabeth, or was a former enslaver always suspect? And what did Elizabeth make of all this? This complicated case exposed a divide within the abolitionist ranks and the inadequacy of the freedom suit scenario. The proceedings and the outcome were embarrassing and dissatisfying for all, and Elizabeth's will and desires seemed beside the point. She was portrayed as "content" at all times, when surely being taken by strangers to another city for months at a time and then abruptly returned must have been traumatic. At the end of the proceedings, she remained a free child, but it is not clear what freedom with her former enslavers really meant: we do not know if she truly was a member of the Bright family or if she was being raised as a future servant.

Med's Death: The Freedom Suit Scenario Turns Tragic

The details of Med's life between the fall of 1836 and the winter of 1838 are unknown. By then, Ellis Gray Loring's correspondence revealed that Med was seriously ill. In March 1838, Med was living in the Samaritan Asylum, and Ellis and his wife Louisa Loring sent a sofa and money for incidentals and offered to hire a full-time nurse if needed. They also arranged for their personal physician to consult with the in-house physician. As Loring wrote to Catherine Sullivan, an active BFASS member, "I have full confidence in the management of the Asylum, and doubt not every thing possible will be done for her health and comfort. I feel a strong interest in her, and most earnestly pray that she and her mother may, one day, be reunited, in freedom."[42]

In 1838, Lydia Maria Child and her husband David Lee Child were working on a sugar beet farm in Northampton, Massachusetts, a quixotic attempt to create an alternative to the "blood-stained" sugar from the South. The Childs did not seem overly concerned about Med's health at first, and she jokes that Loring's aristocratic wife would not be up to the task of farming. In a letter to Loring, she described working in their sugar beet fields at three or four a.m.: "Mr Child says, 'What do you think would tempt Louisa to bestir herself at this hour?' 'Nothing short of saving Ellis' life,' said I, laughing. 'Oh, I guess she would try it twice, for little Med's life.' 'Maybe she would try it once to save little Med,' said I, 'Ellis having a strong desire that Med should survive.'"[43]

Letters from that July reveal that Med did not recover, and she died sometime in the summer. She may have already been ill before she left New Orleans: Slater noted that they brought her on the sea voyage "principally for her health." She was not the only child from the Samaritan Asylum to have died: the Asylum's own circular reported that "thirteen children have been admitted; two of whom have died," and the Weston sisters' correspondence contains plans for the funeral of a girl named Phebe.[44]

This sad news affected everyone involved with the case. The freedom suit scenario was not supposed to end with the premature death of the emancipated child. Child wrote to Loring regarding an awkward visit with the Shaws, during which she had to inform them about Med's death. Justice Shaw, whose decision had changed the course of Med's life, needed reassurance about this sad outcome. Child sought Loring's help in this endeavor:

> Judge and Mrs. Shaw called to see me this summer. He asked whether Med were in a comfortable situation, and was surprised when I told him of her death. He repeated a conversation with a New Orleans gentleman about the cruelty of separating a child from its parents, how dreadfully the mother felt about it, etc. I mention this, thinking you may put Dr. Jackson, or some other person, in the way of convincing the Judge that Med received every possible kindness. He was very reserved on all subjects connected with Anti-Slavery. I suppose on account of his official station.[45]

Loring, in turn, sought Child's assistance in memorializing Med and her legacy: "I am about to erect a grave stone bearing the dates of the birth, freedom & death of little Med. Can you supply me with a short inscription?"[46] The attorney who in court promised a glorious life in freedom—"This child, if freed, will be educated for usefulness and respectability. She will never want a friend, nor the means of improvement and happiness"[47]—could only mourn her premature loss. Loring and the abolitionists might have thought about what might have been without their legal intervention. Might Med have grown to adulthood under the care of her mother? Would an enslaved life in New Orleans have been better than an early death in a Boston institution?

These questions become even more complicated when considering the legal terrain of Louisiana. Had Med returned to Louisiana and found legal advocates there, it is likely that the Louisiana courts would have ruled in her favor. The Supreme Court of Louisiana frequently struggled with the very question considered in *Commonwealth v. Aves*: "Was the status of Louisiana slaves affected by brief sojourns with their owners in states where the law prohibited slavery?" In most cases, as historian Judith Kelleher Schafer notes, the answer was yes: "The Supreme Court of Louisiana ... with few exceptions, granted comity to the laws of northern states in suits for freedom based on transportation to a free state or country, despite the attempt of the Louisiana legislature to restrain the scope of these rulings."[48]

For example, in *Lunsford v. Coquillon* (1824), the "landmark case in suits for freedom based on transportation to a free area," Rebecca Lunsford, an enslaved woman, sued for freedom based on her three-year residence in Ohio; her enslaver then forcibly removed her to Kentucky and sold her to Michel Fortier of Louisiana. The Louisiana Supreme Court upheld the lower court ruling in her favor: "As she was a free woman there [Ohio], she must be held so every where." It was quite telling that both Ellis Gray Loring and Justice Shaw cited *Lunsford* in their arguments: Loring to establish the distinction between fugitives and non-fugitives and Shaw to establish that slavery was a matter for municipal law.[49] And just months before the Med case, in *Marie Louise, f.w.c., v. Marot* (1835, 1836), the Louisiana court "actually *suggested* using transportation to free soil as a potentially successful tactic for a slave seeking her freedom." The petitioner took the court's advice and sued for freedom based on her sojourn in France. Chief Justice George Mathews ruled that "Being free for one moment in France, it was not in the power of her former owner to reduce her again to slavery."[50] This Louisiana variation on the freedom suit scenario offered an alternative legal pathway and might have led to a happier outcome for Med.

Anne: Legal Vengeance against Abolitionists

Despite the tragic outcome of the Med case, abolitionists in Massachusetts continued to use the *Aves* precedent to sue for the freedom of enslaved children in transit. While Anne's 1838 case in Worcester County went unreported, the pamphlet published by the Holden Anti-Slavery Society portrayed the community uproar over slavery in their midst. Olivia Eames had moved with her husband to New Orleans and then returned to visit friends in Holden and Grafton following his death in 1837. She brought Anne, the thirteen-year-old girl she claimed as property, with her to serve as a nurse to her son and general household servant. The Holden report reminded readers of Anne's legal standing following *Aves*: "Of course, as soon as she came into this State, she was as free as any native born citizen of this State, and had the right to remain with or leave her mistress, as she saw fit. The highest tribunal has decided, that, if a person come here on business or pleasure, and bring a slave, the slave becomes free."[51]

At first, things unfolded according to the freedom suit scenario: local abolitionists sued out a writ of personal replevin, which guaranteed trial by jury on questions of personal freedom. This was a brand-new legal strategy, as the writ was part of the state personal liberty law of 1837. Eames and Anne appeared in court, and Eames conceded that Anne was indeed free. As a town history from 1894 recorded, "At the December term of court, 1838, judgment was, by agreement, taken against the defendant, Mrs. Eames, in the sum of one dollar and costs, and thus the freedom of the girl was judicially and finally established."[52]

But Eames was not so quick to give up her "property" and went on the offensive, claiming that the abolitionists had deprived her of her voluntary servant and that Anne had not requested the writ. In other words, according to Eames, the abolitionists were not rescuers but kidnappers, and she filed suit in the Court of Common Pleas in Worcester the next month. In *Commonwealth v. Stratton*, four local men, Samuel Stratton, Samuel Foster, James E. Cheney, and Farnum White Jr., were "charged ... with a conspiracy to defraud Olivia Eames of Holden, of the voluntary services of her servant girl, named Anne, without her consent."[53] As in Elizabeth's case, the question of the former enslaver's intent was important; unlike the five-year-old Elizabeth, the thirteen-year-old Anne was deemed old enough to express her own will and consent. After testimony from neighbors about Anne's mistreatment and Eames's intent to sell her when they returned to New Orleans, as well as Anne's own statement that she wished to be free, the defendants were acquitted. We do not know what happened to Anne, a young teenager now on her own in Massachusetts. In her case the freedom suit scenario held, but with a strange retaliatory second act in which the abolitionists' legal strategies were turned against them.

Rose: "Choosing" Slavery

Sewall, joined by his colleague Ellis Gray Loring, pursued the freedom suit scenario again in the case of the thirteen-year-old Rose in summer 1841. This time the writ was sued out by Joshua Upham of Salem, Massachusetts, and brought before the Supreme Judicial Court and Justice Shaw. The case does not seem to have been reported, but some traces of the case can be found in newspaper articles from the *Salem Register*, *Boston Courier*, and *Boston Atlas*, reprinted in the *Liberator*. The multiple reprintings make it hard to find a stable editorial voice, but the critique of the abolitionists is clear in its mocking tone:

> A colored girl, named Rose, was brought before the Supreme Judicial Court on Saturday, on a writ of Habeas Corpus, sued out in her behalf by those vigilant enemies of slavery, the abolitionists. Ellis Gray Loring and S.E. Sewall, Esquires, represented to the Court, that Rose came on from Mobile as the

hired servant of Mrs. Eliza M. Ticknor—that at Mobile she was a slave—that being under 14, she was not adequate to make her election between slavery and freedom—and that therefore the Court ought not to regard any choice she might make, but let her free, *willy nilly*, on the ground that one who preferred slavery must be incompetent to settle the question for herself.[54]

Here the question of will and consent became central, and as he had done in previous cases, Judge Shaw decided that young teenagers had the capacity to choose for themselves. He went on to report the results of their private interview: "She stated it to be her desire to remain with Mrs. Ticknor, and return to Mobile, where she should see her brothers and sisters.... She was therefore ordered to be discharged, and went her way with Mrs. Ticknor, much to the disappointment of those who thought themselves better friends to her than she was to herself, and presenting a spectacle of the triumph of natural affection over the deep instinctive impulses to freedom." The *Courier* gleefully reported this abolitionist defeat, while at the same time noting the complicated nature of Rose's decision between "natural affection" and "freedom." The *Atlas* went on to report that "the abolitionists appeared to be much disappointed and surprised.... They would probably say that any one who chooses slavery rather than liberty is incompetent to decide.... One colored person attempted to induce her to remain, by depicting to her the horrors of slavery, but without success." The *Atlas* also reported that she was detained by a black man the previous summer in an attempt to keep her from returning to Mobile, portraying the abolitionists as the terrifying kidnappers. It also had this suggestion for abolitionists: "when next they take so strong an interest in other people's affairs, to ascertain *first* the wishes of the object of their sympathy."[55] For the abolitionists, this turn of events was hard to understand: it was inconceivable that anyone would "choose" slavery. They did not understand that enslaved people electing to return were not choosing enslavement but, rather, choosing family and community.

Anson: Too Young to Consent

In *Commonwealth v. Taylor* (1841), Sewall appeared, once again, before Justice Shaw in the Supreme Judicial Court. In this Med case reprise, they would decide the fate of Anson, a little boy about eight years old. His enslaver Mary B. Taylor was a resident of Arkansas, and like Mary Aves Slater, she had brought her slave with her on a visit to Massachusetts. The probate court had issued a writ of habeas corpus ordering Taylor to relinquish custody of

Anson and had appointed guardians. Taylor was represented by a prominent attorney and Democratic Party activist, Benjamin Franklin Hallett, who had previously worked with William Apess, the Pequot Indian author and activist, as counsel for the Mashpee Indians during the Mashpee Revolt of 1833–1834, a protest movement that led to restored self-government for the Mashpee Indians on Cape Cod.[56]

The Supreme Judicial Court ruled that the probate court had acted correctly, and Shaw noted the applicability of the Med case:

> We can perceive no difference in principle between the present case, and that of *Commonwealth v. Aves*. . . . The apparent distinction is, that in that case, the persons, by whom the slave child was brought from Louisiana, explicitly claimed the right of holding the child, and carrying him back to be held as a slave. In the present case, the persons by whom the boy has been brought here, and by whom he was before held in slavery, do not claim the right to hold or regard him as a slave here, or to restrain him of his freedom, and regard him otherwise than as a free boy here; not to remove him to Arkansas, unless by his consent.[57]

In other words, while the Slaters had claimed the right to bring their slave Med home with them, the Taylors were savvy enough about the law to say that Anson was free and that it was all up to him whether he wished to go home to Arkansas and slavery. Sewall's biography notes how the Med case warned traveling slaveholders to change their strategies: "Masters coming into Massachusetts with their slaves tried to evade proof of ownership, or were prepared to set up as a defence that their charges were willing to return."[58]

But Justice Shaw denied that a young child had the capacity to make such decisions: "In point of law, a child of such tender years has no will, no power of judging or electing; and therefore his will and choice are to be wholly disregarded. The natural and strong feelings of a child, which induce him to cling instinctively to those whom he has been accustomed to regard as his natural protectors, cannot be regarded as the exercise of a legal will, or of an excellent choice."[59]

The Massachusetts Anti-Slavery Society praised Shaw's decision and its clarification of the position of children in freedom suits:

> The Supreme Court of Massachusetts, to its honor be it told, has made an advance the past year on the decision in the Med case, and that in regard to a point of considerable practical importance. Nothing is more common than for the wives of slaveholders to bring with them from the South young slaves,

as attendants during their Northern tours. In the case of Commonwealth vs. Taylor... which was the case of a child eight years old, brought into the State by Mrs. Taylor, with the consent of its master, and whom she intended to carry back to Arkansas, if the child should consent, the Court held, "that the consent of so young a child would not authorize his removal into slavery, and ordered him to be delivered to the guardians who had been appointed for him by the Judge of Probate under the revised statutes." The Judge of Probate may appoint such guardians for all under fourteen years of age; and as the Supreme Court appears to have considered his having exercised this right as an important feature of the case, the question may probably be considered settled for all under that age, who shall be claimed as slaves.[60]

In other words, Shaw established fourteen as the age of capacity for consent; younger children would have guardians consent for them. The implication, of course, was that no guardian would ever send a child back to slavery.

A footnote by an unidentified writer in the *Monthly Law Reporter* suggests that Anson did not agree with his guardian's decision:

> Upon declaring the opinion of the court, the person who had been for the custody and appearance of the child, from day to day, was directed to deliver him up to one of the persons named as guardian, who was then in court; when a scene of most painful interest occurred. The boy, who was about ten years old, had, during several successive days, been apparently an unconcerned spectator of the proceedings before the court. He seemed to be a bright, intelligent child, and remarkably cheerful and happy while with his bail. His former owner was also in court at the time the opinion was given. But the moment the child understood that he was to be given up to his new guardian, to remain here, he broke out into most impassioned entreaties to be permitted to go back and see his father and mother and brothers and sisters, weeping bitterly, and pleading with his guardian to let him go. The business of the court was suspended, while the child was led away, shrieking and begging to be suffered to go back to his father and mother.[61]

The dramatic reactions described here form a striking contrast to the legal language of the body of the report. We can only wonder about Med's reaction to her emancipation: the two pamphlets about her case give no indication of her presence in court or her response to the ruling. But the impact on her life was the same, as Edlie Wong notes: "Med and Anson were required to forgo their kin ties to be remade into free northern children."[62]

The Med case was intended to "disinter" and clarify the law of freedom in Massachusetts, and the freedom suit scenario provided the paradigm for events. But the results were complicated, as shown by the subsequent cases involving children. Was there an "age of reason" that would allow children to choose their own fates? And what if they "chose" slavery, which seemed wildly irrational to the abolitionists in addition to being terrible public relations for the cause? The abolitionists did not understand that the power of family ties meant that the "simple" choice between slavery and freedom was anything but. And they did not anticipate that the great writ might be turned against the abolitionist forces. In all, the post-Med cases were a chaotic disappointment: Emma was hidden from the court yet was alleged to have consented to slavery by her cheerful demeanor; Rose chose to return south to her family; Anson was judged too young to decide, but was reportedly devastated by his freedom; Anne's "rescuers" were charged with kidnapping, as were Elizabeth's, and it was never determined to the satisfaction of the community whether Elizabeth were truly free. In the midst of it all, Med's death seemed to have no impact on the abolitionists' legal strategies, and the meaning of freedom for emancipated children remained unsettled.

CHAPTER 4

Maria Sommersett, the American Stewart, and Dred Scott

MARIA SOMMERSETT

Commemorating Med

Shortly after the courtroom victory, the Boston Female Anti-Slavery Society (BFASS) renamed Med "Maria Sommersett." This renaming was chiefly ceremonial and symbolic: it honored her "Uncle Somerset," whose precedent made her freedom possible. The name also honored her "new mothers"— Lydia Maria Child and Maria Weston Chapman—who had spearheaded the case. This renaming was the first step toward her eventual erasure; while it was common for emancipated people to choose new names, in this case, her name was chosen for her. There seemed to be no recognition of the parallel between slavers and abolitionists renaming someone else's child. In addition to renaming Med after the petitioner in the landmark decision, BFASS also compared the lead attorney and judge in her case with their counterparts in the English precedent. As the BFASS annual report proclaimed, "The time is at hand, when even the south, will honor the names of Ellis Gray Loring and Chief Justice Shaw, as they are now honored by all who reverence the worthy memories of Granville Sharp and of Lord Mansfield."[1] These parallels placed Med's case firmly in the tradition of Anglo-American free soil and recast legal men as the driving actors in the freedom suit scenario.

By renaming Med, the moral geography of England so central to the *Somerset* case became inscribed in Med's civil identity and in the identity of New England as well. While the assertion of free soil and pure air was central to vernacular legal arguments, it also fulfilled an important "ego-function" in that antislavery advocates affirmed their own identities at the same time as they addressed external audiences. In other words, moral geography and free soil were as much about the abolitionists as about the enslaved people themselves. "Slaves cannot breathe in England" because of the superior national character; by rejecting slavery, audiences might affirm their own position of moral authority and self-worth. Poet William Cowper's phrasing is striking: it is about creating a space that is moral—that is, free from slavery—but not multiracial. There are no black people in this image and certainly little concern about that fraught and difficult transition from slavery to freedom. Cowper's claim that "They touch our country, and their shackles fall" is compelling but profoundly misleading. Emancipation is a process not easily accomplished by the crossing of a border. This expression of moral geography adopted by Boston abolitionists negated the local experience of slavery, and this assertion of New England as a free place always functioned to shirk responsibility for real people.[2]

In addition to renaming Med after her key legal precedent, BFASS proclaimed August 26, the date of the Med ruling, as an antislavery milestone: "The Patriot should henceforth keep the 26th of August as a holiday. A law of mercy belonged to Massachusetts, and until that day, she was ignorant of it. It was dead, but is now alive. It was lost but is now found." Just as the father of the prodigal son rejoiced in his son's return in the gospel of Luke, on August 26 abolitionists would celebrate the restoration of Massachusetts's revolutionary values.[3]

December 22, the date the Pilgrims were said to have landed at Plymouth in 1620, became another important date for antislavery commemorations. BFASS held its third annual Anti-Slavery Fair on December 22, 1836.[4] Child reported in the *Liberator* that "The choice of that day was accidental; but it was a pleasant and appropriate manner of celebrating the Anniversary of the Pilgrims.... Around the Hall was placed in large letters the motto: 'On this day did our FATHERS *land* on the ROCK OF FREEDOM; let us *stand* firmly on this Rock.'" Plymouth Rock had powerful symbolic meaning for New Englanders, despite the dubious tradition of the Pilgrim landing, and it also became an important site for the free soil of New England. The motto was also an unmistakable allusion to the gospel of Matthew: "Upon this rock I will build my church, and the gates of the netherworld shall not prevail against it."[5] Plymouth Rock, in this schema, was a foundation for democracy and for the Christian character of New England. This "gospel ground" was as much a part of New England's moral geography as its free soil.

In her account of the fair, Child went on to describe the Med case as both a step forward in the cause of human freedom and as a return to the historical values of Massachusetts. At the fair, BFASS sold special Med work-bags as part of the celebration of free soil. These kinds of work-bags were typically made of silk that had been professionally stamped with abolitionist images and texts; they would then be cut out and assembled by antislavery volunteers.[6] They were used to carry embroidery or knitting projects, and they were often filled with antislavery literature for purchasers to read and distribute. While no extant examples of the Med work-bags have been found, Child wrote a detailed description:

> Work-bags were manufactured in commemoration of little Med's case, decided by Judge Shaw, in a manner so honorable to himself and his country. On one side was the representation of a Slave kneeling before the figure of Justice; underneath, these sentences were printed in golden letters: 'Slavery was abolished in Massachusetts, by the adoption of the Bill of Rights as a part of the Constitution, A.D. 1780.' Slavery says of this law, 'Lo, 'tis cold and dead, and will not harm me.' Anti-Slavery replies, 'But with my breath I can revive it!' Then follows, 'The adjudication on the case of a slave brought into Massachusetts from another State, fifty-six years afterward, Aug. 26, A.D. 1836.'[7]

It is interesting that the bag made "in commemoration of little Med's case" did not incorporate her name or image, instead relying on the familiar image of the kneeling slave. Using stock plates for the imagery may have been a matter of efficiency and cost-savings, but it is telling that even the new text seems to negate Med. Rather than referring to "the case of the slave-child, Med," as BFASS did in other places, the case is generically described as "the case of a slave brought into Massachusetts from another State."

The work-bag displayed the new antislavery historiography, establishing 1780 as the date slavery ended in Massachusetts. Justice Shaw had been less certain about the exact date and method, and he had acknowledged the complexities of the timeline in his Med ruling: "How, or by what act particularly, slavery was abolished in Massachusetts, whether by the adoption of the opinion in Sommersett's case, as a declaration and modification of the common law, or by the Declaration of Independence, or by the Constitution of 1780, it is not now very easy to determine, and it is rather a matter of curiosity than of utility; it being agreed on all hands that if not abolished before, it was so by the declaration of rights."[8]

In Child's description, the reverse side of the work-bag firmly links the Med ruling to this revolutionary legacy. It featured the Massachusetts coat of arms above the following verses:

> Old Massachusetts yet
> Retains her earlier fires!
> Still on our hills are set
> The altars of our sires!
>
> Our 'fierce democracies'
> Have yet their strength unshorn!
> And giant power shall see
> Its Gaza-gates uptorn.
>   *August 26, A.D. 1836*[9]

These lines are an excerpt from John Greenleaf Whittier's encomium, "To George Bancroft, Esq. Author of the Worcester Democratic Address." The poem praises Bancroft's speech on behalf of the poor and the enslaved, drawing a tight connection between the oppression of the poor and the practice of slavery, which will be countered by the revolutionary values of Massachusetts. In a jarring shift from Revolutionary fervor to Old Testament wrath, Whittier here compares American democracy to the biblical Samson, who tore down the gates of Gaza before the Philistines cut his hair, thereby sapping his superhuman strength.[10] The implication, perhaps, is that American democracy remains strong, despite its vulnerabilities.

It was thus as descendants of pilgrims and patriots that the BFASS women celebrated both Med's own freedom and the potential of her precedent in their annual report. At the same time, they omitted her name in yet another move toward her erasure: "Those who simply are moved with pity for the poor child, will rejoice that she is unfettered and may drink freely of the fountain of Life. A more enlarged philanthropy will see in this event the safety and freedom, of all colored persons, who may hereafter be brought hither by slaveholders, and their joy will be unspeakable."[11] In other words, BFASS saw Med's case as both a tactical and strategic success: Med was free, and the ruling would prevent Southerners from bringing enslaved people to Massachusetts in the future. But with the repeated omission of her name, we find the erasure of her personhood and her reality as a dependent child.

The neglect of Med's needs as a newly emancipated child was surely a factor in her early death. While Med's case was initially framed as a milestone in antislavery history, her death in the Samaritan Asylum less than two years later brought an immediate end to the celebrations. Med's death disrupted the triumphant narrative: free soil did not live up to its promise; her death had no heroic meaning; and the protectors of children had failed miserably.

Erasing Med

The abolitionists had already started omitting Med's name from her own narrative, and her death accelerated her erasure. Her passing was not publicly mourned as a "good and holy death," the kind commonly found in the genre of elegiacal writing at the time.[12] No one talked about her as being with God or as offering a spiritual example. No one talked about her at all.

It is interesting to note that there was no attempt to frame Med as a Christlike figure whose sacrifice for others should be honored. Med was not Little Eva, Harriet Beecher Stowe's iconic character from *Uncle Tom's Cabin*, the child too good for this world who inspires all to live a Christian life. The Med story, as framed by the freedom suit scenario, was supposed to be about her new life in northern freedom, and her untimely death ruined the plot. As a result, there is no deathbed scene, like Little Eva's, in which Med proclaims her joy at seeing God and inspires witnesses to renew their faith. Med was also no Uncle Tom, the enslaved man who willingly sacrifices himself for the enslaved people on the Shelby and Legree plantations and inspires his young enslaver to free the people he had claimed as property. Stowe thus makes Christ figures out of a little white girl who transcends the racism of her society and an enslaved man who dies rather than harm others. For BFASS, the death of a newly freed black girl had no meaning beyond their failure: her death only strengthened the proslavery position and had to be silenced.

In *Uncle Tom's Cabin*, we might also gain insight into BFASS's actions through the character of Miss Ophelia. She hails from New England and exemplifies the kind of inept parenting demonstrated by the BFASS women: they are all supportive of antislavery missionary work in theory, but their engagement falls far short in practice. Christian love and childrearing require hands-on relationships. Miss Ophelia tries to "educate" the enslaved Topsy as a reluctant duty, but her racism keeps her from loving the child. Topsy senses Miss Ophelia's aversion to her: "She can't bar me, . . . she'd 's as soon have a toad touch her!" There can be no real freedom for Topsy (or Med) without

Christian love and maternal care, which are sacrificed to prejudice and political strategy. In the novel, Miss Ophelia learns Christian love from Eva, and by her death she is transformed and able to offer Topsy the love and nurture she needs. "I can love you; I do, and I'll try to help you to grow up a good Christian girl."[13] The BFASS women are not willing or able to learn these lessons, and Med's passing speaks volumes about the limits of antislavery.

In the world of Uncle Tom's Cabin, as American studies scholar Karen Sánchez-Eppler explains, Stowe used "bereavement ... as the means of forging a sympathetic connection with both the lives of slaves and the lives of her readers."[14] The death of a child created compelling connections among mothers of all races. But the reactions to Med's death did not create sympathy or unite the antislavery community in its bereavement. There was only defensiveness toward suggestions that they had made a mistake and that by freeing Med they had caused her death. The fact that Justice Shaw, whose ruling changed the course of Med's life, was surprised to learn about her death reveals how quiet the abolitionists were about this matter. There was no obituary, and while Ellis Gray Loring eventually planned a gravestone five months later, the location of her grave remains unknown.

The silence surrounding Med's death was even more glaring when we consider that another child who died too young on Beacon Hill was memorialized in a spiritual biography by African American abolitionist and BFASS member Susan Paul. The free-born James Jackson lived on Butolph Street, just one block perpendicular to the Aves house on Pinckney Street. In her 1835 *Memoir of James Jackson, the attentive and obedient scholar, who died in Boston, October 31, 1833, aged six years and eleven months*, Paul hoped that her deceased student's model life might "do something towards breaking down that unholy prejudice which exists against color."[15]

Jackson's biography is an unusual book, and African American studies scholar Lois Brown suggests why there are so few texts of this kind: "The dearth of published eulogies and memoirs about African Americans is explained in part by the fact that antislavery sentiment could be aroused more effectively by reports of black Americans who died gruesome deaths.... The antislavery press regularly published articles about individuals who died in the South at the hands of mercenary over-seers, diabolical owners, or slave catchers who pursued them when they fled north."[16]

Brown's insights perhaps partially explain the absence of an obituary or biographical sketch for Med: an emancipated child who died in northern freedom did not advance the cause. But there may be an additional reason: perhaps there was no sketch because no one took the trouble to get to know her. We have no quotations from Med and no description of her physical appearance or personality. We do not know what food she liked or if she asked for her mother and siblings. We do not know if she was learning to read or liked to play with the other children.

We also lack insight from the people back in New Orleans who knew her best. We do not know if Med's family and the Slaters ever learned about her death, and, if they did, we can only speculate about their reactions. Did Med's mother resent the abolitionists who kept her daughter from returning to New Orleans? Was she comforted by the thought of her daughter in heaven? Did Med's death prove the Slaters' contention that she would have been better off with them in New Orleans?

THE "AMERICAN STEWART" AND THE TEXAS TROUBLES

If Med was the "American Somerset," then it followed that Samuel Slater was the "American Stewart," the enslaver on the losing side of the slave transit ruling. In many ways, Slater's history is also about slave transit. His life was a continuous series of moves between free and slave territories: his residences included Massachusetts, New York, Pennsylvania, Missouri, Illinois, Louisiana, and Texas. Slater, a native New Englander who moved South and claimed people as property, complicates the moral geography of the "Free North" and the "Slave South." Slater's name is not well known, perhaps in part because he was home in New Orleans during the case; it was his father-in-law, Thomas Aves, who represented his interests and whose name appears in the case title.

Like the Boston abolitionists, the Slaters also seemed to forget Med after the ruling. At the very least, they accepted the futility of further legal action as they returned to a private life with their two sons in New Orleans, where they lived until 1839. Glimpses of their life can be found in the historical record. The 1838 New Orleans city directory lists Samuel Slater as a commission merchant, and he also makes occasional appearances in the Historical Notaries' Indexes in New Orleans.[17] Between 1837 and 1839, he sold at least five enslaved people, perhaps in preparation for his 1839 move to Texas. We can only wonder if Med's mother and siblings were among those sold. We also know that he bought land in Texas, and he is listed in Texas tax records.

After the family moved to Galveston in the independent Republic of Texas, he worked at least part-time as a bookkeeper in the U.S. Custom House.[18] The Slaters had seven more children while living in Texas, and all nine of their children survived to adulthood.

We do not know anything specific about Slater's career as a customs bookkeeper in Galveston, but we can surmise that he would have been witness to the rampant illegal foreign slave trade in the Republic of Texas. Given his previous trading experience in New Orleans and Havana, it is not unimaginable that he had some involvement. After the slave trade had been outlawed by the United States in 1808, Galveston in particular became a "hub for foreign traffic." This would change following the annexation of Texas by the United States, which turned the illegal international trade between Texas and the United States into a legal domestic trade, but, as historian Adam Rothman notes, "from the 1820s to the 1840s Texas was a hotbed of slave smuggling, especially of slaves from Louisiana and Cuba."[19]

Circumstances might have changed for the Slaters after Texas became a state at the end of 1845, and we might speculate that the changing political winds put Slater out of a job and led him to sell some extensive land holdings.[20] He may also have moved on from Galveston because of his reportedly failing health. By 1848 the family had moved to ten thousand acres in Henderson County.[21]

After twelve years in Henderson County, Slater was ready for another move: he sold most of his land and planned to move near a railroad. In August 1860, he went to the town of Tyler, Texas, in neighboring Smith County in order to conduct some final business and "found the people greatly excited by the news of the general elections and the success of the Republican party." To his surprise, he "was told by a friend that the Vigilance Committee was trying to find something out against him, that it had been reported he was about leaving the country, and would take a great many negroes with him."[22] Slater was caught up in the "Texas Troubles," the slave insurrection panic of 1860 that would sacrifice an estimated thirty to one hundred lives to vigilante justice and would contribute to the secession movement throughout the South.

The summer of 1860 brought record heat and an extended drought to Texas. On July 8, fires broke out in Dallas, Denton, and a dozen other communities in North Texas. At first the fires were attributed to the extreme temperatures and the new phosphorous matches, which were prone to spontaneous combustion in hot weather. But as the days passed, rumors of an abolitionist conspiracy spread, and the details of the supposed plot were revealed following the interrogation of more than one hundred local enslaved people during the next two weeks. The alleged abolitionists, described as white northerners hiding in plain sight, were said to be planning to devastate North Texas by fire and poison in preparation for a large-scale slave insurrection on the state Election Day, August 6. Election Day passed without incident, but this still did not calm the fears of the white population, who credited their own vigilance for defeating the suspected plot.[23]

The alleged insurrection was investigated by community-elected vigilance committees outside the justice system. In this perceived state of emergency, the speed with which these committees could dispense justice was seen as advantageous, despite the fact that they suspended constitutional rights in order to do so. And while Texas courts did not permit black testimony against white defendants, the extralegal route meant that black testimony would be admissible, which was important because almost all the "evidence" came from the torture of enslaved African Americans. The vigilance committees also focused on finding the secret abolitionists in their midst: "identifying and rooting out white abolitionists became a mania in some parts of the state," as historian Donald Reynolds notes, "and immigrants from northern states often were considered guilty of harboring anti-slavery principles unless they could prove otherwise."[24]

It was in this climate that Slater drew the attention of the Tyler vigilance committee:

> They cited him to appear at the court house. He did so, and found there about forty men, self elected jurors. There was no charge made against Mr. Slater and of course no witnesses, but a little lawyer said: "I'll fix him!" and the trial began. After questioning him some time about where he was born, and the different places he had lived before coming to Texas, they dispatched two men twenty-five miles to search his house for abolition documents, keeping him under guard at Tyler during the time. The two men returned next day with large bundles of the New York Observer, which they called those abolition documents.[25]

In actuality, the *New York Observer* was a conservative Presbyterian newspaper that espoused traditional Calvinist orthodoxy and the preservation of the Union. It would oppose the Emancipation Proclamation, and only converted to antislavery several years into the war.[26] Possession of this newspaper in 1860 was hardly evidence of abolitionist sympathy, but in this heated atmosphere, all northerners and all northern publications were suspect.

In this sham vigilante trial without formal charges, rules of evidence, or first-hand witnesses, Slater was inevitably found guilty, but he was saved by a group of local friends:

> The trial was opened next day, and a Methodist preacher, whom Mr. S. considered his friend, and who secretly was one, was called on to testify. He stated that a third person had told him that Mr. Slater was an abolitionist, and he believed it. This settled the question. The trial closed and he was sent to the Vigilance committee of his own county for punishment, but before arriving at his destination the guard told him of a plan they had formed for his escape. A man who owed Mr. Slater met them at this point and paid him five hundred dollars, besides giving him a good mule to make out his team. He found his wife had made all preparations, and they started Aug. 17, 1860, and traveled ten miles through the woods that night. One of the guard told Mrs. Slater that the committee would have hung her husband the first day had it not been for the Methodist minister, who only testified against Mr. S. to save his own life, and was secretly doing all he could to save Mr. Slater. Some of the guard traveled with them two days and then returned.[27]

The Slater family made their escape on August 17, 1860, twenty-four years to the day after Med had been produced in court by the Boston deputy sheriff. They fled to Alton, Illinois, arriving at long last in October. Other people, such as the Northern Methodist minister Reverend Anthony Bewley, were not as lucky. He was chased all the way to Missouri by a posse and brought back to Texas to be executed for his alleged leadership in the plot. By September, it was clear that there had been no conspiracy and that the men who were hanged were not abolitionist spies but mostly poor migrants to the area, with nothing in common besides their northern origins. At least thirty black and white men were executed based on coerced testimony from enslaved people, and some estimates suggest that the number of victims may be as high as one hundred.[28]

Slater was an outlier in terms of the demographic profiles of the accused. Despite his thirty years' residence in the South, twenty-one of which were spent in Texas, in the eyes of the vigilance committee, he remained a northerner and an outsider. No one remembered his role as the respondent in the landmark *Commonwealth v. Aves*, which might have served as a defense of sorts against charges of abolitionism. Whether Slater had undergone a conversion on the question of slavery or had continued to support slavery is unknown.

In any case, the Texas Troubles almost cost Slater his life, and, on a national level, they had a dramatic effect on political debates in Louisiana, Georgia, and Alabama, where there was significant resistance to secession. The insurrection panic was used to promote the secessionist cause, as Donald Reynolds concludes: "Shrewdly playing upon the public's fears and anxieties, secessionist editors and politicians were able to parlay the fires of July 8 into a psychological conflagration that became the most widespread—and most disastrous—mass panic in southern history."[29]

During the Civil War, Slater served in the Quartermaster Department of the U.S. Army and then worked as a mail agent. In 1868, he bought a farm in Bates County, Missouri, where he and his wife Mary are buried. Slater is now long forgotten, and the memory of his role in the Med case and the Texas Troubles, two watershed moments in the history of U.S. slavery, has fallen into obscurity.[30]

DRED SCOTT AND MED REVISITED

In 1850s Boston, the Med case briefly re-entered political discourse as the city grappled with the impact of the Fugitive Slave Act and the *Dred Scott* decision.

Jane Johnson

In January 1856, Maria Weston Chapman reported with great excitement that the formerly enslaved Jane Johnson had attended the Twenty-Second National Anti-Slavery Bazaar in Boston. Johnson was a national celebrity after her slave transit case in Pennsylvania the previous year. She had claimed her freedom while traveling with her enslaver, Colonel John H. Wheeler of North Carolina, minister to Nicaragua, and her two sons, Daniel and Isaiah. They were headed to New York to catch a ship to Nicaragua, but while in Philadelphia, Johnson got word to the Pennsylvania Abolition Society (PAS) that she wished to claim her freedom. PAS Vigilance Committee leaders William Still and Passmore Williamson, along with five black dockworkers, met the party at their departing ferry, explained that under the laws of Pennsylvania Johnson and her sons were free, and helped them flee to a waiting carriage. Wheeler was quick to pursue legal remedies, and Williamson was summoned with a writ of habeas corpus by a federal judge to produce Johnson and her sons in court. Williamson truthfully denied knowing their whereabouts, but, nevertheless, he was jailed for contempt of court. The story then became a national sensation, and in addition to the contempt charges, Williamson and the dockworkers were charged with riot and assault and battery. Johnson testified at their trial as a surprise witness at great personal risk, given that federal marshals wished to arrest her. Critics contended that federal judge John Kintzing Kane was flouting Pennsylvania law in order to defend slavery in a free state and that there was no role for the federal government given that Johnson was not a fugitive. After three months of mounting pressure, Judge Kane finally cleared Williamson of contempt charges and set him free. Johnson, in the meantime, had settled in Boston and was welcomed by the antislavery community with great enthusiasm.[31]

Chapman and the former BFASS members (the organization having dissolved in 1840) claimed credit for this success and the warm welcome Johnson received in Boston: "All our friends present thronged round to welcome and thank her—the strong-hearted woman, who, amid the thousand paralyzing influences a slave-holding nation brings to bear upon its victims, took advantage of the decision we procured on the 'Med case,' in 1836, and claimed her freedom under it."[32] After almost twenty years of silence, Chapman here mentioned Med in the context of another famous transit case. This case was easier to celebrate, of course: Johnson was an adult woman who exercised her own will and acted on behalf of her children. It is remarkable that decades of reflection still did not lead to any acknowledgment of Med's death. Johnson's presence at the fair was living proof of abolitionist impact, and Med's death remained unspoken. The celebration was short-lived, however, as Johnson's case would soon be followed by the Supreme Court's ruling on the most famous slave transit case in U.S. legal history.

Dred Scott

Dred Scott and Med were both purchased around 1833, and they both entered history when they traveled into free jurisdictions. Dr. John Emerson, a U.S. Army surgeon, purchased Scott in St. Louis before being transferred to the Rock Island Arsenal in the free state of Illinois. During the pivotal month of May 1836, little Med left New Orleans for Boston with Mary

Aves Slater, and the forty-year-old Scott moved again with Emerson to Fort Snelling in free Wisconsin Territory (present-day Minnesota). It was there he would meet his wife, Harriet Robinson, who had already spent ten years in this free territory with her enslaver, Major Lawrence Taliaferro, the U.S. Indian Agent for the Upper Mississippi region. She married Scott soon after his arrival, when she was about seventeen. These residences in free jurisdictions would shape their legal destiny, as historian Adam Arenson explains: "These moves made the case: Scott had been brought into a state and then a federal territory where slavery was prohibited."[33]

The Scotts would sue on the basis of this residence in free territory in 1846, ten years after Med's case. They had every expectation of success, based on three decades of legal precedents in which Missouri courts freed over two hundred enslaved people under similar circumstances. In fact, the state court did free Scott in a second trial after confusion about ownership in the first trial "produced the absurd effect of allowing Mrs. Emerson to keep her slaves simply because no one had proved that they *were* her slaves." But on appeal, in the 1852 *Scott v. Emerson*, the Missouri Supreme Court reversed the decision, claiming that Missouri had no obligation to honor the laws of other states and overturning precedent by claiming that the times had changed. After six years of litigation, Scott's case then headed for the U.S. Supreme Court.[34] It is worth noting that while Med's entire legal proceedings, from writ to ruling, took place in a crisp eleven days, Scott's legal odyssey would last for eleven years. It is also important to note that while the case bears his name only, it also included Harriet Robinson Scott and their two daughters, Eliza and Lizzie, who spent their entire childhoods in the shadow of this case.[35]

The 241-page Supreme Court ruling has puzzled readers since 1857. As historian Don Fehrenbacher notes in his classic study of the case, "Only one thing was absolutely certain. Dred Scott had lost his eleven-year battle for freedom in the last court of appeal. Seven of the nine justices agreed that at law he was still a slave." The case is also remembered for Chief Justice Robert B. Taney's infamous ruling that African Americans were not citizens of the United States, which meant that Dred Scott had no standing to sue in federal court under the diversity of citizenship clause of the Constitution, the provision that allows litigation between citizens of different states. He also ruled that the Missouri Compromise of 1820 was unconstitutional because Congress had no power to prohibit slavery in the territories. This meant that Scott had *not* become a free man during his time in Wisconsin Territory.

In addition, Taney contended that Scott did not gain his freedom by his residence in the free state of Illinois either, because his status depended on Missouri law after his return.[36]

In some ways, the larger slave transit issue—the status of an enslaved person in a free jurisdiction—was not the primary topic of the opinion, since Taney contended that Scott had no standing and that "free territory" was unconstitutional, but these issues did get more substantial treatment in the concurring and dissenting opinions.

In the four concurring opinions by Justices Samuel Nelson, John Catron, John Campbell, and Peter Daniel, the question of whether Dred Scott's residence in free territory was temporary or permanent took on some significance, although there was hardly a definitive conclusion. Justice Nelson argued that an army officer's residence was temporary by definition, but he also then had to grapple with what Fehrenbacher calls the "embarrassing precedent of *Rachel v. Walker*, in which the Missouri supreme court had freed a slave held, like Dred Scott, in free territory by an army officer." Having painted himself into a corner, Nelson simply dropped the point and later concluded: "The question we think too plain to require argument." Justice Catron seemed to return to the old regional compromise in which domicile meant emancipation, while temporary residence did not: "Unless the master becomes an inhabitant of that State, the slaves he takes there do not acquire their freedom; and if they return with their master to the slave State of his domicil, they cannot assert their freedom after their return."[37] In other words, Justice Catron rejected the *Aves* ruling, which gave enslaved people in free jurisdictions for any length of time the chance to claim their freedom.

The concurring opinions also insisted that *Grace* ("reattachment"), the case that denied an enslaved woman's freedom after her return to Antigua from England, rather than *Somerset* ("once free, forever free") was the more relevant precedent. Justice Nelson cited correspondence between Lord Stowell, the judge in the *Slave, Grace* case, and Supreme Court Justice Joseph Story, as evidence. In an exchange of letters in 1828, Story assured Stowell that he agreed with this ruling: "In my native state, (Massachusetts) the state of slavery is not recognized as legal; and yet, if a slave should come hither, and afterwards return to his own home, we should certainly think the local law would re-attach upon him, and that his servile character would be reintegrated."[38] Justices Campbell and Daniel also attacked *Somerset* and upheld *Grace* as the relevant precedent. For Justice Campbell, the *Dred Scott* and

Grace cases were the same, which meant that "reattachment" applied here: "There is no distinguishable difference between the case before us and that determined in the admiralty of Great Britain."³⁹ Justice Daniel agreed that *Grace* was the relevant precedent and that *Somerset* "must be considered as having been overruled by the lucid and able opinion of Lord Stowell in the more recent case of the slave Grace."⁴⁰

These positions were puzzling, as Fehrenbacher notes, because the *Dred Scott* "suit had been based on an assumption of permanent residence in Illinois, while the principal decisions cited against him, such as *Grace* and *Strader*, dealt with instances of temporary residence." Legal historian Paul Finkelman explains the significance of the *Strader* case, heard first in Kentucky and then by the U.S. Supreme Court in 1851: "It became the first major slave-state opinion to support the right of a master voluntarily to employ his slaves in a free state for a short time, and then return to a slave state, where they would remain slaves. As a federal case, *Strader* was used, or perhaps misused, by the United States Supreme Court as a precedent for its decision in *Dred Scott v. Sandford* (1857)." In all, Fehrenbacher concludes, the concurring opinions offered "no authoritative ruling on whether Scott's residence in Illinois was temporary or permanent, and none on whether it made any difference one way or the other."⁴¹

The case is also remembered for Justice Benjamin Robbins Curtis's powerful dissent. With remarkable historical irony, the same young lawyer who had argued against Med's freedom now found himself siding with Dred Scott and sparring with Chief Justice Taney on the issues of citizenship and the Missouri Compromise. The case turned into a family affair, as American studies scholar Albert J. von Frank explains: his brother George Ticknor Curtis was brought in as part of Scott's defense team to argue "the constitutionality of the Missouri Compromise and the power of Congress to determine questions of slavery and freedom in the territories." George T. Curtis was no abolitionist and was known for supporting the enforcement of the Fugitive Slave Act as U.S. Commissioner in Boston. It was seen as strategic to bring in a conservative lawyer given the makeup of the court.⁴²

Justice Curtis tackled the two main contentions of the Taney ruling head on: "I dissent ... from that part of the opinion of the majority of the court, in which it is held that a person of African descent cannot be a citizen of the United States; and I regret I must go further, and dissent both from what I deem their assumption of authority to examine the Constitutionality of the act of Congress commonly called the Missouri compromise act, and the grounds and conclusions announced in their opinion." His rhetoric soon became even more provocative: "I do not hold any opinion of this court, or any court, binding, when expressed on a question not legitimately before it."[43] While Curtis never used the term *obiter dictum*, a judge's incidental expression of opinion, not essential to the decision and not establishing precedent, many Republicans did and contended that the Taney opinion was out of bounds for "reviewing the Dred Scott case on its merits after having decided that the federal courts had no jurisdiction."[44] In Curtis's opinion, the Court could not have it both ways; that is, it could not deny Scott's standing *and* weigh the merits of the case, but, nevertheless, he felt compelled to respond to the entire ruling.

Curtis argued that the descendants of enslaved Africans were indeed citizens of the United States, basing his conclusion "largely on a historical inquiry into who qualified for citizenship when the Constitution was adopted."[45] Here he cited *Commonwealth v. Aves*, the case he had lost back in 1836, to demonstrate that Taney's Massachusetts history was simply wrong and "would be received with surprise by the people of that State, who know their own political history." Contrary to Taney's claims, Curtis countered, "It is true, beyond all controversy, that persons of color, descended from African slaves, were by that Constitution made citizens of the State; and such of them as have had the necessary qualifications, have held and exercised the elective franchise, as citizens, from that time to the present. (See Com. v. Aves, 18 Pick. R., 210.)"[46]

On the issue of slavery in the territories, Curtis interpreted the "territory clause broadly as an express and plenary delegation of power to govern," and noted that he and the majority actually agreed that Congress had the power to govern the territories. The point of disagreement was whether slavery formed an exception to this power. Taney had additionally argued that slave property was protected by due process, but Curtis countered that slavery was not protected and relied on the *Somerset* doctrine requiring positive law. It is interesting to see Curtis use natural law as a basis for the law of slavery here—in the Med case and fugitive cases, he argued that natural rights were not a basis for law—but here he seemed comfortable making a natural rights argument. Curtis also denounced the Supreme Court's overreach: "On so grave a subject as this, I feel obliged to say that, in my opinion, such an exertion of judicial power transcends the limits of the authority of the court, as described by its repeated decisions, and, as I understand, acknowledged in this opinion of the majority of the court."[47]

In addition to his rebuttals to the main two points of the ruling regarding citizenship and the Missouri Compromise, Curtis also addressed Taney's arguments regarding the status of a slave in a free jurisdiction. Both Curtis and his fellow justice John McLean upheld the *Somerset* tradition and contended that Scott's permanent residence in free jurisdictions made him forever free; they rejected the idea that Scott's status "reattached" when he moved back to Missouri. They also contended that the refusal of comity and the claim that *Scott v. Emerson* was now the law of Missouri was simply wrong. Curtis boldly stated, "I do not feel at liberty to surrender my own convictions of what the law requires, to the authority of the decision in 15 Missouri Reports."[48]

Historian Paul Finkelman reminds us that "Although Taney's opinion is most remembered for its effect on slavery in the territories and its statement concerning black citizenship, the decision had profound implications for interstate comity and slave transit." Had the Civil War not occurred so soon after the decision, it is likely that these implications would be better remembered. Finkelman goes on to explain, "Lincoln, and other northerners, saw the *Dred Scott* decision as a first step toward a judicial nationalization of slavery. Such a decision would probably have come through cases involving slave transit or sojourn."[49] Justice Nelson's concurring opinion made it clear that he would welcome the opportunity to rule on "the right of the master with his slave of transit into or through a free State.... When that question arises, we shall be prepared to decide it."[50] Despite these serious threats at the national level, however, it was unlikely that the *Dred Scott* decision would be enforced in cases involving state law in New England.[51] Massachusetts would put this theory to the test just eight months later in *Betty's Case*.

In the meantime, the *Liberator* discussed the *Dred Scott* ruling and its implications for weeks, and William Lloyd Garrison led the way with a fiery protest:

> We are here to enter our indignant protest against the Dred Scott decision—against the infamous Fugitive Slave Law...—against the alarming aggressions of the Slave Power upon the rights of the people of the North—and especially against the existence of the slave system at the South.... We are here to declare that the men who, like Crispus Attucks, were ready to lay down their lives to secure American Independence, and the blessings of liberty... are not the men to be denied the claims of human nature, or the rights of citizenship.... Our work is before us. It is to disseminate light—to change public opinion—to

plead every man with his neighbor—to insist upon justice—to demand equal rights—to crush out slavery wherever it exists in the land. Let Massachusetts lead the van.[52]

It is telling that Garrison referenced Crispus Attucks, the African American man commonly regarded as the first victim of the Boston Massacre, in his first article about the decision. The following year, black activist and historian William Cooper Nell organized March Fifth commemorations, the anniversary of the Boston Massacre, beginning in 1858 and continuing through the Civil War. Given that the *Dred Scott* decision had been handed down on March 6, no one could miss the fact that the celebration of Attucks was also a protest of the *Dred Scott* ruling.[53]

Antislavery lawyer Samuel Sewall also lamented the decision: "The Supreme Court of the United States has just decided that a negro is not a citizen of the United States, and that Southern slaveholders can carry their slaves through the free States without making them free. I feel ashamed of living in a country where there is a such a contemptible President and judges." And he grudgingly gave credit where credit was due for the Curtis dissent: "Is it not remarkable that Judge Curtis has come out on the right side in a very able opinion, but with no more moral feeling than an iceberg? Still he deserves credit for what he has done."[54]

Justice Curtis was no favorite among antislavery forces in Boston, especially after his speech in support of the despised Fugitive Slave Act at an 1850 Constitutional Meeting in Faneuil Hall. And in 1855, two years prior to the *Dred Scott* case, abolitionist minister Theodore Parker had denounced Curtis in the context of the infamous Anthony Burns rendition in 1855. Parker and seven others were indicted for interfering with the arrest of Burns, a fugitive from slavery. The chaotic rescue attempt failed, and the subsequent rendition radicalized many Bostonians. Parker was to be tried under Justice Curtis on the U.S. Circuit Court, and Parker reminded Bostonians of Curtis's role during the Med case. The indictments were squashed on a technicality, but Parker published an extended, book-length version of his planned closing arguments.[55] In *The Trial of Theodore Parker*, he condemned his archenemy Curtis at great length and asserted that his proslavery position dated back to the Med case:

> Gentlemen, Mr. Curtis in 1836 contended for ... the right of the slaveholder to sit down at the foot of Bunker Hill monument with his slaves!

> The slave child Med, poor, fatherless, and unprotected, comes before the Supreme Court of Massachusetts, claiming her natural and unalienable Right to Liberty and the Pursuit of Happiness,—if not granted she is a slave forever. In behalf of her wealthy "owner" Mr. Curtis resists the girl's claim.[56]

For Parker, the Curtis dissent in *Dred Scott* did not make up for a career spent defending compromises with the slave power.

Scott and Med, despite the differences in their ages, agency, and legal journeys, had several remarkable parallels in their experiences. Benjamin Robbins Curtis would frame the legal debate, despite his presence on the losing side in both cases. Med became a test case for Massachusetts abolitionism, and Scott's case was also impacted by antislavery politics in the state. Through a complicated series of deaths and marriages, Scott ended up being enslaved by the Republican Massachusetts representative Calvin Chaffee, who hastily arranged for the manumission of the Scott family by a Missouri resident. Most significantly, freedom for both Med and Scott raised challenging questions: What did it mean to be the free child of an enslaved mother? What did it mean to be a free black man in the wake of the Taney decision denying black citizenship?[57] For both plaintiffs, freedom was complicated and contingent, and neither would have the chance to live out these questions. Like Med, Scott died less than two years after he gained his freedom.

Betty's Case

Eight months after the *Dred Scott* decision and twenty-one years after his Med decision, Justice Shaw ruled on *Betty's Case* in the Massachusetts Supreme Judicial Court. He was seventy-six years old and nearing retirement, and he wrote his decision in the first person, which was a departure from his usual practice. Maria Weston Chapman included the text of the ruling in the 1858 *Liberty Bell*, a gift annual published as a fundraiser for the Massachusetts Anti-Slavery Society. The entry featured the following headnote: "The friends of Freedom hail, as a happy augury, this judicial act of 1857, of the same righteous tribunal, by the same honored name that vindicated the law of Massachusetts, in 1836, in the case of the slave 'Med.' They see in it a strengthening of the dykes so lately tampered with by the Supreme Court of the United States."[58] For the second time in two years, Chapman referred to Med's case in the context of a current slave transit suit. Here, she suggests that Shaw was resisting the *Dred Scott* ruling, which she dismisses as judicial "tampering" by the Supreme Court.

In *Betty's Case*, the Supreme Judicial Court upheld the Med precedent, ruling that "a slave brought by his master into a free State has a right to stay with his master, or not, at his election, and if he elect to remain with his master, no one can interfere with him." Lucy S. Schuyler, of Lawrence, had petitioned for a writ of habeas corpus "setting forth that a colored woman, named Betty, was restrained of her liberty, at said Lawrence, by Sullivan Sweet and his wife." The Sweets' counsel responded that they were from Tennessee and "had been travelling with their servant Betty, in Canada and several of the Northern States, and for the last six weeks had been at Lawrence. That Betty had, during all this time, been aware that she was entitled to her liberty, and had been under no restraint; and that his clients were willing to abide by her choice."[59]

As he had done with so many other cases, Justice Shaw interviewed the enslaved person who was the subject of the case, in this instance the twenty-five-year-old Betty, privately to ascertain her wishes. He found her to be "intelligent" and "capable of judging for herself," and so he accepted her choice to stay with the Sweets and return to her husband in Tennessee. But he also made sure that there was a record of the proceedings for Betty's reference and potential future use should she change her mind about claiming freedom. While it always disappointed the abolitionists when an enslaved person in transit "chose" slavery, this time they celebrated that Shaw followed his own Med precedent rather than apply the new *Dred Scott* ruling, which would have denied any claim to freedom. "Shaw never mentioned that he was defying, or at the very least ignoring, the holding in *Dred Scott*," legal scholar Aviam Soifer explains, "though he clearly seemed to do so by considering whether Betty was free, and by asserting the authority of a Massachusetts court to be sufficient to deprive the Sweets of their property."[60]

The *Liberator* reprinted news coverage of the case, which offers additional details. The *Boston Herald* claimed that the writ was served because Betty expressed a strong desire to remain in the North, but that when she chose to return to Tennessee, antislavery people, black and white, begged her to stay. There were scenes of "intense excitement," such as when Mrs. Simon Grover, who had assisted in the case, "abandoned the case in disgust" when Betty seemed inclined to go back. The *Daily Advertiser* praised Justice Shaw for defying *Dred Scott*: Shaw's ruling "gives us strong ground for entertaining the belief that the monstrous doctrines said by some writers to be supported by the Dred Scott decision are not regarded as law by the Supreme Judicial

Court of Massachusetts. That tribunal expounds the doctrine, that except in the single case of fugitives . . . the free air of Massachusetts makes free all men and women who breathe it; and the freedom which they have thus once acquired, they can never lose, even when they return into a slave State."[61]

A few months later, the *Liberator* reported an exciting turn of events in a brief paragraph: "The Lawrence *American* says that the slave woman, Betty, whose case caused some little excitement in this city some few months ago, and who refused to accept her liberty, after returning with Mrs. Sweet to New York, suddenly left her mistress whom she loved so much, took passage upon the under-ground railroad, and safely escaped to Cincinnati, where she was joined by her husband, who is a free man."[62] We can only wonder about how this all came to pass, but it seems that Betty was able to achieve both freedom and family unity for herself outside of the freedom suit scenario.

While Justice Shaw earned praise for his apparent willingness to ignore the *Dred Scott* decision, he always enforced the Constitution and the Fugitive Slave Act of 1850, and his role in fugitive renditions in Boston was condemned by abolitionists. They were frustrated that Justice Shaw refused to issue a writ of habeas corpus on behalf of Shadrach Wilkins in February 1851, but in response to this judicial resistance, Wilkins was freed by a daring vigilante rescue. In order to prevent another fugitive rescue after the arrest of fugitive Thomas Sims in April 1851, the Court House was barricaded by iron chains, requiring court officials to duck under them in order to enter the building.[63] Abolitionist orator Wendell Phillips gave a scathing critique of Justice Shaw for this literal and symbolic obeisance to the slave power:

> Did he not know that he was making history that hour when the Chief Justice of the Commonwealth entered his own court bowing down like a criminal beneath a chain four feet from the soil? Did he not recollect he was the author of that decision which shall be remembered when every other case in Pickering's Reports is lost, declaring the slave Med a free woman the moment she set foot on the soil of Massachusetts, and that he owed more respect to himself and his own fame than to disgrace the ermine by passing beneath the chain?[64]

Shaw's critics did not sway his legal beliefs: he went on to deny the writ of habeas corpus for Sims and to defend the constitutionality of the Fugitive Slave Act. While Phillips's main claim was that Shaw tarnished his antislavery judicial legacy with his support of fugitive renditions, it is notable that Med was transformed into an adult in his account.

Phillips was not alone in this transformation: for Boston's abolitionists, Med's child martyr status remained too rhetorically untouchable and too historically unusable. Her story of free soil had to be reimagined, reframed, and fictionalized, and in each retelling, the child icon was replaced by an adult.

CHAPTER 5

Free Soil Fictions

Following the death of "the slave-child Med," Boston abolitionists turned to rebels and fugitives for their abolitionist icons. For example, Med's advocates defended the *Amistad* captives, who had rebelled off the coast of Cuba in 1839; established the Latimer Committee in defense of fugitive George Latimer in 1842; and aided fugitives from slavery after the passage of the Fugitive Slave Act in 1850. The free soil principle remained important to the cause, however, and so Med was replaced by adults in various "free soil fictions," thus avoiding all the rhetorical and practical complications of emancipated childhood.

In her 1840 story "Pinda: A True Tale," Maria Weston Chapman erased Med and chose the adult Pinda as a new abolitionist icon. Lydia Maria Child remained silent for decades about the Med case, but in her *Romance of the Republic* (1867), she offered a postbellum revision, in which an adult woman benefits from the Med precedent. While Chapman and Child struggled to exorcise Med's ghost with their accounts of successful slave transit claims by adults, author Herman Melville took the opposite approach in *White-Jacket* (1850), erasing the legal victory in *Commonwealth v. Fitzgerald*. In this 1842 case, Chief Justice Lemuel Shaw, Melville's father-in-law, had expanded the *Commonwealth v. Aves* decision on behalf of an enslaved sailor. Melville seemed to counter that the victorious freedom suits were also problematic for adults; that the answer to the slavery dilemma was not to be found in northern courts; and that consent and freedom under the law were all fictions. While for Chapman and Child, Med's tragedy could be corrected by replacing her with adults, Melville cautioned that even adult freedom is limited and contingent.¹

"PINDA: A TRUE TALE"

Chapman instructed readers about Med's legal legacy in her 1840 story "Pinda: A True Tale," which was published in the *National Anti-Slavery Standard* and the *Monthly Offering,* as well as in a twenty-three-page stand-alone pamphlet.² Chapman, in a sharp departure from her self-congratulatory discussion in the BFASS annual reports, exorcised the ghost of her namesake "Maria Med Sommersett" by anointing the adult Pinda as the new icon for abolitionism. Despite the fact that it was Med's case that made Pinda's freedom possible, the story of an adult avoided all the pitfalls of freedom suits involving children. Pinda could exercise consent, and when she chooses freedom, she supports herself and even contributes to the Massachusetts Anti-Slavery Society.

The story opens in 1836, the year of *Commonwealth v. Aves,* on board the ship *Eli Whitney,* about to sail from Boston Harbor to Savannah: an officer appears with a writ of habeas corpus filed on behalf of Pinda, an enslaved woman on board. Out of concern for her husband Abraham, she declines the legal action and returns to Savannah. While the abolitionists understand that "there might exist a thousand reasons" for this decision, "the proslavery press gleefully reports the case as evidence that slaves 'were wise enough to prefer slavery with their masters.'" Her husband urges her "to never lose another chance for freedom out of regard for me," and on a second trip North the following year, she plans to claim her freedom.³

During this second journey, her enslaver, Mr. Logan, attends the sixth annual meeting of the Massachusetts Anti-Slavery Society and challenges the group to convince him "that slaveholding was condemned by Scripture." After the usual exchange of biblical quotations for and against slavery, he uses Pinda's refusal of freedom as an example of the "felicity" of the enslaved. Some antislavery activists invite Mr. Logan to an evening tea party in the hopes of converting him to their cause; little did he know that his hosts were assisting Pinda and that she would be claim her rights during the said party. No formal legal action is needed: she simply packs her things and walks away. Persuasion and manipulation are the Logans' only remedies, but Pinda is too smart to fall for their threats. Pinda leads a self-sufficient, if lonely, life in Boston, and nineteen months later, the couple is reunited when Abraham escapes. Because their children have died, Abraham and Pinda can take comfort that they "have not left them in slavery." They plan to seek safety in Canada or Guiana, but before they depart, they pay their pledged weekly contribution to the Massachusetts Anti-Slavery Society in advance.[4]

While the story never mentions Med herself, it carefully defines the legal principles from her recent case. In the second paragraph, the story makes it clear that *Commonwealth v. Aves* is indeed the law of the land: "It was . . . an anxious moment for the friends of freedom . . . while they waited to learn the result of a legal process by which they offered to the poor slave-woman the freedom secured by the laws of Massachusetts to all slaves brought under its jurisdiction by their masters." "By their masters" is the key phrase; the story repeatedly reminds readers that the ruling does not apply to fugitive slaves. When Mr. Logan explains to his antislavery hosts how he had sent for Pinda, they note that "here was a case in which a slave might hereafter require their aid to prove her master's acknowledged agency in her transportation." In other words, they could bear witness that Pinda was not a fugitive from slavery and that her enslaver had brought her to free soil of his own volition. Abraham realizes the difference between their legal statuses, and so they plan to move to Canada or Guiana: "Aware that his own case differed from that of his wife, he being a fugitive, and she protected by the law in the enjoyment of her freedom, he laid his plans for safety with acuteness, and followed them out with steadiness."[5] Fugitives from slavery remain at risk in Massachusetts, as the story reminds readers: many antislavery battles remain for the enslaved and the "friends of freedom" on the streets of northern cities. The story also condemns the northern complicity with slavery, especially the financial ties and the failure of the clergy to condemn this most unchristian practice.

The story is based on the life of a real woman named Pinda, who was enslaved by a Mr. and Mrs. Hogan ("Logan" in the story); journal entries and letters among antislavery activists confirm the general outline of these events. Ellis Gray Loring's journal entry for March 27, 1838, revealed that he was the abolitionist host the night of Pinda's escape: "Mr. and Mrs. Hogan, Anne and Deborah [sic] Weston, Mrs. Child, Charles Whipple, Mrs. Bradford and Mrs. Bishop—A very dull evening, made more disagreeable by the conviction that the Hogans had only professed to be affected by the reasonings of the abolitionists.—Mr. Hogan's female slave arrived this morning and went to Mrs. Chapman's saying that her husband had urged her to take her freedom when she should next be at the North."[6] In her "true tale" of Pinda's journey to freedom, Chapman carefully noted geographical locations and street names. Using Pinda and Abraham's real names seems like an insensitive decision given that Abraham was at risk as a fugitive from slavery, especially as she changed the enslavers' names slightly and completely omitted the abolitionists' names, presumably for their own protection.

Chapman also omitted New Bedford in her version of events: as they had done many times before, the Weston sisters used their connections in the whaling city to assist fugitives from slavery. In March 1840, Debora Weston described her encounter with Abraham in a letter to her sister:

> Today at noon Abraham came with your letter. . . . He kept talking about his family, & removing his family. Pinda I suppose he meant. I liked him very much. He wanted me when I wrote to tell you that he got here safe. He wants you to tell Pinda that at the place where he is staying are two old acquaintances of his, who came from the very place he did, Savannah I suppose & that he has not the least trouble in getting along. . . . There is great feeling for runaway slaves here, & it is rather a recommendation than otherwise. I dont doubt he will prosper. I should not think it at all safe though to publish his story, which is a great pity, for there never was a prettier one—Why did he not go to Guiana? He quoted you very often. It was "I and my lady" all the time. I will do everything in my power for him.[7]

Despite Debora Weston's concerns for Abraham's safety, apparently her sister could not resist publishing his "pretty" story despite the risks. Perhaps this is why she completely omitted New Bedford from the story: for his protection and for the protection of the antislavery community. Many months later, Abraham was still living in New Bedford. The Weston sisters continued to look out for his safety and sent a warning message about the Hogans through abolitionist William C. Coffin, who was active in the New Bedford and Nantucket antislavery communities:[8]

> I received your letter requesting me to inform Abraham of the arrival in Boston of the <u>amiable</u> Mr. Hogan by this mornings mail. I immediately went in search of him and informed him of the fact, he did not seem to be at all alarmed—feeling perfectly safe surrounded as he is by kind friends who are willing to do all in their power to prevent his falling into the hands of this christian slave-holder. He thinks it would be better for Pinda to remain where

she is for the present as Hogan might discover his whereabouts if she should attempt to come to him, which I think is good advice. He wished me to say that he was well, and that he should have paid Pinda a visit in a week or two had he not received this information. He wishes to know if Hogan's wife is with him and whether he intends to remain in Boston during the winter.[9]

Chapman's literary decisions—her inclusions, omissions, and revisions—were all shaped by her primary rhetorical purpose: fundraising for the Massachusetts Anti-Slavery Society (MASS), the state-level auxiliary of the new national American Anti-Slavery Society. MASS was seeking a stable source of funding through a new weekly contribution plan, as American studies scholar Teresa Goddu explains: "Modeled on the American Anti-Slavery Society's (AASS) cent-a-week societies which began in 1838, the MASS's weekly contribution plan sought to raise money for the cause through the collection of small donations at regular weekly intervals sent to the society monthly."[10]

Chapman wrote "Pinda: A True Tale" in support of the campaign, and the story first appeared in two parts in the July and August 1840 issues of the *Monthly Offering to the Collectors and Contributors of the Weekly Contribution Plan*. The sixteen-page periodical was a companion to the "Weekly Contribution Plan" collection boxes, and it was also intended as an introduction to the antislavery movement for newcomers. The cover featured the familiar Wedgwood image of the kneeling slave, but instead of the usual rhetorical question, "Am I not a woman and a sister?," the lettering above the image exhorted readers to "Remember your Weekly Pledge." Beneath the image, this action was given biblical justification: "The truth shall make you free" and "Cry aloud, and spare not" encouraged MASS supporters to remain steadfast in what was still an unpopular fringe cause. The corresponding collection box had the same image of the supplicant slave, but the biblical verse below the image was even more pointed than the exhortations from John and Isaiah: "Upon the first day of the week, let every one of you lay by him in store, as GOD hath prospered him."[11]

The last page of the August issue reminds readers about the Pinda story: "Fail not to read the interesting narrative of PINDA which is concluded in this number.... The reader may be assured that even the minutest of its details are facts."[12] Readers who completed Pinda's story found that it concluded with a description of "the savings banks of the cause" and Pinda and Abraham's generous donation: "The little boxes of the Massachusetts

Anti-Slavery Society, the savings banks of the cause, have the aperture made too narrow for the reception of any but small coins; and the contributors to the West street box blushed to think, that the first time that the size of a donation rendered it necessary to raise the cover for its admission, was when Pinda brought her discolored Mexican dollar, (yet encrusted with the sand of its Savannah hiding-place,) to carry on the operations of the Massachusetts Society against slavery."[13]

After the story's summer debut in Massachusetts, it was then reprinted for a national audience on the back page of the *National Anti-Slavery Standard* on October 29, 1840. This paper was newly launched by the American Anti-Slavery Society in June 1840, after the schism between different factions of the antislavery movement over issues of religious tolerance, political engagement, and women's rights. A notice on the inside third page of the paper praised the "Tale of Pinda":

> The story of this fugitive from southern bondage, so touchingly and beautifully told by Mrs. Chapman . . . is worth more than all the works of fiction which literary dandies and butterflies have ever produced. Some would-be delicate and refined persons will, probably, think it exceedingly vulgar, and altogether beneath their notice, because IT IS TRUE. There are those, however, whose hearts will be cheered and warmed by its thrilling incidents, and who will bless the Providence by whose favor Abraham and Pinda are now enjoying the sweets of liberty.[14]

The writer seems to have missed the key legal nuance of the story—that Pinda was not a fugitive from slavery but had been brought to Massachusetts by her enslaver—but the American Anti-Slavery Society believed that this true story was powerful for their cause: "We are happy to state, that an edition of this story, in pamphlet form, will be issued at the Anti-Slavery Office, 143 Nassau street, in a few days. It will no doubt have a wide circulation."[15]

This assertion of "truth in fiction" is a commonplace in early American literature, in which titles regularly proclaimed themselves as "a tale of truth" or "founded in fact." Such true tales were even more important when the subject was slavery. Chapman needed to write about Pinda because the true tale of Med's freedom and subsequent early death could not be told. Through Pinda, Chapman both celebrated the impact of the *Aves* decision and erased the dead child, creating a self-sufficient adult hero who could model the desired behavior of weekly donations.

Almost thirty years later, Lydia Maria Child would revisit Pinda's tale in an 1868 column for the *National Anti-Slavery Standard*. Her "Anti-Slavery Reminiscence" clearly drew on Chapman's story as a main source, and she also identified herself as a principal actor in the events. Child's intention is to remember the "glorious days, wherein souls were refreshed by living for an earnest purpose, and strengthened by fearless conflict with falsehood. They were filled with thrilling tragedies, not unfrequently relieved by amusing comedies. One incident in particular frequently occurs to my mind and always produces a smile."[16] She remembered the "exquisite comedy" caused by the dramatic irony of the party scene, during which time the Hogans discussed the contentment of their slaves while at the same time Pinda was claiming her freedom. One big difference was that Child named the abolitionists in her version, and it reads like a "who's who" of Boston's abolitionist community: Ellis Gray Loring was the host of the Hogan party, which was attended by William Lloyd Garrison, Child and her husband David Lee Child, Chapman and her husband Henry Grafton Chapman, and several other abolitionists. Prior to the party, African American activist and historian William Cooper Nell encountered Pinda on the street and brought her to the Chapman residence, where BFASS officer Mary Parker and Child were present.

Child and Chapman erased Med and used the Pinda story for different purposes in different historical moments: Chapman's 1840 version seems haunted by Med and is intended to support the fundraising campaign in the moment. Child's postbellum version offers a nostalgic look back at the movement as part of her efforts to win the peace, that is, win the struggle for the meaning of the Civil War. Like Frederick Douglass, Child understood that "historical memory ... was the prize in a struggle between rival versions of the past, a question of will, of power, of persuasion."[17] Toward that end, there was no room for Med in Child's reminiscence and no accounting for antislavery failures, except perhaps obliquely in her mention of the "thrilling tragedies" of slavery relieved by "amusing comedies." Child could remember Pinda's true story and smile, while Med's story remained an unspeakable memory, with the inescapable bitter irony of her early death in northern freedom.

A ROMANCE OF THE REPUBLIC

A year before her Reminiscence column, Child published her ambitious postbellum novel, *A Romance of the Republic* (1867). She dedicated the novel to the parents of Colonel Robert Gould Shaw of the Fifty-Fourth Massachusetts Infantry, one of the first African American regiments in the Civil War. As she explained in a letter to Francis Shaw, "Having fought against slavery till I saw it go down in the Red Sea, I wanted to do something to undermine prejudice."[18] Beyond this stated purpose, careful readers will find that it was also the text in which she rewrote the Med case and affirmed the free soil principle.

A Romance of the Republic returns to the "tragic mulatta" theme Child had developed in her abolitionist fiction twenty-five years earlier. The novel features two sisters, Rosa and Flora, who live with their widowed father on the outskirts of antebellum New Orleans. Upon their father's death, the young women find out that their "Spanish mother" was actually a "quadroon" and enslaved; they too are claimed as property, scheduled to be sold at auction to pay their father's debts.

The villain of the novel, Gerald Fitzgerald, seizes this opportunity to control the sisters: he helps them escape on a ship to Nassau, marries Rosa in a sham ceremony (she is somehow unaware that marriage to an enslaved person is illegal in Louisiana), secretly buys them, and settles them in a secluded sea island cottage in Georgia. His consequent power leaves the sisters vulnerable to abuse: he makes advances to his sister-in-law Flora (causing her to fake her death and run away) and marries a white bride, Lily Bell, despite his purported marriage to Rosa. Rosa then asks Gerald to manumit her, because she is pregnant and knows the "bitter significance of the law" that the child follows the condition of the mother.[19] He never frees her, but in a crazed moment, Rosa gets her revenge. The legal Mrs. Fitzgerald has also given birth to a baby boy, Gerald Jr., and Rosa switches the babies so hers is raised as the Fitzgerald heir while the legal heir is sold into slavery.

As the plot progresses, both sisters are helped by white friends to escape from slavery. They also both marry white men: Rosa marries the proper Bostonian Alfred King, her father's friend's son (modeled after Ellis Gray Loring), and Flora marries the German Franz Blumenthal, her father's former clerk.

Previous scholarship on Child's *Romance of the Republic* emphasizes these racial border crossings: interracial liaisons drive the plot, and the novel explores intermarriage as the key to the nation's future.[20] What has been overlooked are the novel's *geographic* border crossings, in which enslaved people are transported to free jurisdictions *by their enslavers*. These episodes fictionalize major legal rulings about the status of enslaved people in free jurisdictions, such as *Somerset's Case* and *Commonwealth v. Aves*. While the courts focused narrowly on the question of wrongful detainment, the characters repeatedly voice the popular interpretation that the free soil of England (and New England) was transformative, freeing all who crossed its borders. The novel also inverts the mother-daughter dynamics of the Med case and rewrites the tragedy with a happy ending.

In one example, the sisters Rosa and Flora are said to be free based on their brief sojourn on British free soil. Following their father's death, Fitzgerald's decision to help them escape the auction block by sailing from New Orleans to Nassau in the British West Indies proves significant. This is an essential legal point: as the lawyer Willard Percival later advises, Fitzgerald could not claim them as property because "British soil has the enviable distinction of making free whosoever touches it." Flora is believed to be safe in her new Boston home, as "no court in the Free States could help deciding that, if he sent her to Nassau, she became free."[21]

Nassau as a free soil haven would be familiar to Child and her readers as the destination of the ship *Creole* following a slave rebellion. In November 1841, the enslaved people on a ship from Virginia bound for New Orleans revolted and forced the first mate to sail for Nassau. Child praised the Creole rebels during her editorship of the *National Anti-Slavery Standard* in the early 1840s. She also wrote a biographical sketch of the rebellion's leader Madison Washington in the *Freedmen's Book* (1865), describing how the fugitives "sprang out upon free soil" upon their safe arrival in Nassau.[22]

The free soil of Massachusetts also offers legal protection in the novel. In a moment of foreshadowing, the King family's country landlord Joe Bright notes that he watches visiting Southerners carefully: "If they've brought any blacks with 'em, I shall let 'em know what the laws of Massachusetts are; and then they may take their freedom or not, just as they choose."[23] Bright understands that free soil was not magically transformative: enslaved people had to claim their rights under the law.

When this scenario comes to pass and the King family discovers that their former slave Tulee is living with Southern boarders right next door, Rosa and Alfred King explain the laws of Massachusetts according to the ruling in the Med case. Rosa's explanation of the law is less nuanced at first, as she tells Tulee: "You became free the moment they brought you to Massachusetts." But she goes on to explain that Tulee had a choice: "Remember you are not a slave here. You can walk away at mid-day and tell them you are going to live with us."[24] "Here" is the operative word: Tulee's status depends on her geographic location and her consent to be restrained in a free state.

Tulee's decision is complicated by the fact that she has left several children behind in Carolina (Child does not offer a specific state): "Do you think ... if I don't go back with 'em, they'll let me have my chil'ren?" Here Child might also be thinking about the enslaved woman named Rosa she had met in Northampton in 1838, who faced a similar dilemma of "choosing" slavery or abandoning her children. In this case, Tulee opts for freedom and avoids this severe consequence, as Alfred Royal King negotiates for her children on her behalf. King tells Tulee's enslaver: "I came to inform you that Tulee does not wish to go back to Carolina; and that by the laws of Massachusetts she has a perfect right to remain here." Her enslavers protest, but King reiterates calmly, "Tulee chooses to take her freedom, and any court in Massachusetts will decide that she has a right to take it."[25] The dilemma of motherhood is solved by King's wealth: he offers to compensate her enslavers for Tulee, even though she is already free, if and only if, they allow him to buy her children's freedom as well. And so there is a happy ending: Tulee claims her legal rights, and she is reunited with her children for a new life in freedom.

Med's family was never reunited like Tulee's: while Med was freed, her mother and siblings remained in slavery, and she was left in the anomalous position as the free child of an enslaved mother. Child and her BFASS colleagues could only plead with her owner to do the right thing, but their pleas went unanswered. Three decades after Med's death, Child broke her silence about this tragic case and rewrote the ending. She inverted the mother/daughter roles: the adult Tulee is able to speak for herself and claim her freedom with the help of her benefactors. And this time, Ellis Gray Loring, who could only provide doctors and ultimately a headstone for Med, is able to provide the fairy-tale ending. In the character of Royal King, he uses his wealth to buy Tulee's children's freedom and reunite the family. Tulee was then able to support herself and educate her children. The free soil principle works precisely because she is an adult and because the Kings provide employment for all of them. The fictional King family recognizes that emancipation is a process, not just a transformative moment in time, and that they have a responsibility to Tulee and her family.

The other formerly enslaved characters in the King household are well aware of the difference in their status: the fugitives Tom and Chloe know they are at risk from the Fugitive Slave Act, but Tulee does not share in their anxiety: "She had got beyond Mount Pisgah into the Canaan of freedom; and her happiness was unalloyed."[26]

The legal distinction between enslaved people in transit and fugitives from slavery seemed like a moot point in 1867: What was the relevance of the free soil principle for postbellum readers? And it seems telling that Child pointedly overlooked the *Slave, Grace* (1827) and *Dred Scott* (1857) decisions that overturned the "once free, forever free" principle of free soil in favor of the "reattachment" theory of enslavement.[27]

So why would Child discuss two landmark legal cases while not incorporating the proslavery cases that undercut them? One possibility is that this historical legal education was part of Child's fight to win the peace by preserving the war's antislavery legacy, protecting former slaves, and documenting abolitionist activism.[28] As biographer Carolyn Karcher notes, "At a time when lifelong antiabolitionists were parading as allies of those they had so fiercely persecuted, numerous vignettes recall the insults, ostracism, and mob violence that abolitionists had had to endure from 'gentlemen of property and standing.'" The novel pays "nostalgic tribute" to antislavery heroes through cameo appearances by William Lloyd Garrison, Francis Jackson, Samuel Sewall, and Reverend Samuel Snowden. Others appear in "fictional guise": Willard Percival as Wendell Phillips; Joseph Houseman as Joseph Carpenter; and Alfred Royal King as Med's lawyer Ellis Gray Loring.[29] Child remembered who was on the right side of history from the very beginning, and she wanted her readers to remember as well.

Child's revisioning of the Med case was part of her plea for remembrance during the Reconstruction era. But we are left with a major interpretive problem: the people she left out of the novel. The BFASS women are nowhere to be found, and there is virtually no mention of the African American community, which played an essential role in the Med case and all antislavery efforts in Boston. At a time when she is trying to valorize antislavery heroes and prove African Americans as worthy of citizenship (see, for example, her *Freedmen's Book*), the African American heroes are erased except for a very brief mention of Reverend Snowden on Belknap Street.[30]

The reception of *A Romance of the Republic* suggests that Child's contemporary readers were also puzzled by the novel, and her letters are filled with her bitter disappointment: "I had some expectations, quite modest, at the time I published 'The Romance of the Republic'; but I found out then what the interest of friends amounted to, and I shall never dream again, not even the merest little bit of a dream."[31] Child did get some positive reviews in the abolitionist press, and Robert Purvis, one of the African American founders of the American Anti-Slavery Society, praised her work. T. W. Higginson described the novel as "in some respects her best fictitious work" and noted that "it will always possess value as one of the few really able delineations of slavery in fiction."[32] If, like Frederick Douglass, her "intention was to forge enduring historical myths that could help win battles in the present," then this was important praise indeed.[33] Despite the novel's shortcomings and omissions, Child's portrayal of slavery and the abolitionist movement offer twenty-first-century readers insight into this precarious historical moment, and careful readers can find Med hidden in this story of New Orleans and Boston. Careful readers might also be disappointed in Child, who showed no regret for Med's death in her retelling of the story.

WHITE-JACKET: OR, THE WORLD IN A MAN-OF-WAR

Herman Melville was not an abolitionist activist like Child and Chapman, and yet he found himself linked to the slave transit case *Commonwealth v. Fitzgerald* (1842) through his father-in-law Justice Shaw and his enslaved shipmate Robert Lucas. But unlike Child, who rewrote the Med case to create a successful outcome, Melville took the opposite approach in his novel *White-Jacket* and erased the antislavery legal victory.

White-Jacket: or, The World in a Man-of-War fictionalizes Melville's fourteen months as an ordinary seaman in the U.S. Navy on the frigate *United States*, August 1843–October 1844. During his voyage, he witnessed over 150 floggings, and his novel protests this inhumane practice. The antiflogging campaign had been underway for almost a decade by the time Melville entered the conversation, and his position merely affirmed public opinion. Indeed, *White-Jacket*, composed at an incredible pace during July–August 1849 and published in March 1850, seemed "ripped from the headlines" with its topicality. In September 1850, Congress abolished flogging in the U.S. Navy. Melville was thrilled by the prospect of naval reform, as he wrote to his friend, the editor and publisher Evert Duyckinck: "I am offering up devout jubilations for the abolition of the flogging law."[34]

September 1850 also marked the passage of the Fugitive Slave Act; the issues of slavery and naval flogging were closely connected in the public mind. The antislavery Senator John P. Hale of New Hampshire spearheaded the campaign against flogging, which he denounced as a "relic of feudalism and barbarity."[35] For Melville, the Fugitive Slave Act would change the course of his next novel in progress, *Moby-Dick*, published the following year. Literary scholar Jeffrey Hole argues, "*Moby-Dick* is not a work that explicitly voices opposition to the Fugitive Slave Act, but it does open up a number of important questions about 1850, about law and property, about imperial conquest, about religion and commerce, about the intelligence of 'property' (including slaves) that can retaliate, as does the white whale."[36]

Following the publication of *White-Jacket*, Melville's initial reviewers seemed relieved to see him return to his previous terrain of the seaman's narrative, after the critical failure of *Mardi* (1849). While the critics were pleased, Melville wrote disparagingly of his efforts in *White-Jacket* and *Redburn*, an earlier novel published in 1849: "But no reputation that is gratifying to me, can possibly be achieved by either of these books. They are two *jobs*, which I have done for money—being forced to it, as other men are to sawing wood.... It is my earnest desire to write those sort of books which are said to 'fail.'"[37] Despite Melville's own reservations, *White-Jacket* enjoyed "nearly universal critical approval" at the time of publication. British reviewers liked his "praise of British seamen" and "descriptions of shipboard life," while "Americans were more interested, naturally, in Melville's attack on naval abuses. They also approved the humanitarian tone of the work and its strong defense of democracy."[38] Antebellum critics did not seem to notice his discussion of slavery, despite the common comparisons made between sailors and slaves in antebellum sea narratives.

Current critics are more likely to read the condemnation of flogging in the navy as a critique of slavery and racism. For twenty-first-century readers, as literary scholar Samuel Otter explains, *White-Jacket* becomes "a book about the extension of black slavery to the decks of United States naval frigates and to the backs of white sailors." The novel might also be read as a reflection on the issues of slave transit, free soil, and moral geography at the heart of the Med case. Melville reminds us that sailors can only claim their rights as consenting citizens on land: they have no rights at sea. Their rights are contingent upon their location, just as the rights of slaves were contingent upon their location in free or slave jurisdictions. As historian T. K. Hunter notes in her discussion of slave transit litigation, the question becomes not "what is the law?" but "where is the law?"[39] Furthermore, at sea, the sailors are like children under the guardianship of the patriarchal captain, and they can only reclaim their adulthood and full citizenship on land. But the key difference, of course, is that for white sailors, once they disembark, all land is free soil.

The narrator, White-Jacket, is named after the white duck jacket he sews for himself because the uniform pea-jackets were no longer available at the end of a three years' cruise. The world he describes on the fictional ship *Neversink* demonstrates that all is not well on the American ship of state: "*White-Jacket* depicts abuses of power in the United States Navy as a microcosm of the modern political world," notes biographer Laurie Robertson-Lorant. As Otter describes it, in ninety-four short chapters, White-Jacket chronicles "the structures of order, the varieties of labor, and the social relations in ship and state" that readers might expect from the genre, but he also recounts a world in which the officers abuse their authority and enlisted men are flogged for even minor offenses.[40] Over the course of four chapters, Melville built his case against flogging, the main claims being evident from the chapter titles: Chapter 33: A Flogging; Chapter 34: Some of the Evil Effects of Flogging; Chapter 35: Flogging Not Lawful; and Chapter 36: Flogging Not Necessary. White-Jacket denounces this physical abuse and psychological humiliation with great passion:

> We assert that flogging in the navy is opposed to the essential dignity of man . . . ; that it is oppressive, and glaringly unequal in its operations; that it is utterly repugnant to the spirit of our democratic institutions; indeed, that it involves a lingering trait of the worst times of a barbarous feudal aristocracy; in a word, we denounce it as religiously, morally, and immutably wrong.
>
> No matter, then, what may be the consequences of its abolition; no matter if we have to dismantle our fleets, and our unprotected commerce should fall prey to the spoiler, the awful admonitions of justice and humanity demand that abolition without procrastination. . . . It is not a dollar-and-cent question of expediency; it is a matter of right and wrong. And if any man can lay his hand on his heart, and solemnly say that this scourging is right, let that man but once feel the lash on his own back, and in his agony you will hear the apostate call to the heavens that it is wrong.[41]

This call for the abolition of flogging reads like a classic argument for the abolition of slavery. Abolitionists and naval reformers made similar arguments: that slavery and flogging are undemocratic and unchristian; that economic questions cannot outweigh these moral imperatives; that neither practice can withstand the challenge of the golden rule.

While over fifty pages of the novel deal directly with flogging, for Melville, "the practice was itself only a symptom of the anti-democratic nature of the Navy." In addition to his lengthy denunciation of flogging, White-Jacket extends his equation of sailors and slaves through an analysis of seamen's legal status. He argues against the suspension of habeas corpus and considers the claims of natural law. As White-Jacket describes, "In the American Navy there is an everlasting suspension of the Habeas Corpus. Upon the bare allegation of misconduct, there is no law to restrain the Captain from imprisoning a seaman, and keeping him confined at his pleasure." White-Jacket concedes that the metaphorical ship of state and actual naval ships operate under different conditions: "Certainly the necessities of navies warrant a code for its government more stringent than the law that governs the land; but that code should conform to the spirit of the political institutions of the country that ordains it. It should not *convert into slaves* [emphasis mine] some of the citizens of a nation of freemen." "The law of our soil," White-Jacket laments, does not follow sailors to sea. For both sailors and slaves, White-Jacket concludes, "our Revolution was in vain" and "our Declaration of Independence is a lie."[42]

Ironically, White-Jacket sees Guinea, a "Virginian slave regularly shipped as a seaman," as more free than the free white sailors on the *Neversink*. Guinea "belonged to the Purser, who was a Southern gentleman; he was employed as his body servant." Observing Guinea's privileges on board ship makes White-Jacket painfully aware of his own second-class citizenship: "Never did I feel my condition as a man-of-war's-man so keenly as when seeing this Guinea freely circulating about the decks in citizen's clothes, and through the influence of his master, almost entirely exempted from the disciplinary degradation of the Caucasian crew. Faring sumptuously in the wardroom; sleek and round, his ebon face fairly polished with content: ever gay and hilarious; ever ready to laugh and joke, that African slave was actually envied by many of the seamen. There were times when I almost envied him myself."[43] On the *Neversink*, Guinea is enslaved but relatively free, while the white sailors are virtually enslaved.

Guinea is a minor character in the novel, and he presumably returns with his owner to a life in slavery when the fictional voyage ended in Norfolk, Virginia. It is puzzling to read White-Jacket's praise of the Purser in this regard:

"Upon our arrival home, his treatment of Guinea, under circumstances peculiarly calculated to stir up the resentment of a slave-owner, still more augmented my estimation of the Purser's good heart."[44]

The character Guinea is based on Robert Lucas, Melville's shipmate and the petitioner in *Commonwealth v. Fitzgerald* (1844), an enslaved man enlisted in the navy by his enslaver Edward Fitzgerald in Virginia and freed by Justice Shaw when the *United States* sailed into Boston. Shaw, Melville's formidable father-in-law and Med's emancipator, would spend thirty years as the chief justice of the Massachusetts Supreme Judicial Court, and wrote 2,200 opinions, "including some the most important in the formative era of American law." Shaw "was the embodiment of the law," as scholar Michael Rogin notes, "and his decisions decisively shaped the histories both of American slavery and of Melville's fiction."[45]

Previously in *Commonwealth v. Aves*, Shaw had to decide "the status of a slave brought only *temporarily* into a free state" and ruled that enslaved people brought to Massachusetts by their enslavers could not be brought out of the state against their will. In the Lucas case, Shaw expanded the Med precedent: he ruled Fitzgerald had lost legal control of Lucas once they sailed from Virginia and that Lucas was free once he entered Massachusetts.[46]

Melville had sailed with Lucas on the USS *United States* and arrived with him in Boston in October 1844, when the *United States* sailed into the Charlestown Navy Yard within sight of the newly completed Bunker Hill monument. Two of Lucas's shipmates brought his case to abolitionist lawyers, who filed a writ of habeas corpus.[47] Fitzgerald's attorney, Benjamin F. Hallet, who had also represented Mary Taylor in her attempt to keep the enslaved child Anson (see chapter 3), argued that the Med precedent did not apply in the case, as Finkelman explains, "because Fitzgerald did not voluntarily bring Lucas into the state." Abolitionist lawyer Samuel Sewall countered that the Med case did indeed apply because when his enslaver enlisted him in the navy "he thereby consented that he should go anywhere the ship might be lawfully ordered to, and took the chance of his being sent to a free port." Justice Shaw agreed with Sewall that Lucas had been brought to Massachusetts by his enslaver, and in his ruling further argued that slaves could not be enlisted because they could not enter contracts. Lucas was thus freed from both slavery and naval service.[48] Legal historian Leonard Levy put it best: "Discharging Lucas from the service of both his master and the federal government, Shaw concluded with a precise and sweeping formulation of the law on the subject at issue: 'Where a slave is in Massachusetts casually, not being a runaway, whether he is brought here voluntarily by his master or not, there is no law here to authorize his restraint.'"[49]

The questions of consent and will were complicated here: Shaw ruled, on the one hand, that slaves could not enter contracts, but, on the other hand, that they could consent to a writ of habeas corpus on their own behalf. The *Liberator* reported on Shaw's approach to his decision:

> Chief Justice Shaw first made inquiry of the party apart, whether the process was instituted at his request, and ascertained that it was not, but that as it had gone so far, he now desired it should proceed. This was deemed a sufficient authority for the parties who took out the habeas corpus to act for him. Lucas also desired to know what would be the effect of his discharge here if he returned to Virginia, but the chief justice said he could not advise him on that point, in case he was not released by the master.[50]

As he did in previous freedom suits based on transit, Shaw interviewed Lucas in private and learned that, while he had not initiated the proceedings, Lucas was indeed willing to pursue his case. Like previous enslaved litigants, Lucas was concerned that freedom would also mean separation from his home and wondered if returning to Virginia would be an option. The freedom suit scenario worked because Lucas was an adult and able to take charge of his own life; as an adult free man on free soil, he lacked the complicated status of a "free child" or a "sailor at sea." The *Liberator* noted the significance of his adulthood: "Lucas was accordingly discharged from custody, and being of full age, was left to return to Virginia or remain, as he might elect."[51]

In both the Med and Lucas cases, Justice Shaw ruled in favor of freedom. And yet Melville's fictional ship *Neversink* ends its voyage in Norfolk, Virginia, rather than in Boston, leaving the Guinea/Lucas character in a life of slavery. This ending creates a significant interpretive problem: why would Melville write so passionately about habeas corpus rights only to ignore Lucas's successful exercise of these rights in *Commonwealth v. Fitzgerald*? Why does his novel erase Lucas's legal victory, praise the "good heart" of the enslaver, and deny his father-in-law's antislavery ruling?

Perhaps Melville understood that the answer to the slavery dilemma was not to be found in northern courts, and so he declined to conclude his book with a celebration of Lucas's freedom. He predicted that Shaw's narrow legalisms were nothing to celebrate; this pessimism was borne out by his father-in-law's infamous fugitive renditions of Shadrach Wilkins and Thomas Sims in 1851. Melville would go on to explore the failure of law in greater depth in later works such as *Benito Cereno* and *Billy Budd*.[52] Slavery was not America's only problem, according to Melville: "freedom" remained elusive for people of all races. As Brook Thomas observes, "For Melville, slavery was only one case, if the most obvious, of America's failure to live up to the promises inscribed in the Declaration of Independence to offer liberty to all of its people." As Ishmael would famously ask in Melville's next novel, *Moby-Dick*, "Who aint a slave?"[53]

Melville's critique was nothing new: his ideas were anticipated by eighteenth-century writers and activists such as Olaudah Equiano and Ottobah Cugoano, who questioned the "*Somerset* myth" of a free England following the Mansfield ruling.[54] As Melville was disappointed in the failure of the United States to live up to its ideals, so Equiano and Cugoano were disappointed to find that the *Somerset* myth was just that. In direct defiance of the Mansfield ruling, the forced deportation of enslaved people continued despite the myth of English "free air." English freedom meant little when there was slavery in the rest of the empire.[55] And in Melville's analysis, American freedom was also undermined by American slavery, a profound failure of the law.

The immoral nature of slavery was clear, but Melville knew that there were no easy answers. He remained concerned about the role of the legal system in that process. As Rogin notes, "Shaw's rulings separated the abstract, natural rights of slaves from their social and personal consequences. Melville saw the futility and danger of that split. Emancipation from slave and familial masters, he implied against Shaw, was no simple matter of the stroke of a pen."[56] The freedom suit scenario, which seemed to work well in Lucas's case, ignored the complications of forging new lives in freedom. Melville could not even imagine how this could be accomplished writ large.

In the final chapter of Melville's novel, White-Jacket exclaims: "Oh, shipmates and world-mates, all round! we the people suffer many abuses" but "in vain . . . do we appeal" to higher authorities. It is surprising to hear White-Jacket, this stout defender of constitutional rights, go on to explain that the law cannot remedy the injustices in our society: "Yet the worst of our evils we blindly inflict upon ourselves; our officers cannot remove them, even if they would. From the last ills no being can save another; therein each man must be his own saviour."[57]

It is a somber homecoming for the sailors and slaves on the *Neversink*: the novel simultaneously appeals for justice and recognizes the futility of that appeal. Justice Shaw, who freed Med, Robert Lucas, and other enslaved people in transit, would soon become infamous for his role in renditions under the Fugitive Slave Act. And while *White-Jacket* was in press, Shaw would develop the "separate but equal" concept in the Sarah Roberts school segregation ruling.

CONCLUSION

Sarah, Ruby, and Med

"SEPARATE BUT EQUAL"

On November 14, 1960, first-grader Ruby Bridges integrated the William Frantz school in the Ninth Ward of New Orleans. The photos of little Ruby in her white starched dress with a ribbon in her hair are iconic images of the civil rights movement, and Norman Rockwell's 1963 painting *The Problem We All Live With* further solidified her cultural legacy.[1] Rockwell depicted Ruby walking to school under the protection of four U.S. marshals, anonymous agents of the law whose heads are cropped by the top edge of the image. The protestors remain off stage, but their menacing presence is implied by a racial epithet and a smashed tomato on the wall.

In 1847, four-year-old Sarah Roberts attempted to integrate the Otis School in Boston. While law enforcement would protect Ruby Bridges on her way to school, in Sarah's case, a Boston police officer removed her from the designated whites-only school. There are no extant images of this event, but Susan Goodman's recent picture book, *The First Step: How One Girl Put Segregation on Trial*, transposes the Rockwell image to illustrate this scene in antebellum Boston. Illustrator E. B. Lewis alludes to the iconic Rockwell painting to tell the story and, in so doing, offers commentary through the contrasting scenes (figure 7). In Lewis's picture, which extends across two pages, Sarah and the police officer are in profile against a wall. They face right, in the opposite direction of Ruby and her bodyguards. The large officer remains faceless and motionless with his fists clenched, his head cropped

FIGURE 7. Sarah Roberts. © Susan E. Goodman (author), E. B. Lewis (illustrator), 2016, *The First Step: How One Girl Put Segregation on Trial*, Bloomsbury Publishing, Inc.

from the image like the federal marshals in the Rockwell painting. In this image, there are no implied crowds or protestors on the lonely, empty street. Sarah walks downhill with downcast eyes. She carries a book like Ruby, but she has the face and body of a four-year-old. By the time her lawsuit got to court, she would have looked more like Ruby, with the longer legs and narrower face of a first-grade child. We have no image or description of Med, but we might imagine she had a similar appearance at this age as well.[2]

Med's journey from New Orleans to Boston made her a free child; Sarah and Ruby's test cases, spanning over a century, asked Boston and New Orleans to define what freedom meant. Boston's antebellum abolitionists understood that northern prejudice sustained the system of southern slavery, and so school segregation cases, along with campaigns against the intermarriage ban and segregated transportation, were essential to the antislavery cause. These cases raised fundamental questions about northern freedom: Did free soil mean the absence of slavery or did it mean true equality and citizenship? Segregation cases created another layer of moral geography, challenging communities to consider who belonged within free soil boundaries.

Sarah's presence at the white Otis School violated the moral geography of the Boston School Committee, which operated separate schools for black students. Her "proper" place was the Abiel Smith School on Beacon Hill, the same neighborhood that had rallied around Med's cause. When Sarah was denied an admission ticket from the school committee to her desired local school, Sarah's father Benjamin Franklin Roberts, a Boston printer descended from generations of activists, boldly enrolled her anyway. This defiance soon came to the attention of school officials: Sarah was abruptly removed by a police officer, as portrayed in the Goodman book, and the Roberts family found that litigation was their only recourse.[3]

The Roberts family lost their lawsuit, *Sarah C. Roberts v. the City of Boston* (1850), despite the efforts of their African American attorney, Robert Morris, who had studied under Med's advocate Ellis Gray Loring, and his co-counsel Charles Sumner, who would be elected to the Senate in 1851. The case was heard by the Supreme Judicial Court, and so once again, Chief Justice Lemuel Shaw would decide the fate of a little girl and establish a legal precedent. The case is mostly remembered for Sumner's assertion of "equality before the law," eighteen years before the equal protection clause of the Fourteenth Amendment, and Shaw's development of the "separate but equal" doctrine that would prove so damaging in future civil rights cases such as *Plessy v. Ferguson* (1896). While slave transit was not the issue, it is interesting to note that Sumner cited the historical arguments from the Med case, making a direct link between southern slavery and northern prejudice. He strategically cited *Aves* to support his argument that the Massachusetts Declaration of Rights prohibited segregation just as it had abolished slavery: "Slavery was abolished in Massachusetts, by virtue of the declaration of rights in our constitution, without any specific words of abolition in that instruction, or in any subsequent legislation.... The same words, which are potent to destroy slavery, must be equally potent against any institution founded on caste."[4] For Sumner, Article I of the Declaration of Rights settled the matter: "All men are born free and equal, and have certain natural, essential, and unalienable rights."[5]

In his ruling, Justice Shaw initially stated that he agreed with Sumner's "equality before the law" concept, but it was clear that his version of equality was something altogether different:

> But, when this great principle [equality before the law] comes to be applied to the actual and various conditions of persons in society, it will not warrant the assertion, that men and women are legally clothed with the same civil and political powers, and that children and adults are legally to have the same functions and be subject to the same treatment; but only that the rights of all,

as they are settled and regulated by law, are equally entitled to the paternal consideration and protection of the law, for their maintenance and security.[6]

"Equality before the law" for Shaw, in other words, meant that everyone had the equal chance to have white men determine their rights under the guise of paternalism and protection. Shaw was not alone in this belief: Sarah, like all antebellum children, was part of what literary scholar Lesley Ginsberg describes as "a category of the disenfranchised, like women, slaves, and animals, who could only trust in the 'paternal' arm of the law to guarantee what rights the law deemed worthy to bestow upon them."[7]

Shaw's framing of "equality" in this manner set up his "separate but equal" conclusion: "Conceding, therefore, in the fullest manner, that colored persons, the descendants of Africans, are entitled by law, in this commonwealth, to equal rights, constitutional and political, civil and social, the question then arises, whether the regulation in question, which provides separate schools for colored children, is a violation of any of these rights." His restrictive definition of equality allowed him to conclude that the answer was no. The Boston School Committee could indeed exclude black children from white schools as long as it provided other schools for them. Prejudice, Shaw concluded, "is not created by law, and probably cannot be changed by law." While Sarah's lawsuit was defeated, black leaders used this defeat to rally the community around the equal schools campaign and the successful petition to the state legislature. In 1855, Massachusetts passed the first law in the United States desegregating public schools: "No distinction shall be made on account of the race, color, or religious opinions, of the applicant or scholar."[8]

This was not the end of the story for Boston, of course. The struggle for educational equity has been a fraught, contested process that dates back to Prince Hall's 1787 petition to the Boston School Committee and continues to this day. The narrow media focus on the 1974 busing crisis obscures this lengthy history and erases generations of black activism. "Maintaining the 'Boston busing crisis' frame," as scholars Matthew Delmont and Jeanne Theoharis explain, "serves to reduce Boston's racism to working class ethnic parochialism, . . . and obfuscates the long history of systematic racial inequality in the Cradle of Liberty that led to a decades-long protest movement in the city. . . . It maintains a dangerous fiction that what happened in Boston was far different from what happened in Little Rock or Birmingham."[9] In other words, resistance to "forced busing" created a more respectable veneer for the Boston School Committee's resistance to desegregation and for the framing of segregation as a southern problem. In reality, students were placed on the front lines of civil rights battles, North and South, while all sides claimed to be "for the children."

"THEY NEVER SAW A CHILD"

Charles Sumner presented a dramatic David versus Goliath scenario in the Sarah Roberts lawsuit: "On the one side is the city of Boston, strong in its wealth, in its influence, in its character; on the other side is a little child, of a degraded color, of humble parents, still within the period of natural infancy, but strong from her very weakness, and from the irrepressible sympathies of good men, which, by a divine compensation, come to succor the weak. This little child asks at your hands her personal rights." It was Sarah's father and "next friend," of course, who was asking the court for Sarah's "personal rights." Sumner intentionally opened his remarks in this fashion because he knew that the sentimental appeal of children could be useful for the cause. As American studies scholar Anna Mae Duane describes, when we think about children, "it seems only natural that their weakness will translate into a certain power over adults who feel compelled to care for them. . . . In this model, the rights of the powerless . . . come into existence solely through the feelings they evoke in the powerful."[10] And yet, as Duane notes, this model is highly problematic: "personal rights" dependent on pathos and paternalism are not rights at all.

Sarah had turned six by the time Morris and Sumner made their arguments before the Supreme Judicial Court, about the same age as Ruby and Med when they became test cases. Their very young ages raise questions about consent and involvement in legal proceedings they could not possibly understand. Sarah did not leave behind any letters or personal papers, so we can only wonder what she thought about her summary removal from school and the litigation that followed. Med did not live past these tender years, so we can never know what she thought about her new home among strangers. Ruby Bridges, in contrast, has become an activist and author in adulthood, and her books offer rich insight into her childhood experiences. Despite the wide gap in time and circumstances, we might consider how her experiences can help us understand Sarah and Med's lives as well.

Bridges reflects on the event that changed her life in a remarkable 1999 photobook, *Through My Eyes*. While the book jacket promises "an amazing story of innocence, courage, and forgiveness," American studies scholar Katharine Capshaw rightfully observes that "*Through My Eyes* is a quietly furious book," as Bridges both celebrates her historical legacy and constructs "her younger self as an unwilling and unknowing participant in the integration effort." The book opens with the following lines: "When I was six years old, the civil rights movement came knocking at the door. It was 1960, and history pushed in and swept me up in a whirlwind." She recalls that she passed a special test given to black kindergarteners by the school board and that the National Association for the Advancement of Colored People (NAACP) pushed her family to send her to a white school: "They pressured my parents and made a lot of promises."[11]

By 1960, the lawsuit responsible for Ruby's admission to the William Frantz school, *Bush v. Orleans Parish School Board*, was older than the little girls who would carry out the judge's order. The lead plaintiff, "Earl Benjamin Bush . . . had been sixteen when the suit was filed in 1952, two years before the United States Supreme Court had announced in *Brown v. Board of Education of Topeka* that racial segregation in public schools violated the federal Constitution."[12] The *Bush* suit had stalled in anticipation of the *Brown* ruling; the plaintiffs then filed an amended suit in 1955 following the rejection of "separate but equal" by the U.S. Supreme Court under Chief Justice Earl Warren. The New Orleans case dragged on for another five years, concluding when Earl Bush was a twenty-four-year-old man, long gone from the school system. It would be left to four little first-grade girls to implement the court ruling.

Reflecting on that historic day in November 1960, Bridges remembers her mother's advice to behave herself at her new school. She wondered if all the crowds were there for Mardi Gras and reports going home after her first day of school and skipping rope to the "Two, four, six, eight, we don't want to integrate" chant she had learned, having no idea what the words meant. There is a heartbreaking innocence here as she tries to make sense of the protests, with their strange air of festivity and danger. Bridges also has a distinct, terrifying memory: "Most of all I remember seeing a black doll in a coffin, which frightened me more than anything else." In this memory, Ruby is not the "brave girl" of civil rights legend but a child facing death threats. The black doll in a coffin, Capshaw explains, represents "white menace" and complicates "the trope of the martyred child that is so central to the consensus memory of the civil rights movement." Like Capshaw, I cannot find any noble purpose here.[13] The parading of a doll in a coffin before the living child it represents is an undeniable threat.

While Ruby Bridges remains a civil rights icon, Med and Sarah Roberts have been reduced to historical footnotes, and the archives provide no sense of them as people or historical actors. Their places in academic and public history are somewhat different: *Commonwealth v. Aves* can be found in the legal scholarship, but Med and her case are not part of Boston African American National Historic Site run by the National Park Service (NPS). In contrast, Sarah Roberts is featured on the NPS Black Heritage Trail, but there is surprisingly little scholarship about her case, besides brief mentions of the case as a precursor to the *Brown* decision.[14] Sarah was also conspicuously omitted from the celebrations following the passage of the 1855 legislation desegregating schools in Massachusetts. The success of the equal schools campaign in many respects was owing to the tireless efforts of William Cooper Nell. At a formal celebration honoring him in December of that year, Nell praised the efforts of Benjamin Roberts, Charles Sumner, and Robert Morris, but strangely omitted Sarah from his list of tributes.[15] Nell deserved this recognition for his years of activism, but surely the little girl who served as the test case deserved to be named as well.

In contrast, Ruby Bridges remains a household name not only because of the powerful twentieth-century media and the Rockwell painting, but also because her story can be made to fit the consensus civil rights narrative, which defines events between 1954 and 1968 as a triumph of American democracy and erases the complexity and lengthy history of the movement. The celebration of the lone Ruby Bridges, furthermore, glosses over the experiences of the "McDonogh Three," the three other first-grade girls who were also part of the "designed to fail" token integration of the New Orleans Public Schools. Leona Tate, Tessie Prevost, and Gail Etienne attended the McDonogh School under the protection of federal marshals (although the school was practically empty owing to a boycott by white students), but the girls went on to integrate the Thomas Jefferson Semmes school in third grade without the protection of law enforcement. This time, although there was no white boycott, many teachers and students made it clear that they were unwelcome. New Orleans officials would celebrate the city's nominal, "non-violent" integration success, but, as adults reflecting back on their experiences, the

McDonogh Three tell a very different story. They describe "a living hell" in which they were targeted by protestors, classmates, and teachers.[16]

What does it mean to put young black girls on the front lines of a controversial desegregation plan? These little girls were chosen because of their academic abilities and gender; smart, well-behaved African American girls were perceived as non-threatening compared to African American boys. In Sumner's words, the girls were "strong from [their] very weakness" and the desire of all good people to "succor the weak." But we know that their vulnerability did not inspire protection and have to wonder how people justified their attacks on children. Dr. Robert Coles, the child psychiatrist who worked with the New Orleans children during the school desegregation crisis, asks important questions about the courage required by test cases in his *Children of Crisis:* "How can a child of six survive such an ordeal? What lends ordinary people like Ruby, her parents, and the parents of the other children who accompanied her the courage and endurance to outface a mob?" But I think Capshaw asks more fundamental questions in her discussion of Bridges's book: "Why should a child—an innocent—have to be brave in the face of incomprehensible racial terror? Why should a child take on the role of warrior when she does not understand the political landscape?" There was a real human cost for the New Orleans children: the girls all recall stress, loneliness, nightmares, and loss of appetite. Bridges had virtually stopped eating after one of the "cheerleaders" (the white mothers who protested at the school) threatened to poison her on a daily basis.[17]

Looking back, Bridges is proud of her historic role and yet laments, "I feel as if I lost my childhood." In a recent PBS documentary, Bridges tries to explain the behavior of the protestors and concludes that they had a kind of moral blindness: "They didn't see a child. They saw change and what they thought was being taken from them. They never saw a child."[18]

"AS THOUGH IT HAD NEVER HAPPENED"

Just as Med was abandoned by the Boston Female Anti-Slavery Society after the court victory, Bridges recounts being abandoned by her teacher, the NAACP, and the U.S. marshals after first grade. The silence was confusing for her: "No one spoke about the previous year. It was as though it had never happened." Looking back as an adult, "she felt that the NAACP knew what was going to happen and failed to warn the participants. She had a lingering feeling of being used. 'After that they never even looked at us. They never cared if we finished school.'" As a child, Ruby did not understand her historical impact: she did not recognize herself in the 1987 *Eyes on the Prize* documentary, and she explains, "It's taken me a long time to own the early part of my life."[19]

No one spoke about Med either; while the freedom suits continued, there was only silence about her short life and death. "They never saw a child" in many ways also applies to Med's experience. I would argue that all parties failed to see Med as a child: enslavers wanted her for her market value, while abolitionists wanted her for her legal precedent and iconic value. What happened to Med might best be explained through contradiction: the abolitionists did not see her as a child, and yet, it was as a child that she disrupted the freedom suit scenario, leading to her vulnerable, short life in freedom.

Med embodies many overlapping histories: Boston history, antislavery history, legal history, literary history, and the history of childhood. Her story is the story of a child who entered history and was erased from history by adults who made decisions about her life, claiming parental authority without taking on the care and nurture a young child needs.

Med is also the missing historical and legal link between James Somerset and Dred Scott. History remembers the adult men who exercised their own rights, capacity, and agency through the freedom suits that "freed all the slaves in England" and "caused the Civil War." Abolitionists excelled at this kind of ceremonial, commemorative rhetoric, but in Med's case they could not claim virtue and could not avoid responsibility. Remembering Med forces a kind of moral accounting, one that we have avoided through the mythologies of Boston as the birthplace of abolition and the cradle of liberty. Remembering Med makes it harder to cast abolitionism as a "satisfying morality tale."[20] Her life and death remind us that human rights work cannot lose sight of individual humanity.

NOTES

PREFACE

1. Boston Female Anti-Slavery Society, *Right and Wrong in Boston, in 1836. Annual Report of the Boston Female Anti-Slavery Society, being a concise history of the cases of the slave child, Med, and of the women demanded as slaves of the Supreme Judicial Court of Mass. with all the other proceedings of the society* (Boston: Isaac Knapp, 1836).
2. Lydia Maria Child, *Letters of Lydia Maria Child* (Boston: Houghton Mifflin, 1882); Lydia Maria Child, *The Collected Correspondence of Lydia Maria Child, 1817–1880*, ed. Patricia G. Holland, Milton Meltzer, and Francine Krasno (Millwood, NY: KTO Microform, 1979); Britt Rusert, "Disappointment in the Archives of Black Freedom," *Social Text* 33, no. 4 (December 2015): 27; Saidiya Hartman, "Venus in Two Acts," *Small Axe* 12, no. 2 (July 17, 2008): 1–14.
3. Don E. Fehrenbacher, *The Dred Scott Case: Its Significance in American Law and Politics* (New York: Oxford University Press, 1978); Paul Finkelman, *An Imperfect Union: Slavery, Federalism, and Comity* (Chapel Hill: University of North Carolina Press, 1981); Leonard W. Levy, *The Law of the Commonwealth and Chief Justice Shaw* (New York: Oxford University Press, 1957); T. K. Hunter, "Geographies of Liberty: A Brief Look at Two Cases," in *Prophets of Protest: Reconsidering the History of American Abolitionism*, ed. Timothy Patrick McCarthy and John Stauffer (New York: The New Press, 2006); Stuart Streichler, *Justice Curtis in the Civil War Era: At the Crossroads of American Constitutionalism* (Charlottesville: University of Virginia Press, 2005); Sue Peabody and Keila Grinberg, "Introduction. Free Soil: The Generation and Principle of an Atlantic Legal Principle," *Slavery and Abolition* 32, no. 3 (September 2011): 332; Sue Peabody, *"There Are No Slaves in France": The Political Culture of Race and Slavery in the Ancien Régime* (New York: Oxford University Press, 1996); Edlie Wong, *Neither Fugitive nor Free: Atlantic Slavery, Freedom Suits, and the Legal Culture of Travel* (New York: New York University Press, 2009); Carolyn L. Karcher, *The First Woman in the Republic: A Cultural Biography of Lydia Maria Child* (Durham: Duke University Press, 1994); Lee V. Chambers, *The Weston Sisters: An American Abolitionist Family* (Chapel Hill: University of North Carolina Press, 2014).

4. Anna Mae Duane, ed., *Child Slavery before and after Emancipation: An Argument for Child-Centered Slavery Studies* (New York: Cambridge University Press, 2017); Karen Sánchez-Eppler, *Dependent States: The Child's Part in Nineteenth-Century American Culture* (Chicago: University of Chicago Press, 2005); Robin Bernstein, *Racial Innocence: Performing Childhood from Slavery to Civil Rights* (New York: New York University Press, 2011); Nazera Sadiq Wright, *Black Girlhood in the Nineteenth Century* (Urbana: University of Illinois, 2016); Katharine Capshaw, *Civil Rights Childhood: Picturing Liberation in African American Photobooks* (Minneapolis: University of Minnesota Press, 2014).

INTRODUCTION: THE SAID MED

1. Don E. Fehrenbacher, *The Dred Scott Case: Its Significance in American Law and Politics* (New York: Oxford University Press, 1978), 54.
2. Samuel Slater, "Refuge of Oppression," *Liberator*, October 15, 1836. The Samuel Slater mentioned in this paragraph is no relation to the famous English-American industrialist Samuel Slater, known as the "Father of the American Industrial Revolution."
3. Lydia Maria Child to Esther Carpenter, September 4, 1836, *Letters of Lydia Maria Child* (Boston: Houghton Mifflin, 1882), 20–21.
4. *Case of the Slave-Child, Med. Report of the Arguments of Counsel, and of the Opinion of the Court, in the Case of Commonwealth vs. Aves; Tried and Determined in the Supreme Judicial Court of Massachusetts* (Boston: Isaac Knapp, 1836), 3.
5. *Case of the Slave-Child, Med*, 3; "History," Boston Police Department News, http://bpdnews.com/history/. A "Leven L. Harris" does appear in the Boston Athenæum's *Directory of African Americans in Boston, 1820–1865* database, which suggests that he was still a resident of Boston in 1855. https://www.bostonathenaeum.org/library/electronic-resources/boston-athenaeum-directory-african-americans-in-boston-1820-1865.
6. Frederick Douglass, *Narrative of the Life of Frederick Douglass*, in *Classic Slave Narratives*, ed. Henry Louis Gates Jr. (New York: Penguin, 1987), 258–59; Harriet Jacobs, *Incidents in the Life of a Slave Girl*, in Gates, *Classic Slave Narratives* (New York: Penguin, 1987), 341; *Case of the Slave-Child, Med*, 4; Douglass, *Narrative*, 255. Nazera Sadiq Wright notes that age six is a particularly important age for black girls in antebellum literature: "The youthful and unknowing girl represents a blank slate with the capacity to undergo transformation through intellectual agency and achievement." Nazera Sadiq Wright, *Black Girlhood in the Nineteenth Century* (Urbana: University of Illinois, 2016), 61.
7. John Carroll Power, comp., *History of the Early Settlers of Sangamon County, Illinois—1876* (1999), http://sangamon.illinoisgenweb.org/1876/slatere.htm; *Case of the Slave-Child, Med*, 4, including quotations.
8. *Case of the Slave-Child, Med*, 4.
9. *Case of the Slave-Child, Med*, 4.
10. Leonard W. Levy, *The Law of the Commonwealth and Chief Justice Shaw* (New York: Oxford University Press, 1957), 68; Paul Finkelman, *An Imperfect Union: Slavery, Federalism, and Comity* (Chapel Hill: University of North Carolina Press, 1981), 127. See also Edlie Wong, *Neither Fugitive nor Free: Atlantic Slavery, Freedom Suits, and the Legal Culture of Travel* (New York: New York University Press, 2009), chap. 2.
11. Stephen Kendrick and Paul Kendrick, *Sarah's Long Walk: The Free Blacks of Boston and How Their Struggle for Equality Changed America* (Boston: Beacon Press, 2004),

xvi–xvii. We do not know for sure which house was inhabited by the Aves family because street numbering could be fluid in the 1830s. The legal documents from the Med case and *Stimpson's Boston Directory* list the Aves address as #21 Pinckney Street, but there is some tentative evidence that today the building might be #25. An exploration of the Suffolk Registry of Deeds was inconclusive because the deeds from the time period did not include street numbers; the alternate numbering hypothesis is based solely on descriptions of properties and later maps.

12. See *Greenwood v. Curtis*, 6 Mass. 358, March 1810. Curtis was sued for failing to fulfill a contract to deliver slaves. See also Finkelman, *Imperfect Union*, 80–81, and Albert J. Von Frank, *The Trials of Anthony Burns: Freedom and Slavery in Emerson's Boston* (Cambridge: Harvard University Press, 1998), 299–300.
13. *Case of the Slave-Child, Med.* The informal case name remained in common usage. See, for example: "The case of the slave child Med, decided by the Supreme Court of this state, on a habeas corpus, has settled the question that this class of persons cannot be reclaimed as fugitives." Samuel E. Sewall, "Speech of the Hon. S. E. Sewall of Middlesex, in the Senate on the Bill to Protect Personal Liberty," *Frederick Douglass' Paper*, June 24, 1852. Med is never referred to as "Med Slater," after her owners. Her unusual name, "Med," remains mysterious. Slave names were very often classical names or place names, and thus Med may be short for Medford.
14. However, as Anna Mae Duane observes, while it is difficult to recover "the authentic experience of children," we can "elicit the hidden voices of children in texts in ways that can reveal children's presence as historical actors" by listening "creatively to both adult representations of children and the influence children may have had on those representations." Anna Mae Duane, *Suffering Childhood in Early America: Violence, Race, and the Making of the Child Victim* (Athens: University of Georgia Press, 2010), 9.
15. P. Gabrielle Foreman et al., "Writing about Slavery/Teaching about Slavery: This Might Help," community-sourced document, https://docs.google.com/document/d/1A4TEdDgYslX-hlKezLodMIM71My3KTNozxRvoIQTOQs/mobilebasic.
16. Karen Sánchez-Eppler, "'Remember, Dear, when the Yankees came through here, I was only ten years old': Valuing the Enslaved Child of the WPA Slave Narratives," in *Child Slavery before and after Emancipation: An Argument for Child-Centered Slavery Studies*, ed. Anna Mae Duane (New York: Cambridge University Press, 2017), 29, 42, 43; Anna Mae Duane, "Introduction: When Is a Child a Slave?," in Duane, *Child Slavery before and after Emancipation*, 5.
17. Douglass, *Narrative*, 294; Sarah L. H. Gronningsater, "Born Free in the Master's House: Children and Gradual Emancipation in the Early American North" in Duane, *Child Slavery before and after Emancipation*, 124–27.
18. Kidada E. Williams, "Maintaining a Radical Vision of African Americans in the Age of Freedom," *The Journal of the Civil War Era* 7, no. 1 (March 2017), https://www.journalofthecivilwarera.org/forum-the-future-of-reconstruction-studies/maintaining-a-radical-vision/.

CHAPTER 1: BEFORE MED

1. Vincent Carretta, *Phillis Wheatley: Biography of a Genius in Bondage* (Athens: University of Georgia Press, 2014), 7; Jennifer Thorn, "Phillis Wheatley's Ghosts: The Racial Melancholy of New England Protestants," *The Eighteenth Century* 50, no. 1 (2009): 71.

2. Thorn, "Phillis Wheatley's Ghosts"; Lucia Hodgson, "Infant Muse: Phillis Wheatley and the Revolutionary Rhetoric of Childhood," *Early American Literature* 49, no. 3 (2014): 663–82; June Jordan, "The Difficult Miracle of Black Poetry in America," Poetry Foundation (August 15, 2006), https://www.poetryfoundation.org/articles/68628/the-difficult-miracle-of-black-poetry-in-america.
3. Phillis Wheatley, *The Collected Works of Phillis Wheatley* (New York: Oxford University Press, 1989), 74.
4. Eric Robert Papenfuse, "From Redcompense to Revolution: *Mahoney v. Ashton* and the Transfiguration of Maryland Culture, 1791–1802," *Slavery and Abolition* 15, no. 3 (1994): 42; *Smith v. Brown & Cooper*, (1701) 2 Ld. Raym. 1274; *Smith v. Gould*, (1705) S.C. Salk. 666, pl.2.
5. Norman Poser, *Lord Mansfield: Justice in the Age of Reason* (Montreal and Kingston: McGill-Queen's University Press, 2013), 289.
6. T. K. Hunter, "Publishing Freedom, Winning Arguments: *Somerset*, Natural Rights, and Massachusetts Freedom Cases, 1772–1836" (PhD diss., Columbia University, 2005), 4. *Somerset* might additionally be understood, as George Van Cleve argues, as "an imperial conflict of laws case." In other words, arguments about "how a slave's status changed when the slave came to England" were often also "arguments about imperial governance." George Van Cleve, "*Somerset's Case* and Its Antecedents in Imperial Perspective," *Law and History Review* 24, no. 3 (Fall 2006): 603.
7. Tim Cresswell, "Moral Geographies," in *Cultural Geography: A Critical Dictionary of Key Concepts*, ed. David Atkinson et al. (New York: Palgrave Macmillan, 2005), 128; Sue Peabody and Keila Grinberg, "Introduction. Free Soil: The Generation and Principle of an Atlantic Legal Principle," *Slavery and Abolition* 32, no. 3 (Sept. 2011): 331–32. See also Francis Hargrave, *An Argument in the Case of James Sommersett* (Boston: Russell, 1774); T. K. Hunter, "Transatlantic Negotiations: Lord Mansfield, Liberty, and *Somerset*," *Texas Wesleyan Law Review* 13, no. 2 (March 2007): 712.
8. *Somerset v. Stewart* [*Somerset's Case*], (1772) Lofft 1, 500, 506, 509.
9. *Somerset v. Stewart* [*Somerset's Case*], 510.
10. M. S. Weiner, "Notes and Documents—New Biographical Evidence on *Somerset's Case*," *Slavery and Abolition* 23, no. 1 (2002): 124–26; Hunter, "Transatlantic Negotiations," 725.
11. William M. Wiecek, "*Somerset*: Lord Mansfield and the Legitimacy of Slavery in the Anglo-American World," *University of Chicago Law Review* 42, no. 1 (Autumn 1974): 87, 106, 141. One caution: cases brought before the King's Bench in the eighteenth century were not recorded; decisions were given orally, and they only survive if someone in the audience was taking notes. See Wiecek, "*Somerset*," 145–46.
12. *West's Encyclopedia of American Law, Edition 2.* s.v. "Positive Law," http://legal-dictionary.thefreedictionary.com/Positive+Law; Van Cleve, "*Somerset's Case*," 644. The ruling also created a new premise of human rights: "Somerset's humanity gave him legal protection from being physically removed from England by Stewart. This human right was not qualified by his race, birthplace or subjectship. . . . In this sense, the case contributed to the abstraction of English liberty into a human right. Still, it remained a liberty available to people *in England* rather than everywhere. . . . The empire's legal pluralism allowed Mansfield to rationalize the brutality of slavery while locating it offshore." Daniel J. Hulsebosch, "Nothing but Liberty: *Somerset's Case*

and the British Empire," *Law and History Review* 24, no. 3 (Fall 2006): 656–57. See also Eliga H. Gould, "Zones of Law, Zones of Violence: The Legal Geography of the British Atlantic, circa 1772," *William and Mary Quarterly* 60, no. 3 (July 2003): 471–510.

13. Vernacular law, this "general notion of legal principles and procedures that are understood and acted upon by a community, sometimes independent of—and even in opposition to—more formal or statist political or juridical powers," seems to be a perfect description of what happened following the *Somerset* case. Sue Peabody, "La Race, l'esclavage et 'la francité,': L'affaire Furcy," trans. Cyril Le Roy, in *Français? La nation en débat entre colonies et métropole, XVIe-XIXe siècle*, ed. Cécile Vidale (Paris: les Editions de l'EHESS, 2014), 189–210. Vernacular law was particularly influential in eighteenth-century England because most criminal cases and everyday legal business were judged and administered by local justices of the peace, who were influenced by local values. Their decisions often diverged from those of the legal establishment. "The interpretation and enforcement of the law . . . was not a matter for the judges alone. The majority of criminal cases and much routine administrative business was left to the local justices of the peace. These justices were representatives of the county elite, chosen for their status rather than for their legal knowledge. Some did have formal legal training, but for the most part they administered justice with the aid of manuals and treatises, local knowledge, advice from colleagues and a hefty dollop of what could be termed (depending on one's perspective) either common sense or social prejudice. The decisions they took were not necessarily congruent with the law as conceived by trained jurists." Ruth Paley, "After *Somerset*: Mansfield, Slavery, and the Law in England, 1772–1830," in *Law, Crime, and English Society, 1660–1830*, ed. Norma Landau (Cambridge: Cambridge University Press, 2002), 179.

14. Prince Hoare, *Memoirs of Granville Sharpe* (London: Henry Colburn, 1828), I, 115–16, 134, quoted in F. O. Shyllon, *Black Slaves in Britain* (New York: Oxford University Press, 1974), 92, 106; Paley, "After *Somerset*," 183.

15. Carretta, *Phillis Wheatley: Biography*, 128; Joanna Brooks, "Our Phillis, Ourselves," *American Literature* 82, no. 1 (January 1, 2010): 5; Patricia Bradley, "Slavery in Colonial Newspapers: The *Somerset Case*," *Journalism History* 12, no. 1 (Spring 1985): 4; Steven M. Wise, *Though the Heavens May Fall: The Landmark Trial That Led to the End of Human Slavery* (Cambridge: DaCapo Press, 2005), 200–201.

16. Wiecek, "Somerset," 115.

17. Van Gosse, "'As a Nation, the English Are Our Friends': The Emergence of African American Politics in the British Atlantic World, 1772–1861," *American Historical Review* 113, no. 4 (October 2008): 1008.

18. Margot Minardi, *Making Slavery History: Abolitionism and the Politics of Memory in Massachusetts* (New York: Oxford University Press, 2012), 37. For an extended discussion of *Somerset* and *Aves*, see Leonard W. Levy, *The Law of the Commonwealth and Chief Justice Shaw* (New York: Oxford University Press, 1957; Paul Finkelman, *An Imperfect Union: Slavery, Federalism, and Comity* (Chapel Hill: University of North Carolina Press, 1981); T. K. Hunter, "Geographies of Liberty: A Brief Look at Two Cases," in *Prophets of Protest: Reconsidering the History of American Abolitionism*, ed. Timothy Patrick McCarthy and John Stauffer (New York: The New Press, 2006); Wiecek, "Somerset."

19. David Waldstreicher, "Ancients, Moderns, and Africans: Phillis Wheatley and the Politics of Empire and Slavery in the American Revolution," *Journal of the Early Republic* 37, no. 4 (2017): 709–10; Vincent Carretta, "Phillis Wheatley, the Mansfield Decision of 1772, and the Choice of Identity," in *Early America Re-Explored: New Readings in Colonial, Early National, and Antebellum Culture*, ed. Fritz Fleischmann and Klaus H. Schmidt (New York: Lang, 2002), 202, 208.
20. Wheatley, *Collected Works*, 119.
21. Carretta, *Phillis Wheatley: Biography*, 135–36.
22. Carretta, *Phillis Wheatley: Biography*, 136–37.
23. Carretta, *Phillis Wheatley: Biography*, 137–45.
24. Phillis Wheatley to Samson Occom, February 11, 1774, in Wheatley, *Collected Works*, 176–77; Philip Gould, "Slavery in the Eighteenth-Century Literary Imagination," in *Cambridge Companion to Slavery in American Literature*, ed. Ezra F. Tawil (New York: Cambridge University Press, 2016), 27.
25. Phillis Wheatley to Samson Occom, February 11, 1774, in Wheatley, *Collected Works*, 176–77.
26. Wheatley, *Collected Works*, 149–50.
27. Carretta, *Phillis Wheatley: Biography*, 176, 196; quotations from Brooks, "Our Phillis, Ourselves," 16–17; Ignatius Sancho, *Letters of the Late Ignatius Sancho, An African. In Two Volumes. To Which Are Prefixed, Memoirs of His Life, Vol. 1.* (London: J. Nichols, 1782), 176, http://docsouth.unc.edu/neh/sancho1/sancho1.html.
28. Minardi, *Making Slavery History*, 102.
29. Jeffrey Bilbro, "Who Are Lost and How They're Found: Redemption and Theodicy in Wheatley, Newton, and Cowper," *Early American Literature* 47, no. 3 (2012): 583; Matthew Wyman-McCarthy, "Rethinking Empire in India and the Atlantic: William Cowper, John Newton, and the Imperial Origins of Evangelical Abolitionism," *Slavery and Abolition* 35, no. 2 (April 3, 2014): 310. Contemporary poet and scholar Honorée Fanonne Jeffers makes the connection between Wheatley and Cowper in her forthcoming collection, *The Age of Phillis*. Jeffers's poem "The Transatlantic Progress of Sugar in the Eighteenth Century" uses a stanza from Cowper's "Pity for Poor Africans" as an epigraph. Jeffers is one of the few current scholars to note Wheatley's influence on evangelical rhetoric and British abolitionism.
30. Karen O'Brien, "'Still at Home': Cowper's Domestic Empires," *Early Romantics: Perspectives in British Poetry from Pope to Wordsworth*, ed. Thomas Woodman (New York: Macmillan, 1998), 134. The *Zong* massacre galvanized the abolitionist movement in the late eighteenth century. In 1781, about 130 enslaved people were thrown overboard because of a water shortage on the slaving ship *Zong*. Activists Granville Sharp and Olaudah Equiano advocated for murder charges, but the case, *Gregson v. Gilbert*, was only heard as a maritime insurance claim regarding "jettisoned cargo." The underwriters, who did not wish to pay for the insured, murdered enslaved people, successfully appealed to Lord Mansfield on the King's Bench for a second trial. He granted the new trial because heavy rains had alleviated the water shortage; note that no one was ever prosecuted for murder. See Shyllon, *Black Slaves in Britain*, 184–209.
31. Suvir Kaul, *Poems of Nation, Anthems of Empire: English Verse in the Long Eighteenth-Century* (Charlottesville: University of Virginia Press, 2000), 1; James Thomson, "Rule, Britannia!," in *Complete Poetical Works of James Thomson* (London: Oxford University Press, 1908), 422–23. Readers of Harriet Jacobs will remember her famous chapter "The Loophole of Retreat," in which she hides in her grandmother's attic

crawlspace and watches the world go by, a clear nod to Cowper's lines in book IV of the poem:

> 'Tis pleasant, through the loopholes of retreat,
> To peep at such a world; to see the stir
> Of the great Babel, and not feel the crowd;
> To hear the roar she sends through all her gates
> At a safe distance, where the dying sound
> Falls a soft murmur on the uninjur'd ear.

William Cowper, *The Task: A Poem, In Six Books* (London: J. Johnson, 1785), bk. 4, lines 88–93.
32. Cowper, *The Task*, bk. 2, lines 40–42.
33. Cowper, *The Task*, bk. 2, lines 6–28.
34. Brycchan Carey, *British Abolitionism and the Rhetoric of Sensibility* (New York: Palgrave Macmillan, 2005), 18.
35. Cowper, *The Task*, bk. 2, lines 37–47.
36. Christopher Brown, *Moral Capital Foundations of British Abolitionism* (Chapel Hill: University of North Carolina Press), 27. "The new British Empire, post-dating the slave trade, is to be defined by its power *and* its mercy," as Suvir Kaul explains, "a winning combination of military and moral authority." Kaul, *Poems of Nation*, 239. See also Wyman-McCarthy, "Rethinking Empire," 312.
37. "Sonnet Addressed to William Wilberforce, Esq." (1792) hints at the power of British free soil, a place where Africans might find freedom "fenc'd with British laws."
38. William E. Channing, *The Duty of the Free States, or remarks suggested by the case of the Creole* (Boston: William Crosby, 1842).
39. *Case of the Slave-Child, Med. Report of the Arguments of Counsel, and of the Opinion of the Court, in the Case of Commonwealth vs. Aves; Tried and Determined in the Supreme Judicial Court of Massachusetts* (Boston: Isaac Knapp, 1836), 27.
40. *Case of the Slave-Child, Med*, 27. The *Vermont Telegraph* celebrated the Med ruling by quoting another section of Cowper: "Be it known that any slave coming to a free state with the consent of his master, whether in the way of accompanying him on a visit or otherwise is 'emancipate and loosed' the moment his feet are on our soil." Quoted in "Judge Shaw Declares Freedom for Child, Med," *Liberator*, October 22, 1836.
41. Richard S. Newman, "'Lucky to be born in Pennsylvania': Free Soil, Fugitive Slaves and the Making of Pennsylvania's Anti-Slavery Borderland," *Slavery and Abolition* 32, no. 3 (September 2011): 16, 415.
42. Richard S. Newman, *The Transformation of American Abolitionism: Fighting Slavery in the Early Republic* (Chapel Hill: University of North Carolina Press, 2002), 61. See also Richard S. Newman, "The PAS and American Abolitionism: A Century of Activism from the American Revolutionary Era to the Civil War," *Pennsylvania Abolition Society Digital Exhibit*, Historical Society of Pennsylvania, http://hsp.org/sites/default/files/legacy_files/migrated/newmanpasessay.pdf, 1; Christopher Densmore, "Seeking Freedom in the Courts: The Work of the Pennsylvania Society for promoting the Abolition of Slavery, and for the Relief of Free Negroes unlawfully held in Bondage, and for improving the Condition of the African Race, 1775–1865," *Pennsylvania Legacies* (November 2005): 16–19. Lydia Maria Child was very familiar with these practices through her friendship and collaboration with Quaker PAS member Isaac Hopper. Her 1853 biography of Hopper, written in tribute after

his death, contains a series of sketches of slaves who gained their freedom through residence in Pennsylvania, through habeas corpus actions, and by running away. See Lydia Maria Child, *Isaac T. Hopper: A True Life* (Boston: John P. Jewett, 1853). See also Isaac T. Hopper, *Kidnappers in Philadelphia: Isaac Hopper's Tales of Oppression, 1780–1843*, comp. Daniel E. Meaders (New York: Garland Pub., 1994).

43. Newman, "'Lucky to be born in Pennsylvania,'" 424; Finkelman, *Imperfect Union*, 65, 67, 242–43; *Butler v. Hopper*, 4 F. Cas. 904 (1806); *Commonwealth v. Holloway*, 2 S. &R. (Pa.) 305 (1816); *Ex parte Simmons*, 22 F. Cas. 151 (1823).

44. Meredith McGill, "Poetry of Slavery," in *Cambridge Companion to Slavery in American Literature*, ed. Ezra F. Tawil (New York: Cambridge University Press, 2016), 124; Jennifer Rene Young, "Marketing a Sable Muse: Phillis Wheatley and the Antebellum Press," in *New Essays on Phillis Wheatley*, ed. John C. Shields and Eric D. Lamore (Knoxville: University of Tennessee Press, 2011), 223; Karen Weyler, *Empowering Words: Outsiders and Authorship in Early America* (Athens; London: University of Georgia Press, 2013), 73; Lydia Maria Francis Child, *An Appeal in Favor of That Class of Americans Called Africans* (Boston: Allen and Ticknor, 1833), 171. Wheatley was also reprinted in abolitionist and black newspapers in the 1850s, including *Freedom's Journal*, *Coloured American*, *North Star*, and *Frederick Douglass' Paper*. Young, "Marketing a Sable Muse," 224.

45. Margaretta Matilda Odell, *Memoir and Poems of Phillis Wheatley, a Native African and a Slave. Dedicated to the Friends of the Africans* (Boston: George W. Light, 1834), 5; Phillis Wheatley et al., *Memoir and Poems of Phillis Wheatley, a Native African and a Slave: Also, Poems by a Slave* (Boston: Isaac Knapp, 1838); McGill, "Poetry of Slavery," 124.

46. Catherine Clinton and Sean Qualls, *Phillis's Big Test* (Boston: Houghton Mifflin, 2008); Maryann N. Weidt and Mary O'Keefe Young, *Revolutionary Poet: A Story about Phillis Wheatley*, A Carolrhoda Creative Minds Biography (Minneapolis: Carolrhoda Books, 1997); Afua Cooper, *My Name Is Phillis Wheatley: A Story of Slavery and Freedom* (Toronto: KCP Fiction, 2009).

47. Kidada E. Williams, "Maintaining a Radical Vision of African Americans in the Age of Freedom," *The Journal of the Civil War Era* 7, no. 1 (March 2017), https://journalofthecivilwarera.org/forum-the-future-of-reconstruction-studies/maintaining-a-radical-vision/.

CHAPTER 2: SLAVES CANNOT BREATHE IN BOSTON

1. John C. McConnell, "A History of Superior Court Architecture in Massachusetts" (2002), http://vintage.socialaw.com/renovation/houseslawmconn.htm; Isaac Smith Homans, *Sketches of Boston, Past and Present* (Cambridge: Metcalf, 1851), 169; William W. Wheildon, *Memoir of Solomon Willard, Architect and Superintendent of the Bunker Hill Monument* (Boston: Monument Association, 1865), 230; "New Court House in Boston," *American Magazine of Useful and Entertaining Knowledge* 3, no. 3 (December 1836): 89–90; John K. Hastings, "Anti-Slavery Landmarks in Boston," *Boston Transcript*, September 1, 1897, 3–4.

2. Elizabeth Heyrick, *Immediate, not gradual abolition, or, An inquiry into the shortest, safest and most effectual means of getting rid of West-Indian slavery* (London: R. Clay, 1824); Richard S. Newman, *The Transformation of American Abolitionism: Fighting Slavery in the Early Republic* (Chapel Hill: University of North Carolina Press, 2002),

86, 104, 100; Manisha Sinha, *The Slave's Cause: A History of Abolition* (New Haven: Yale University Press, 2016), 219–21, 223–28.
3. New England Anti-Slavery Society, *First Annual Report of the Board of Managers of the New-England Anti-Slavery Society* (Boston: Garrison and Knapp, 1833), 45–47; Leonard W. Levy, *The Law of the Commonwealth and Chief Justice Shaw* (New York: Oxford University Press, 1957), 61.
4. Barbara Bennett Woodhouse, *Hidden in Plain Sight: The Tragedy of Children's Rights from Ben Franklin to Lionel Tate* (Princeton: Princeton University Press, 2008), 26; Anna Mae Duane, "The Child as a Pivot Point between Consent and Complicity," in *Child Slavery before and after Emancipation: An Argument for Child-Centered Slavery Studies*, ed. Anna Mae Duane (New York: Cambridge University Press, 2017), 151.
5. *In re Francisco*, 9 Am. Jr. 490 (1833).
6. Levy, *Law of the Commonwealth*, 62.
7. *Case of the Slave-Child, Med. Report of the Arguments of Counsel, and of the Opinion of the Court, in the Case of Commonwealth vs. Aves; Tried and Determined in the Supreme Judicial Court of Massachusetts* (Boston: Isaac Knapp, 1836), 25.
8. Debra Gold Hansen, *Strained Sisterhood: Gender and Class in the Boston Female Anti-Slavery Society* (Amherst: University of Massachusetts Press, 1993), 28, 64–65. See also Shirley J. Yee, *Black Women Abolitionists: A Study in Activism, 1828–1860* (Knoxville: University of Tennessee Press), 90, 130; Newman, *Transformation of American Abolitionism*, 170–71; Debra Gold Hansen, "The Boston Female Anti-Slavery Society and the Limits of Gender Politics," in *The Abolitionist Sisterhood: Women's Political Culture in Antebellum America*, ed. Jean Fagan Yellin and John C. Van Horne (Ithaca: Cornell University Press, 1994), 45–46.
9. Lee V. Chambers, *The Weston Sisters: An American Abolitionist Family* (Chapel Hill: University of North Carolina Press, 2014), 5, 146–47.
10. Lydia Maria Child to Lucretia Mott, March 5, 1839, in *Lydia Maria Child: Selected Letters*, ed. Milton Meltzer and Patricia G. Holland (Amherst: University of Massachusetts Press, 1982), 107; Carolyn L. Karcher, *The First Woman in the Republic: A Cultural Biography of Lydia Maria Child* (Durham: Duke University Press, 1994), 182–94, 217.
11. Karcher, *First Woman in the Republic*, 227.
12. Karcher, *First Woman in the Republic*, 227; Lydia Maria Child to Louisa Loring, August 15, [1835], in *The Collected Correspondence of Lydia Maria Child, 1817–1880*, ed. Patricia G. Holland, Milton Meltzer, and Francine Krasno (Millwood, NY: Kraus Microform, 1980), microfiche 3/80.
13. Karcher, *First Woman in the Republic*, 228.
14. Anne Warren Weston to Aunt Mary Weston, October 22, 1835, Ms. A.9.2.4.26, Weston Family Papers, Anti-Slavery Manuscripts, Boston Public Library; Anne Warren Weston to Aunt Mary Weston, October 27, 1835, Ms. A.9.2.7.71, Weston Family Papers, Anti-Slavery Manuscripts, Boston Public Library; Anne Warren Weston to Aunt Mary Weston, October 30, 1835, Ms. A.9.2.7.72, Weston Family Papers, Anti-Slavery Manuscripts, Boston Public Library. For an account of Garrison's capture and rescue, see Nina Moore Tiffany, *Samuel E. Sewall: A Memoir* (Boston: Houghton Mifflin, 1898), 45–52.
15. Boston Female Anti-Slavery Society, *Right and Wrong in Boston: Report of the Boston Female Anti-Slavery Society; with a concise statement of events, previous and subsequent*

to the Annual Meeting of 1835 (Boston: Isaac Knapp, 1836), 39; Harriet Martineau, *The Martyr Age of the United States* (Boston: Weeks, Jordan, 1839), 3.

16. "Meteorological," *American Railroad Journal* 23 (New York: John H. Shuze, 1850), 260; Raymond S. Bradley, Jon K. Eischeid, and Philip T. Ives, *The Climate of Amherst, Massachusetts, 1836–1985*, Contribution No. 50, (Amherst: University of Massachusetts, Department of Geology and Geography, 1987), http://www.geo.umass.edu/research/Geosciences%20Publications/v50BradleyetalCovered.pdf, pp. 97, 101.

17. Chambers, *Weston Sisters*, 20, 25; Boston Female Anti-Slavery Society (BFASS), *Right and Wrong in Boston, in 1836. Annual Report of the Boston Female Anti-Slavery Society, being a concise history of the cases of the slave child, Med, and of the women demanded as slaves of the Supreme Judicial Court of Mass. with all the other proceedings of the society* (Boston: Isaac Knapp, 1836), 32. This petition campaign would continue for twenty-five years. See also Susan Zaeske, "Signatures of Citizenship: The Rhetoric of Women's Antislavery Petitions," *Quarterly Journal of Speech* 88, no. 2 (May 2002): 147–68.

18. BFASS, *Right and Wrong in Boston, in 1836*, 40–41.

19. BFASS, *Right and Wrong in Boston, in 1836*, 41–48.

20. BFASS, *Right and Wrong in Boston, in 1836*, 47–48. See also the broadside, "A Proclamation for a Day of Public Thanksgiving and Praise, by Lt. Governor of the Commonwealth of Massachusetts," October 3, 1835, http://www.classicapologetics.com/special/thanks/Armstrong.Mass.TP.10-03-1835.pdf

21. Maria Weston Chapman to Debora Weston, 1836 [?], Ms. A.9.2. 3.29, Weston Family Papers, Anti-Slavery Manuscripts, Boston Public Library; Anne Warren Weston to Maria Weston Chapman, August 1, 1836, Weston Family Papers, Anti-Slavery Manuscripts, Boston Public Library, Digital Commonwealth, http://ark.digitalcommonwealth.org/ark:/50959/vm417g186. The Debora Weston quotation is contained within the Anne Warren Weston letter.

22. BFASS, *Right and Wrong in Boston, in 1836*, 49.

23. Tiffany, *Samuel E. Sewall*, 62–64; BFASS, *Right and Wrong in Boston, in 1836*, 47–48.

24. BFASS, *Right and Wrong in Boston, in 1836*, 48–52; Leonard W. Levy, "The 'Abolition Riot': Boston's First Slave Rescue," *New England Quarterly* 25, no. 1 (March 1952): 85–92.

25. BFASS, *Right and Wrong in Boston, in 1836*, 52.

26. BFASS, *Right and Wrong in Boston, in 1836*, 52.

27. Tiffany, *Samuel E. Sewall*, 62–64.

28. BFASS, *Right and Wrong in Boston, in 1836*, 62.

29. Letter to the Portage County [Ohio?] Female Anti-Slavery Society, BFASS Letterbook, August 27, 1836, P-176, microfilm reel 1, Ms. N-1887, Massachusetts Historical Society.

30. Letter to Sewall, Esq., The Abolition Lawyer, August 2, 1836, Robie-Sewall Family Papers, 1611–1905, Massachusetts Historical Society; William A. Clarke to Samuel E. Sewall, Esq., August 9, 1836, Robie-Sewall Family Papers, Massachusetts Historical Society. Several weeks after the case, a U.S. naval officer from Baltimore went to Sewall's office and assaulted him with a whip, in a scene eerily prescient of the caning attack on Senator Charles Sumner on the Senate floor in May 1856 by Representative Preston Brooks of South Carolina. See Levy, *Law of the Commonwealth*, 92.

31. "Case of the Colored Women," *New York Emancipator*, August 25, 1836, 2.

32. BFASS, *Right and Wrong in Boston, in 1836*, 63–64.
33. Francis Hilliard, *The Elements of Law: being a comprehensive summary of American civil jurisprudence. For the use of students, men of business, and general readers* (Boston: Hilliard, Gray and Company, 1835), 29.
34. Lesley Ginsberg, "Of Babies, Beasts, and Bondage: Slavery and the Question of Citizenship in Antebellum American Children's Literature," in *The American Child: A Cultural Studies Reader*, ed. Caroline F. Levander and Carol J. Singley (New Brunswick: Rutgers University Press, 2003), 94.
35. BFASS, *Right and Wrong in Boston, in 1836*, 64–65.
36. Lydia Maria Child to Esther Carpenter, September 4, 1836, in Holland, *Collected Correspondence*, microfiche 4/103.
37. BFASS, *Right and Wrong in Boston, in 1836*, 64–66.
38. Edlie Wong, *Neither Fugitive nor Free: Atlantic Slavery, Freedom Suits, and the Legal Culture of Travel* (New York: New York University Press, 2009), 88. BFASS knew this narrative from the abolitionist press, which often portrayed black girls as "objects of white benevolence" to be rescued by white women. Nazera Sadiq Wright, *Black Girlhood in the Nineteenth Century* (Urbana: University of Illinois, 2016), 41.
39. "Another Slave Case," *New Bedford Mercury*, August 26, 1836, 1.
40. BFASS, *Right and Wrong in Boston, in 1836*, 67.
41. "The Slave Case," *Liberator*, September 3, 1836, 143. Rufus Choate became hostile to the antislavery movement later in his life.
42. Joseph Story to Ellis Gray Loring, November 5, 1836, A-115, box 1, folder 17, Ellis Gray Loring Family Papers, Schlesinger Library, Radcliffe Institute, Harvard University; *Case of the Slave-Child, Med*, 35. For a useful legal explication, see also Stuart Streichler, *Justice Curtis in the Civil War Era: At the Crossroads of American Constitutionalism* (Charlottesville: University of Virginia Press, 2005).
43. Lydia Maria Child to Esther Carpenter, September 4, 1836, *Letters of Lydia Maria Child* (Boston: Houghton Mifflin, 1882), 20–21; *Case of the Slave-Child, Med*, 5. See also Octavius Pickering, *Reports of Cases Argued and Determined in the Supreme Judicial Court of Massachusetts* (Boston: Little and Brown, 1840), vol. xviii, 193–225; *Case of the Slave-Child, Med*, 25.
44. *Case of the Slave-Child, Med*, 13.
45. *Case of the Slave-Child, Med*, 13.
46. *Case of the Slave-Child, Med*, 13.
47. Levy, *Law of the Commonwealth*, 63.
48. *Case of the Slave-Child, Med*, 35.
49. *Case of the Slave-Child, Med*, 11–12.
50. *The Slave, Grace*, 2 Hagg. Adm. (G.B.) 94 (1827); Paul Finkelman, *An Imperfect Union: Slavery, Federalism, and Comity* (Chapel Hill: University of North Carolina Press, 1981), 185–86; William M. Wiecek, "Somerset: Lord Mansfield and the Legitimacy of Slavery in the Anglo-American World," *University of Chicago Law Review* 42, no. 1 (Autumn 1974): 111; T. K. Hunter, "Publishing Freedom, Winning Arguments: Somerset, Natural Rights, and Massachusetts Freedom Cases, 1772–1836" (PhD diss., Columbia University, 2005), 256. See also Patricia Hagler Minter, "'The State of Slavery': Somerset, The Slave, Grace, and the Rise of Pro-Slavery and Anti-Slavery Constitutionalism in the Nineteenth-Century Atlantic World," *Slavery and Abolition* 36, no. 5 (2015): 603–17.

51. *Case of the Slave-Child, Med*, 5; Finkelman, *Imperfect Union*, 187.
52. *Case of the Slave-Child, Med*, 17, 23, 29, 33.
53. Finkelman, *Imperfect Union*, 3–4.
54. *Case of the Slave-Child, Med*, 6, 10.
55. *Case of the Slave-Child, Med*, 20–21.
56. *Case of the Slave-Child, Med*, 11.
57. *Case of the Slave-Child, Med*, 17, 11.
58. *Case of the Slave-Child, Med*, 18, 19.
59. *Case of the Slave-Child, Med*, 19.
60. Deuteronomy 23:15; *Case of the Slave-Child, Med*, 23. Loring wanted to make sure that Shaw understood his point here. In a personal letter to Shaw on August 26, 1836, he reiterated his argument: "In remarking on the article touching fugitive slaves, I said it was indeed my opinion, that the northern states, in their concessions to slavery, particularly in pledging their active interposition for the restoration of runaway slaves, had made a compromise of principle—a surrender of conscience,—terms nearly equivalent to Judge Story's milder expression of our 'many sacrifices of opinion and feeling.' Still (I continued) when, as in the case of fugitive slaves the law of God, (Deuteronomy, XXIII.15) and the law of man conflict, I shall not urge this court to disregard or annul the human law. I only claim that when we get beyond the sphere or limits of the human enactment, the court [sic] are at liberty there to look to the will of God, alone." Ellis Gray Loring to Lemuel Shaw, August 29, 1836, P-206, reel 11, folder 1, microfilm edition of the Lemuel Shaw Papers, Massachusetts Historical Society.
61. William Cowper, *The Task: A Poem, In Six Books* (London: J. Johnson, 1785), bk. 2, lines 40–44.
62. *Case of the Slave-Child, Med*, 27.
63. Lydia Maria Child to Esther Carpenter, September 4, 1836, *Letters of Lydia Maria Child*, 20–21.
64. *Case of the Slave-Child Med*, 35. See also Lemuel Shaw, *Minutes of the Supreme Judicial Court of Massachusetts*, P-206, reel 37, vol. 15, pp. 229–40, microfilm edition of the Lemuel Shaw Papers, Massachusetts Historical Society.
65. *Case of the Slave-Child Med*, 36.
66. *Case of the Slave-Child Med*, 38.
67. *Case of the Slave-Child Med*, 40.
68. *Case of the Slave-Child Med*, 40.
69. *Case of the Slave-Child, Med*, 26.
70. Levy, *Law of the Commonwealth*, 68; Finkelman, *Imperfect Union*, 127; BFASS, *Right and Wrong in Boston, in 1836*, 68–69. See also Wong, *Neither Fugitive nor Free*, ch. 2.
71. BFASS, *Right and Wrong in Boston, in 1836*, 70.
72. "Important Decision," *Annual Report of the Board of Managers of the Massachusetts Anti-Slavery Society* (Boston: Isaac Knapp, 1837), 70.
73. *Liberator*, September–October 1836; *Liberator*, September 24, 1836; *Liberator*, September 3, 1836.
74. *Liberator*, September 10, 1836; "Decision of Judge Shaw," rep. in *Liberator*, October 8, 1836.
75. *Liberator*, September 24, 1836; BFASS, *Right and Wrong in Boston, in 1836*, 67.
76. *Case of the Slave-Child, Med*, 14. See also Sarah L. H. Gronningsater, "Born Free in

the Master's House: Children and Gradual Emancipation in the Early American North," in Duane, *Child Slavery before and after Emancipation*, 123–50.

CHAPTER 3: ALL GIRLS ARE BOUND TO SOMEONE

1. Caroline Weston to Debora Weston, after September 5, 1836[?], Ms. A.9.2.3.30, Weston Family Papers, Anti-Slavery Collection, Boston Public Library.
2. Nancy Prince, *A Narrative of the Life and Travels of Mrs. Nancy Prince* (Boston: N. Prince, 1850); Thomas B. Hilton, "Reminiscences: Woodfork and Nancy Prince," *Women's Era* I, no. 5 (August 1894); Sarah Brusky, "Nancy Prince and Her Gothic Odyssey: A Veiled Lady," in *Gender, Genre, and Identity in Women's Travel Writing*, ed. Kristi Siegel (New York: Peter Lang, 2004), 168. Ships were running regularly from New Orleans to northern cities. See John Hope Franklin, *A Southern Odyssey: Travelers in the Antebellum North* (Baton Rouge: Louisiana State University Press, 1976).
3. *Constitution of the Samaritan Asylum for Indigent Children* (Boston: Isaac Knapp, 1836), 3.
4. *Constitution of the Samaritan Asylum*. It is not clear how long the asylum stayed open, but the state dissolved its charter in 1917, along with hundreds of other corporations and charities, in what was likely a cleanup of Massachusetts legal records and tax reform. See *Public Documents of Massachusetts: Being the Annual Reports of Various Public Officers and Institutions for the Year 1917*, vol. XIV, xii.
5. See, for example, Anne Warren Weston's account of a controversial vote: "The meeting of our society was held. It was quite a full one and Miss Sullivan presided.... Mrs. Shipley then introduced the motion that we give this year $500 to the Samaritan Asylum. Ann Chapman made a very good speech opposing it, shewing [sic] that our enemies would maintain that, but that we must do for the Society. Mrs. Shipley however persisted and had it put to vote, we are all voting against it. We had the majority and it was not passed." Anne Warren Weston to Debora Weston, January 16, 1837, Ms. A.9.2.9.7, Weston Family Papers, Anti-Slavery Manuscripts, Boston Public Library, http://ark.digitalcommonwealth.org/ark:/50959/wm117v339.
6. "To the editor of the Liberator," *Liberator*, May 16, 1835; Isaiah 54:2.
7. T. K. Hunter, "Publishing Freedom, Winning Arguments: *Somerset*, Natural Rights and Massachusetts Freedom Cases, 1772–1836" (PhD diss., Columbia University, 2005), 288n276. Hunter explains Knapp's role in the proceedings: "As she was a minor under fourteen (stated in the petition), and had no relatives, Knapp functioned as her 'next friend,' a legal term meaning he served as one who safeguarded her interests." Med did have a mother in New Orleans, of course, but her enslaved status kept her from consideration here. Louis Ruchames explains that Knapp's numerous personal and business problems made him an unlikely guardian, and he died seven years later at the age of thirty-nine. See Louis Ruchames, ed. *The Letters of William Lloyd Garrison, Volume II: A House Dividing against Itself* (Cambridge: Belknap Press, 1971), xxvi.
8. Barbara Bennett Woodhouse, "Dred Scott's Daughters: Nineteenth Century Urban Girls at the Intersection of Race and Patriarchy," *Buffalo Law Review* 48 (Fall 2000): 673. Woodhouse also discusses Douglass and Dred Scott's daughters in *Hidden in Plain Sight: The Tragedy of Children's Rights from Ben Franklin to Lionel Tate* (Princeton: Princeton University Press, 2008), 65.

9. Sarah L. H. Gronningsater, "Born Free in the Master's House: Children and Gradual Emancipation in the Early American North," in *Child Slavery before and after Emancipation: An Argument for Child-Centered Slavery Studies*, ed. Anna Mae Duane (New York: Cambridge University Press, 2017), 123–25. Gronningsater goes on to explain, "The American Patriots' emphasis on reasoned consent as the source of just political authority could cut both ways for black children. On the one hand, some elites explicitly compared slaves, women, paupers, and the insane to children in order to explain their necessary subordination within republican government; all lacked the capacity to reason. On the other hand, some theorizers claimed that black children, just like white children, could become consenting adult citizens as long as they received proper training." Gronningsater, 133.
10. Boston Female Anti-Slavery Society, *Right and Wrong in Boston in 1837* (Boston: Isaac Knapp, 1837), 112; Boston Female Anti-Slavery Society, *Right and Wrong in Boston in 1838* (Boston: Isaac Knapp, 1838), 6.
11. Harriet E. Wilson, *Our Nig: Or, Sketches from the Life of a Free Black, in a Two-Story White House, North. Showing that Slavery's Shadows Fall Even There. by "Our Nig,"* ed. Henry Louis Gates Jr. and Richard J. Ellis, Facsimile, Expanded edition (New York: Vintage, 2011).
12. Barbara A. White, afterword to *Our Nig*, by Harriet E. Wilson, xx–xxvi.
13. Lisa E. Green, "The Disorderly Girl in Harriet E. Wilson's Our Nig," in *Harriet Wilson's New England: Race, Writing, and Region*, ed. JerriAnne Boggis, Eve Allegra Raimon, and Barbara A. White (Durham: University of New Hampshire Press, 2007), 140, 142–43, 152.
14. Anne Warren Weston to Debora Weston, October 22, 1836, Ms. A.9.2 8.93, Weston Family Papers, Anti-Slavery Manuscripts, Boston Public Library.
15. The *Liberator* explained to new subscribers the purpose of the department of the paper called "Refuge of Oppression": "By the term 'Refuge of Oppression', we mean, of course, a retreat into which the enemies of freedom are gathered, in their distinctive character, and for an evil purpose; and we thus put the brand of condemnation on every article found in that department." *Liberator*, January 8, 1847, 2.
16. Samuel Slater, "Refuge of Oppression," *Liberator*, October 15, 1836.
17. Slater, "Refuge of Oppression."
18. Slater, "Refuge of Oppression."
19. Lydia Maria Child, Henrietta Sargent, and Maria W. Chapman to Mrs. [Mary] Slater, September 5, 1836, Henrietta Sargent folder, A/S 245h, Schlesinger Library, Radcliffe Institute, Harvard University.
20. Matthew 7:12.
21. Child, Sargent, and Chapman to Slater, September 5, 1836, Henrietta Sargent folder, A/S 245h, Schlesinger Library, Radcliffe Institute, Harvard University.
22. Child, Sargent, and Chapman to Slater, September 5, 1836, Henrietta Sargent folder, A/S 245h, Schlesinger Library, Radcliffe Institute, Harvard University.
23. Child, Sargent, and Chapman to Slater, September 5, 1836, Henrietta Sargent folder, A/S 245h, Schlesinger Library, Radcliffe Institute, Harvard University.
24. Leslie Harris, "Motherhood, Race, and Gender: The Rhetoric of Women's Antislavery Activism in the *Liberty Bell* Giftbooks," *Women's Studies in Communication* 32, no. 3 (Fall 2009): 298, 302.
25. See Anne Warren Weston to Debora Weston, October 22, 1836, Ms. A.9.2.8.63,

Weston Family Papers, Anti-Slavery Manuscripts, Boston Public Library; Kenneth Burke, *A Rhetoric of Motives* (Berkeley: University of California Press, 1969), iv; Richard B. Gregg, "The Ego-Function of the Rhetoric of Protest," *Philosophy and Rhetoric* 4, no. 2 (Spring 1971): 74.

26. Sue Peabody, "Microhistory, Biography, Fiction: The Politics of Narrating the Lives of People under Slavery," *Transatlantica* 2 (2012): 11.
27. Tim Cresswell, "Moral Geographies," in *Cultural Geography: A Critical Dictionary of Key Concepts*, ed. David Atkinson et al. (New York: Palgrave Macmillan, 2005), 132.
28. Diana Taylor, *The Archive and the Repertoire: Performing Cultural Memory in the Americas* (Durham: Duke University Press, 2003), 28.
29. Nazera Sadiq Wright, *Black Girlhood in the Nineteenth Century* (Urbana: University of Illinois, 2016), 10.
30. As Taylor reminds us, "Scenarios, by encapsulating both the setup and the action/behaviors, are formulaic structures that predispose certain outcomes and yet allow for reversal, parody, and change." Taylor, *Archive and the Repertoire*, 31.
31. "Kidnapping in Boston," *Liberator*, October 29, 1836. In 1849, Judge Merrill would go on to play a minor role in Boston's "trial of the century," issuing the arrest warrant for Dr. John White Webster for the murder of Dr. George Parkman.
32. Nina Moore Tiffany, *Samuel E. Sewall: A Memoir* (Boston: Houghton Mifflin, 1898), 69. See also Edlie Wong, *Neither Fugitive nor Free: Atlantic Slavery, Freedom Suits, and the Legal Culture of Travel* (New York: New York University Press, 2009), 91
33. *Commonwealth v. John Robinson and Sophia Robinson*, Thach. Cr. Case 488, December 1837; Helen Catterall, *Judicial Cases Concerning American Slavery and the Negro*, vol. 4 (Washington, DC: Carnegie Institution of Washington, 1936), 501–5.
34. Anne Marie Reardon, "The Peculiar Kidnapping Case of Elizabeth Bright," *Massachusetts Historical Review* 8 (2006): 38–41.
35. Ellis Gray Loring to John Robinson, November 4, 1837, letterpress copybook, MSAm1554, Houghton Library, Harvard University.
36. "The Case of Kidnapping," *Boston Courier*, December 25, 1837.
37. Debora Weston to Anne Warren Weston, November 19, 1837, Ms. A.9.2.9.88, Weston Family Papers, Anti-Slavery Manuscripts, Boston Public Library.
38. Increase S. Smith to Caroline Weston, December 25, 1837, Ms. A.9.2.9.107, Weston Family Papers, Anti-Slavery Manuscripts, Boston Public Library.
39. "Case of Kidnapping" *Boston Daily Advertiser*, December 21, 1837.
40. "Kidnapping Case in Boston," *New Bedford Mercury*, January 5, 1838.
41. "The Kidnapped Child," *Boston Courier*, December 28, 1837.
42. Ellis Gray Loring to Catherine M. Sullivan, March 8, 1838, letterpress copybook, MSAm1554, Houghton Library, Harvard University.
43. Lydia Maria Child to Ellis Gray Loring, July 10, 1838, A-115, box 2, folder 122, Ellis Gray Loring Papers, Schlesinger Library, Radcliffe Institute.
44. Lydia Maria Child to Ellis Gray Loring, July 10, 1838, A-115, box 2, folder 122, Ellis Gray Loring Papers, Schlesinger Library, Radcliffe Institute; Slater, "Refuge of Oppression"; *Constitution of the Samaritan Asylum*, 2. "Little Phebe at the asylum is dead, and Maria is all worn out making arrangements for the funeral, which took place 2 hours before the appointed time so none of us went." Debora Weston to Anne Warren Weston, June 10–17, 1836, Ms. A.9.2.8.31, Weston Family Papers, Anti-Slavery Manuscripts, Boston Public Library.

45. Lydia Maria Child to Ellis Gray Loring, December 5, 1838, in Lydia Maria Child, *The Collected Correspondence of Lydia Maria Child, 1817–1880*, ed. Patricia G. Holland, Milton Meltzer, and Francine Krasno (Millwood, NY: Kraus Microform, 1980), microfiche 6/154.
46. Ellis Gray Loring to Lydia Maria Child, December 31, 1838, in Holland, *Collected Correspondence*, microfiche 6/160.
47. *Case of the Slave-Child, Med. Report of the Arguments of Counsel, and of the Opinion of the Court, in the Case of Commonwealth vs. Aves; Tried and Determined in the Supreme Judicial Court of Massachusetts* (Boston: Isaac Knapp, 1836), 13.
48. Judith Kelleher Schafer, *Slavery, the Civil Law, and the Supreme Court of Louisiana* (Baton Rouge: Louisiana State University Press, 1994), 250, 262–63.
49. *Lunsford v. Coquillon* (No. 815, 2 Mart. (N.S.) 401 (La. 1824); Schafer, *Slavery, the Civil Law, and the Supreme Court of Louisiana*, 265; *Case of the Slave-Child, Med*, 22, 38.
50. Schafer, *Slavery, the Civil Law, and the Supreme Court of Louisiana*, 271.
51. Board of Directors of the Holden Anti-Slavery Society, *Report of the Holden Slave Case* (Worcester: Colton and Howland, 1839), 5.
52. Leonard W. Levy, *The Law of the Commonwealth and Chief Justice Shaw* (New York: Oxford University Press, 1957), 80–81; David Foster Estes, *History of Holden, Massachusetts, 1684–1894* (Worcester: C. F. Lawrence, 1894), 50.
53. Board of Directors, *Report of the Holden Slave Case*, 5.
54. "Love's Labor Lost," *Liberator*, August 6, 1841.
55. "Love's Labor Lost."
56. Benjamin Franklin Hallett (1797–1862) was a prominent lawyer and Democratic Party activist. He would become chairman of the Democratic National Committee and was appointed by President Franklin Pierce to be U.S. Attorney for Massachusetts (1853–1857). See *Rights of the Marshpee Indians: argument of Benjamin F. Hallett, counsel for the memorialists of the Marshpee tribe, before a joint committee of the legislature of Massachusetts, Messrs. Barton and Strong of the Senate, and Dwight of Stockbridge, Fuller of Springfield and Lewis of Pepperell, of the House, to whom the complaints of the Indians for a change of government and redress of grievances were referred, published at the request of Isaac Coombs, Daniel Amos and William Apes, the Marshpee delegation, March 1834* (Boston: J. Howe, printer, 1834).
57. *Commonwealth v. Mary B. Taylor*, 3 Metcalf 72 (1841).
58. Tiffany, *Samuel E. Sewall*, 68–69.
59. *Commonwealth v. Mary B. Taylor*, 3 Metcalf 72 (1841).
60. *Annual Report of the Board of Managers of the Massachusetts Anti-Slavery Society* (Boston: Oliver Johnson, 1843), 76.
61. *Commonwealth v. Taylor*, Monthly Law Reporter 4 (November 1841): 274.
62. Wong, *Neither Fugitive nor Free*, 93.

CHAPTER 4: MARIA SOMMERSETT, THE AMERICAN STEWART, AND DRED SCOTT

1. Boston Female Anti-Slavery Society (BFASS), *Right and Wrong in Boston, in 1836. Annual Report of the Boston Female Anti-Slavery Society, being a concise history of the cases of the slave child, Med, and of the women demanded as slaves of the Supreme Judicial Court of Mass. with all the other proceedings of the society* (Boston: Isaac Knapp,

1836), 67. Shortly after the *Somerset* case, an enslaved man named Dublin claimed his freedom upon the advice of his "Unkle Somerset." See Mark S. Weiner, "Notes and Documents—New Biographical Evidence on *Somerset's Case*," *Slavery and Abolition* 23, no. 1 (2002): 125.

2. Richard B. Gregg, "The Ego-Function of the Rhetoric of Protest," *Philosophy and Rhetoric* 4, no. 2 (Spring 1971): 74. See also Joanne Pope Melish, *Disowning Slavery: Gradual Emancipation and "Race" in New England* (Ithaca: Cornell University Press, 1998).

3. BFASS, *Right and Wrong in Boston, in 1836*, 68; Luke 15:24. The 26th was the date of the oral arguments; the ruling was handed down the following day. While August 26 is no longer associated with Med's case, today we remember August 26 as Women's Equality Day, the anniversary of the signing of the Nineteenth Amendment in 1920.

4. The Old Colony Club established "Forefathers Day" in 1769, which was then discontinued during the revolutionary era. The celebrations were re-established by the Pilgrim Society for the bicentennial in 1820. The antislavery fair was a success—it netted $540 for the Massachusetts Anti-Slavery Society. See Debra Gold Hansen, *Strained Sisterhood: Gender and Class in the Boston Female Anti-Slavery Society* (Amherst: University of Massachusetts Press, 1993), 127. For more on antislavery fairs, see Lee Chambers-Schiller, "'A Good Work among the People': The Political Culture of the Boston Antislavery Fair," in *The Abolitionist Sisterhood: Women's Political Culture in Antebellum America*, ed. Jean Fagan Yellin and John C. Van Horne (Ithaca: Cornell University Press, 1994); Deborah Van Broekhoven, "'Better than a Clay Club': The Organization of Anti-Slavery Fairs, 1835–60," *Slavery and Abolition* 19, no. 1 (1998): 24–45.

5. Lydia Maria Child, "The Ladies Fair," *Liberator*, January 2, 1837; Matthew 16:18. It was telling that the following year the American Anti-Slavery Society chose December 22 to commemorate the martyrdom of Elijiah Lovejoy, the abolitionist newspaper editor murdered by a proslavery mob in Alton, Illinois, making a tight connection between the abolitionists and the Pilgrims. See *Liberator*, December 22, 1837. According to American Studies scholar John Seelye, "Historians now generally agree that the Pilgrims' storied landing on the Rock never actually took place—the tradition having emerged more than a century after the arrival of the *Mayflower*.... Different political, religious, and social groups used the image of the Rock on behalf of their own specific causes and ideologies." John Seelye, *Memory's Nation: The Place of Plymouth Rock* (Chapel Hill: University of North Carolina Press, 1998), 211.

6. Alice Taylor, "'Fashion has extended her influence to the cause of humanity': The Transatlantic Female Economy of the Boston Antislavery Bazaar," in *The Force of Fashion in Politics and Society: Global Perspectives from Early Modern to Contemporary Times*, ed. Beverly Lemire (Burlington, VT: Ashgate, 2010), 115–18.

7. Child, "The Ladies Fair."

8. *Case of the Slave-Child, Med. Report of the Arguments of Counsel, and of the Opinion of the Court, in the Case of Commonwealth vs. Aves; Tried and Determined in the Supreme Judicial Court of Massachusetts* (Boston: Isaac Knapp, 1836), 36.

9. Child, "The Ladies Fair."

10. Sadly, it seems that Bancroft was not a strong supporter of the antislavery cause. Child was sorry to report that he declined to sign a petition to end slavery in the District of Columbia, because "he did not think it right to throw such an apple of

discord into Congress." Lydia Maria Child to Ellis Gray Loring, December 5, 1838, in Lydia Maria Child, *The Collected Correspondence of Lydia Maria Child, 1817–1880*, ed. Patricia G. Holland, Milton Meltzer, and Francine Krasno (Millwood, NY: Kraus Microform, 1980), microfiche 6/154; Judges 16:1–3.

11. BFASS, *Right and Wrong in Boston, in 1836*, 68.
12. Lois Brown, "Memorial Narratives of African Women in Antebellum New England," *Legacy* 20, no. 1/2 (2003): 39.
13. Harriet Beecher Stowe, *Uncle Tom's Cabin*, 2nd ed. (New York: W. W. Norton and Company, 2010), 217, 258–59, 273.
14. Karen Sánchez-Eppler, *Dependent States: The Child's Part in Nineteenth-Century American Culture* (Chicago: University of Chicago Press, 2005), 106.
15. Susan Paul, *Memoir of James Jackson, the attentive and obedient scholar, who died in Boston, October 31, 1833, aged six years and eleven months*, ed. Lois Brown (Cambridge: Harvard University Press, 2000), 67.
16. Brown, "Memorial Narratives," 3.
17. John Carroll Power, comp., *History of the Early Settlers of Sangamon County, Illinois—1876*, http://sangamon.illinoisgenweb.org/1876/slatere.htm. A commission merchant buys and sells products for a percentage of the sales price. *Gibson's Guide and Directory of the State of Louisiana, and the Cities of New Orleans and Lafayette* (New Orleans: John Gibson, 1838), 190. The New Orleans Notarial Archives Research Center, has Historical Notaries' Indexes available online, http://www.orleanscivilclerk.com/research.htm.
18. Sale of slave. Samuel Slater to John Rollins (January–April 1838), William Christy Indexes, vol. 31, p. 41, Historical Notaries' Indexes, New Orleans Notarial Archives Research Center, http://www.orleanscivilclerk.com/wchristyindexes/christy_william_vol_31.pdf; Sale of slave. Samuel Slater to Stanford W. Waters (1839), William Christy Indexes, vol. 34, p. 343, Historical Notaries' Indexes, New Orleans Notarial Archives Research Center, http://www.orleanscivilclerk.com/wchristyindexes/christy_william_vol_34.pdf; Sale of slave[s?]. Slatter (Samuel) by John Greene (1837), Horatio Davis Indexes, vol. 1, p. 118, Historical Notaries' Indexes, New Orleans Notarial Archives Research Center, http://www.orleanscivilclerk.com/hdavisindexes/davis_horatio_w_vol_1.pdf; Sale of slave. Slater (Samuel) to Andrews [?] (1838), Horatio Davis Indexes, vol. 3, p. 40, Historical Notaries' Indexes, New Orleans Notarial Archives Research Center, http://www.orleanscivilclerk.com/hdavisindexes/davis_horatio_w_vol_3.pdf; Sale of Texas land to Slater (Sml) from J. A. Roberts, 17; Sale of Texas land to Slater (Sml) from J. A. Roberts, 18; Sale of Texas land to Slater (Sml) from J. A. Roberts, 19; Sale of Texas land to Slater (Sml) from J. A. Roberts 20. (1837–1839), Horatio Davis Indexes, vol. 2, Historical Notaries' Indexes, New Orleans Notarial Archives Research Center, http://www.orleanscivilclerk.com/hdavisindexes/davis_horatio_w_vol_2.pdf. See the Texas Tax List Index, 1840–1849, Texas, Compiled Census and Census Substitutes Index, 1820–1890, Ancestry.com. Note that Texas won independence from Mexico in 1836 and was annexed by the United States in 1845.
19. Ernest Odadele-Starks, *Freebooters and Smugglers: The Foreign Slave Trade in the U.S. after 1808* (Fayetteville: University of Arkansas Press, 2007), 88, 94; Adam Rothman, review of *Freebooters and Smugglers: The Foreign Slave Trade in the United States after 1808*, by Ernest Odadele-Starks, *Journal of Southern History* 75, no. 2 (May 2009): 438–39.

20. The Texas, Land Title Abstracts database in Ancestry.com indicates that Slater was involved in at least thirteen land transactions in 1846–1847. Ancestry.com, *Texas, Land Title Abstracts,1700–2008* [database on-line] (Provo, UT: Ancestry.com Operations, Inc., 2000). Original Data: Texas General Land Office. Abstracts of all original Texas Land Titles comprising Grants and Locations, Austin, TX.
21. Slater's landholdings and move to Henderson County are recounted in Power, *History of the Early Settlers*.
22. Power, *History of the Early Settlers*.
23. Donald E. Reynolds, *Texas Terror: The Slave Insurrection Panic of 1860 and the Secession of the Lower South* (Baton Rouge: Louisiana State University Press, 2007), 39; Donald E. Reynolds, "Texas Troubles," in *Handbook of Texas Online*, pub. Texas State Historical Commission, http://www.tshaonline.org/handbook/online/articles/vetbr; Reynolds, *Texas Terror*, 42–51, 54. In the Texas state elections that year, the Democrats defeated the Constitutional Unionists.
24. Reynolds, *Texas Terror*, 65.
25. Power, *History of the Early Settlers*.
26. Lewis G. Vander Velde, *The Presbyterian Churches and the Federal Union, 1861–1869* (Cambridge: Harvard University Press, 1932), 178–80.
27. Power, *History of the Early Settlers*.
28. Reynolds, *Texas Terror*, 151–52, 120–21; Reynolds, "Texas Troubles."
29. Reynolds, *Texas Terror*, 193–95, 212.
30. Power, *History of the Early Settlers*; Julia Barton, "Troubled Times," *Texas Observer*, August 10, 2010, https://www.texasobserver.org/troubled-times/.
31. Phil Lapansky, "The Liberation of Jane Johnson," Library Company of Philadelphia, http://www.librarycompany.org/JaneJohnson/; William Still, *The Underground Rail Road. A record of facts, authentic narratives, letters, &c., narrating the hardships, hairbreadth escapes, and death struggles of the slaves in their efforts for freedom, as related by themselves and others, or witnessed by the author; together with sketches of some of the largest stockholders, and most liberal aiders and advisers, of the road* (Philadelphia: Porter and Coates, 1872), 86–97.
32. Maria Weston Chapman, "The Twenty-Second National Anti-Slavery Bazaar," *Liberator*, January 25, 1856.
33. Lea VanderVelde and Sandhya Subramanian, "Mrs. Dred Scott," *Yale Law Journal* 106, no. 4 (January 1997): 1042; Adam Arenson, "Freeing Dred Scott," *Common-place* 8, no. 3 (April 2008), http://www.common-place-archives.org/vol-08/no-03/arenson/.
34. Lea VanderVelde, *Redemption Songs: Suing for Freedom before Dred Scott* (New York: Oxford University Press, 2014), 10; Don E. Fehrenbacher, *The Dred Scott Case: Its Significance in American Law and Politics* (New York: Oxford University Press, 1978), 254; Duane Benton, "Lessons for Judges from *Scott v. Emerson*," in *The "Dred Scott" Case: Historical and Contemporary Perspectives on Race and Law*, ed. David Thomas Konig et al. (Athens: Ohio University Press, 2010), 204; Fehrenbacher, *Dred Scott Case*, 264.
35. The ages of the girls are reported differently by different sources. Lea VanderVelde, a leading authority on the Scott family, reports that Eliza was eight and Lizzie was three at the time of the initial lawsuit, which would mean that they were nineteen and fourteen by the time of the Supreme Court ruling. Lea VanderVelde, *Mrs. Dred Scott: A Life on Slavery's Frontier* (New York: Oxford University Press, 2009), 232.

36. *Dred Scott v. John F. A. Sandford*, 19 Howard 393 (1857); Fehrenbacher, *Dred Scott Case*, 322–23.
37. Fehrenbacher, *Dred Scott Case*, 392, 396; *Dred Scott v. John F. A. Sandford*, 19 Howard 393 (1857): 175.
38. *Dred Scott v. John F .A. Sandford*, 19 Howard 393 (1857): 73; William Story, *Life and Letters of Joseph Story*, vol.1 (Boston: Charles Little and James Brown, 1851), 554–55.
39. *Dred Scott v. John F .A. Sandford*, 19 Howard 393 (1857): 106.
40. Fehrenbacher, *Dred Scott Case*, 397–98; *Dred Scott v. John F.A. Sandford*, 19 Howard 393 (1857): 106, 92.
41. Fehrenbacher, *Dred Scott Case*, 399; Paul Finkelman, *An Imperfect Union: Slavery, Federalism, and Comity* (Chapel Hill: University of North Carolina Press, 1981), 196.
42. Albert J. Von Frank, *The Trials of Anthony Burns: Freedom and Slavery in Emerson's Boston* (Cambridge: Harvard University Press, 1998), 318; Fehrenbacher, *Dred Scott Case*, 293–94.
43. *Dred Scott v. John F. A. Sandford*, 19 Howard 393 (1857): 194–96.
44. Fehrenbacher, *Dred Scott Case*, 331.
45. Stuart Streichler, *Justice Curtis in the Civil War Era: At the Crossroads of American Constitutionalism* (Charlottesville: University of Virginia Press, 2005), 125.
46. *Dred Scott v. John F. A. Sandford*, 19 Howard 393 (1857): 180.
47. Fehrenbacher, *Dred Scott Case*, 409–10; Streichler, *Justice Curtis*, 142–43; *Dred Scott v. John F. A. Sandford*, 19 Howard 393 (1857): 194–95.
48. Fehrenbacher, *Dred Scott Case*, 411–13; *Dred Scott v. John F. A. Sandford*, 19 Howard 393 (1857): 210.
49. Finkelman, *Imperfect Union*, 281–83.
50. *Dred Scott v. John F. A. Sandford*, 19 Howard 393 (1857): 74.
51. Fehrenbacher, *Dred Scott Case*, 431.
52. William Lloyd Garrison, "Dred Scott and Disunion," *Liberator*, March 12, 1858.
53. Margot Minardi, *Making Slavery History: Abolitionism and the Politics of Memory in Massachusetts* (New York: Oxford University Press, 2012), 162. Garrison had likely learned about Attucks from Nell's books: "William C. Nell, more than anyone, was responsible for resuscitating Attucks's memory and thrusting him into antebellum public discourse surrounding black citizenship. Nell's *Services of Colored Americans in the Wars of 1776 and 1812* (1851) and *The Colored Patriots of the Revolution* (1855) were pathbreaking works of African American history, as well as important abolitionist tracts that publicized the military role blacks had played in the nation's founding and defense." Mitch Kachun, "From Forgotten Founder to Indispensable Icon: Crispus Attucks, Black Citizenship, and Collective Memory, 1770–1865," *Journal of the Early Republic* 29, no. 2 (Summer 2009): 269.
54. Samuel E. Sewall to Simon B. Robie, March 8, 1857, in Nina Moore Tiffany, *Samuel E. Sewall: A Memoir* (Boston: Houghton Mifflin, 1898), 102–3; Samuel E. Sewall to Samuel J. May, April 9, 1857, in Tiffany, *Samuel E. Sewall*, 102–3.
55. Streichler, *Justice Curtis*, 46–47; Dean Grodzins, "'Slave Law' versus 'Lynch Law' in Boston: Benjamin Robbins Curtis, Theodore Parker, and the Fugitive Slave Crisis, 1850–1855," *Massachusetts Historical Review* 12 (2010): 1–24. As Streichler explains, "In this day every member of the U.S. Supreme Court served as a circuit justice for a particular region of the country.... Curtis had the New England circuit." Streichler, *Justice Curtis*, 52.

56. Theodore Parker, *The Trial of Theodore Parker, for the "Misdemeanor" or A Speech in Faneuil Hall against Kidnapping, before the Circuit Court of the United States, at Boston, April 3, 1855. With The Defence*, by Theodore Parker (New York: Negro Universities Press, 1970), 160–61.
57. Arenson, "Freeing Dred Scott."
58. "Habeas Corpus in Relation to a Slave," in *Liberty Bell* (Boston: Boston Anti-Slavery Bazaar, 1858), 310–17.
59. *Betty's Case*, Monthly Law Reporter 10, no. 8 (December 1857): 455.
60. *Betty's Case*, Monthly Law Reporter 10, no. 8 (December 1857): 457; Aviam Soifer, "Status, Contract, and Promises Unkept," *Yale Law Journal* 96, no. 8 (July 1987): 1923.
61. "Another Slave Case in Boston," *Liberator*, November 13, 1857, 183.
62. "Slave Betty," *Liberator*, February 19, 1858, 31.
63. Leonard W. Levy, *The Law of the Commonwealth and Chief Justice Shaw* (New York: Oxford University Press, 1957), 87–108.
64. Wendell Phillips, "Surrender of Sims," in *Speeches, Lectures, and Letters* (Boston: Lee and Shepherd, 1894), 62.

CHAPTER 5: FREE SOIL FICTIONS

1. Maria Weston Chapman, *Pinda: A True Tale* (New York: American Anti-Slavery Society, 1840); Lydia Maria Child, *A Romance of the Republic* (Boston: Ticknor, Fields, 1867); Herman Melville, *White-Jacket: or, The World in a Man-of-War* in *Herman Melville: Redburn, White-Jacket, Moby-Dick* (New York: Library of America, 1983); *Commonwealth v. Fitzgerald*, 7 Monthly Law Reporter 379 (1844).
2. Chapman, *Pinda: A True Tale*; "Pinda," *National Anti-Slavery Standard*, October 19, 1840; "Pinda," *Monthly Offering to the Collectors and Contributors of the Weekly Contribution Plan* 1, no. 1 (July 1840): 11–16 and 1, no. 2 (August 1840): 20–27.
3. Chapman, *Pinda: A True Tale*, 4–5.
4. Chapman, *Pinda: A True Tale*, 7, 18.
5. Chapman, *Pinda: A True Tale*, 3, 13, 19. Harriet Jacobs also describes this distinction within her family: her brother John S. Jacobs and her children were brought to the North by their enslavers, but Harriet was a fugitive from slavery. Harriet Jacobs, *Incidents in the Life of a Slave Girl*, in *Classic Slave Narratives*, ed. Henry Louis Gates Jr. (New York: Penguin, 1987), 652.
6. *Journal of Ellis Gray Loring*, Loring Papers, MCR-S, Schlesinger Library, Harvard University, reprinted in its entirety in Len Gougeon, "1838: Ellis Gray Loring and a Journal for the Times," *Studies in the American Renaissance* 1 (1990): 41.
7. Debora Weston to Maria Weston Chapman, March 4, [1840?], Ms. A.9.2.14.88, Weston Family Papers, Anti-Slavery Manuscripts, Boston Public Library.
8. "In the spring of 1841, during an anti-slavery meeting at the Black Episcopal Methodist Zion chapel of New Bedford, William C. Coffin, a Nantucket banker, heard a young Frederick Douglass briefly describe his experience as a slave. Coffin was so impressed with the man's oratorical ability that he invited Douglass to visit the island and be a guest at Nantucket's first Anti-Slavery Convention." "The Abolitionist Movement," *Nantucket Atheneum*, https://www.nantucketatheneum.org/the-abolitionist-movement/.
9. William C. Coffin to Maria Weston Chapman, September 5, 1840, Ms. A.9.2.14.16, Weston Family Papers, Anti-Slavery Manuscripts, Boston Public Library.

10. Teresa A. Goddu, "The Massachusetts Anti-Slavery Society's Weekly Contribution Box," *Common-place* 15, no. 1 (Fall 2014), http://www.common-place-archives.org/vol-15/no-01/ares/. MASS had its origins in the New England Anti-Slavery Society and the General Colored Association; it was then reorganized as MASS in 1835 as the newly formed national American Anti-Slavery Society decided to create state-level auxiliaries.
11. "Pinda," *Monthly Offering*; John 8:32; Isaiah 58:1; 1 Corinthians 16:1.
12. *Monthly Offering* 1, no. 2 (August 1840): 32.
13. Chapman, *Pinda: A True Tale*, 23. For a description of the coin box, see Goddu, "Massachusetts Anti-Slavery Society's Weekly Contribution Box."
14. *National Anti-Slavery Standard*, October 29, 1840.
15. *National Anti-Slavery Standard*, October 29, 1840.
16. Lydia Maria Child, "Anti-Slavery Reminiscence," *National Anti-Slavery Standard*, August 15, 1868. "Mrs. Chapman once wrote an account of Mr. Hogan's slave 'Pinda.' Do you happen to own a copy of it? I have tried in vain to procure one. It was a funny affair, and I had thoughts of writing my recollection of it for the Standard." Lydia Maria Child to Wendell Phillips, July 5, 1868, in Lydia Maria Child, *The Collected Correspondence of Lydia Maria Child, 1817–1880*, ed. Patricia G. Holland, Milton Meltzer, and Francine Krasno (Millwood, NY: Kraus Microform, 1980), microfiche 96/2561.
17. David Blight, "'For Something beyond the Battlefield': Frederick Douglass and the Struggle for the Memory of the Civil War," *Journal of American History* 75, no. 4 (March 1989): 1159. For additional discussion of abolitionist memory, see Julie Roy Jeffrey, *Abolitionists Remember: Antislavery Autobiographies and the Unfinished Work of Emancipation* (Chapel Hill: University of North Carolina Press, 2008).
18. Lydia Maria Child, *A Romance of the Republic*; Lydia Maria Child [to F. G. Shaw], July 28, 1867, in *Collected Correspondence*, microfiche, 67/1789.
19. Child, *A Romance of the Republic*, 185.
20. See, for example, Karen Woods Weierman, *One Nation, One Blood: Interracial Marriage in American Fiction, Scandal, and Law, 1820–1870* (Amherst: University of Massachusetts Press, 2005).
21. Child, *A Romance of the Republic*, 156–58.
22. Lydia Maria Child, "The Iron Shroud," *National Anti-Slavery Standard*, March 3, 1842; Lydia Maria Child, *Freedmen's Book* (Boston: Ticknor and Fields, 1865), 154. See also George Hendrick and Willene Hendrick, *The Creole Mutiny: A Tale of Revolt Aboard a Slave Ship* (Chicago: Ivan R. Dee, 2003).
23. Child, *A Romance of the Republic*, 367.
24. Child, *A Romance of the Republic*, 373–74.
25. Child, *A Romance of the Republic*, 375–77; Carolyn L. Karcher, *The First Woman in the Republic: A Cultural Biography of Lydia Maria Child* (Durham: Duke University Press, 1994), 253. See also Milton Meltzer and Patricia G. Holland, *Lydia Maria Child: Selected Letters* (Amherst: University of Massachusetts Press, 1982), 87–88.
26. Child, *A Romance of the Republic*, 399.
27. See Patricia Hagler Minter, "'The State of Slavery': *Somerset, The Slave, Grace*, and the Rise of Pro-Slavery and Anti-Slavery Constitutionalism in the Nineteenth-Century Atlantic World," *Slavery and Abolition* 36, no. 5 (2015): 603–17.
28. Senator Henry Wilson also tried to control the postbellum narrative in his

two-volume *Rise and Fall of the Slave Power in America* (Boston: James Osgood, 1872), 370. Toward that end, he celebrated the Med case: "Other facts cheered and encouraged the friends of the slave. In the month of August, 1836, the Supreme Judicial Court of Massachusetts unanimously decided, in the case of the slave-child, Med, ... that 'an owner of a slave in another State, where slavery is warranted by law, voluntarily bringing such slave into this State, has no authority to retain him against his will, or to carry him out of the State against his consent, for the purpose of being held in slavery.' This important opinion was delivered by Justice Shaw. The suit had been prosecuted with unfaltering zeal by the Boston Female Antislavery Society. Samuel E. Sewall and Ellis Gray Loring, assisted by Rufus Choate, conducted the case for the Commonwealth. The argument of Mr. Loring was pronounced a masterly and exhaustive effort, worthy of the cause he advocated and the great tribunal before which it was delivered."

29. Karcher, *First Woman in the Republic*, 510.
30. Child, *A Romance of the Republic*, 270.
31. Lydia Maria Child to Eliza Scudder, July 8, 1869, in *Collected Correspondence*, microfiche 71/1901.
32. Lydia Maria Child to Robert Purvis, August 14, 1868, *Selected Letters*, 482–83; Thomas Wentworth Higginson, "Lydia Maria Child" (1868), in *The Writings of Thomas Wentworth Higginson*, vol. 2, *Contemporaries* (Boston: Houghton Mifflin, 1900), 137–38.
33. Blight, "'For Something beyond the Battlefield,'" 1161. Eliza Wigham, the Scottish suffragist and abolitionist, mentions the case in her book *The Anti-Slavery Cause in America and Its Martyrs* (London: A.W. Bennett, 1863), 34–35. Wigham's intent is to keep Great Britain out of the war. Her brief description of the case does not name Med or the case name, and she refers to "the child" as "he."
34. Melville, *White-Jacket*; Hershel Parker, *Herman Melville, A Biography*, vol. 1, *1819–1851* (Baltimore: Johns Hopkins University Press, 1996), 262, 651; Robert K. Wallace, *Douglass and Melville: Anchored Together in Neighborly Style* (New Bedford: Spinner Publications, 2005), 85; Jay Leyda, *The Melville Log: A Documentary Life of Herman Melville, 1819–1891*, vol. 1 (New York: Gordian Press, 1969), 396. Melville also drew from many print sources. See Howard P. Vincent, *The Tailoring of Melville's White-Jacket* (Evanston: Northwestern University Press, 1970).
35. *Congressional Globe*, 30th Cong., 2d Sess., 20:507 (February 12, 1849), statement of Sen. Hale, CMS 14.286–287. Note that Hale's role in the abolition of both slavery and flogging is given equal weight on his memorial statue on the grounds of the New Hampshire State Capitol: "First Anti-Slavery U.S. Senator. He Secured the Abolition of Flogging and the Spirit Ration in the Navy." *The Statue of John P. Hale Erected in Front of the Capitol and Presented to the State of New Hampshire* (Concord, NH: Republican Press Association, 1892), 6.
36. Jeffrey Hole, "Herman Melville, the Fugitive Slave Act of 1850, and U.S. Empire," interview by Thomas Durwood, *Journal of Empire Studies* (August 2013), http://empirestudies.com/2013/08/17/herman-melville-the-fugitive-slave-act-of-1850-and-u-s-empire/.
37. Brian Higgins and Hershel Parker, eds., *Herman Melville: The Contemporary Reviews* (New York: Cambridge University Press, 1995); Herman Melville to Lemuel Shaw, October 6, 1849, in *Correspondence: Herman Melville*, ed. Lynn Horth, *The Writings*

of Herman Melville, Northwestern-Newberry Edition, vol. 14 (Evanston and Chicago: Northwestern University Press and Newberry Library, 1993), 138–39.
38. Willard Thorp, "Historical Note," in *White-Jacket, The Writings of Herman Melville*, Northwestern-Newberry Edition, vol. 5 (Evanston and Chicago: Northwestern University Press and Newberry Library, 1970), 435.
39. Samuel Otter, *Melville's Anatomies* (Berkeley: University of California Press, 1999), 50; T. K. Hunter, "Geographies of Liberty: A Brief Look at Two Cases," in *Prophets of Protest: Reconsidering the History of American Abolitionism*, ed. Timothy Patrick McCarthy and John Stauffer (New York: The New Press, 2006), 41.
40. Laurie Robertson-Lorant, *Melville: A Biography* (Amherst: University of Massachusetts Press, 1996), 209; Otter, *Melville's Anatomies*, 24.
41. Melville, *White-Jacket*, 500.
42. H. Edward Stessel, "Melville's *White-Jacket*: A Case against the 'Cat,'" *Clio* 13, no. 1 (1983): 39; Melville, *White-Jacket*, 497–98.
43. Melville, *White-Jacket*, 746–47.
44. Melville, *White-Jacket*, 747–48.
45. Brook Thomas, *Cross-examinations of Law and Literature: Cooper, Hawthorne, Stowe, and Melville* (Cambridge: Cambridge University Press, 1987), 93; Michael Paul Rogin, *Subversive Genealogy: The Politics and Art of Herman Melville* (New York: Alfred P. Knopf, 1983), 10.
46. Leonard W. Levy, *The Law of the Commonwealth and Chief Justice Shaw* (New York: Oxford University Press, 1957), 63; *Commonwealth v. Fitzgerald*, 7 *Monthly Law Reporter* 379 (1844): 115.
47. Higgins and Parker, *Herman Melville*, 289; Wallace, *Douglass and Melville*, 89–90.
48. Paul Finkelman, *An Imperfect Union: Slavery, Federalism, and Comity* (Chapel Hill: University of North Carolina Press, 1981), 115; *Commonwealth v. Fitzgerald*, 7 *Monthly Law Reporter* 379–80 (1844); Finkelman, *Imperfect Union*, 115–16.
49. Levy, *Law of the Commonwealth*, 70.
50. "Important Decision. Discharge of a Slave from service on Board an U. States vessel," *Liberator*, October 18, 1844.
51. "Important Decision. Discharge of a Slave from service on Board an U. States vessel."
52. *Benito Cereno* was first serialized in *Putnam's Monthly Magazine* (October–December 1855), then republished in *The Piazza Tales* (New York: Dix and Edwards, 1856). *Billy Budd* was published posthumously in 1924 (London: Constable and Co., 1924). Steven L. Winter contends that "Billy Budd is—at its heart—a book about Lemuel Shaw and the failure of the judicial process in confronting slavery and other forms of state sanctioned violence." Steven L. Winter, "Failure of the Word: Melville, Slavery, and the Failure of the Judicial Process," *Cardozo Law Review* 26 (May 2005): 2473.
53. Thomas, *Cross-examinations of Law and Literature*, 151. Ishmael asks his famous question in the first chapter, "Loomings." Herman Melville, *Moby-Dick; or, The Whale* (New York: Harper and Brothers, 1851), 5. Jeannine DeLombard posits a different reading of the plot: "Returning the *Neversink* to Norfolk, *White-Jacket* makes it easy to tell just who is—and aint—a slave." Jeannine Marie DeLombard, "*White-Jacket*: Telling Who Is—and Aint—a Slave," *New Cambridge Companion to Herman Melville*, ed. Robert S. Levine (New York: Cambridge University Press, 2014), 64–65.
54. F. O. Skyllon reminds us of the real story of the ruling: it established that habeas

corpus applied to blacks as well, but it wasn't enforced. "The pride of generations of Englishmen, that Lord Mansfield first established in the Somerset case the grand doctrine that the air of English has long been too pure for a slave, and that from that day forward a slave was free the moment he touched English soil, is woefully unfounded." F. O. Skyllon, *Black Slaves in Britain* (New York: Oxford University Press, 1974), 176.
55. Edlie Wong, *Neither Fugitive nor Free: Atlantic Slavery, Freedom Suits, and the Legal Culture of Travel* (New York: New York University Press, 2009), 32–36.
56. Rogin, *Subversive Genealogy*, 100.
57. Melville, *White-Jacket*, 769.

CONCLUSION: SARAH, RUBY, AND MED

1. The painting "first appeared as an illustration in the January 14, 1964, issue of *Look* magazine." Katharine Capshaw, *Civil Rights Childhood: Picturing Liberation in African American Photobooks* (Minneapolis: University of Minnesota Press, 2014), 248.
2. Susan Goodman, *The First Step: How One Girl Put Segregation on Trial* (New York: Bloomsbury, 2016), 4; Benjamin Roberts, "Equal School Privileges. Enthusiastic Meeting of the Colored Citizens of Boston," *Liberator*, April 4, 1851. Contemporary artist Philip Maysles also engages with the iconic painting in his "The Comfort of Enlightenment" series, which addresses the failures of white artists to undermine racial hierarchy. See "Phillip Maysles, The Comfort of Enlightenment," http://www.montevistaprojects.com/past-1/2017/2/5/2009. The "Ruby" in the Rockwell painting is actually Lynda Gunn, an eight-year-old girl from Stockbridge, Massachusetts, who modeled for Rockwell. Like Ruby, she was the only black girl at her school. See Rebecca Mead, "Model Student," *New Yorker*, November 28, 2011, http://www.newyorker.com/magazine/2011/11/28/model-student.
3. George R. Price and James Brewer Stewart, "The Roberts Case, the Easton Family, and the Dynamics of the Abolitionist Movement in Massachusetts, 1776–1870," *Massachusetts Historical Review* 4 (2002): 89–115; Roberts, "Equal School Privileges."
4. *Argument against the constitutionality of separate colored schools, in the case of Sarah C. Roberts vs. The City of Boston* (Boston: B. F. Roberts, 1849), 26. Note that the pamphlet was published by Sarah's father. Robert Morris was one of the first African American attorneys in the United States. Charles Sumner served as U.S. Senator from 1851 until his death in 1874. After Sumner's fiery "Crime against Kansas" speech in 1856, Representative Preston Brooks nearly beat him to death on the Senate floor. "The Caning of Senator Charles Sumner," *United States Senate*, https://www.senate.gov/artandhistory/history/minute/The_Caning_of_Senator_Charles_Sumner.htm.
5. Massachusetts Declaration of Rights, art. I, available at https://malegislature.gov/Laws/Constitution.
6. *Sarah C. Roberts v. The City of Boston*, 59 Mass (5 Cush.) 198 (1850).
7. Lesley Ginsberg, "Of Babies, Beasts, and Bondage: Slavery and the Question of Citizenship in Antebellum American Children's Literature," in *The American Child: A Cultural Studies Reader*, ed. Caroline F. Levander and Carol J. Singley (New Brunswick: Rutgers University Press, 2003), 101–2.
8. *Sarah C. Roberts v. The City of Boston*; Zebulon Vance Miletsky, "Before Busing: Boston's Long Movement for Civil Rights and the Legacy of Jim Crow in the 'Cradle of Liberty,'" *Journal of Urban History* 43, no. 2 (March 2017): 208; "An Act in Amendment

of 'An Act Concerning Public Schools,'" Massachusetts Acts and Resolves, 1855 Chap. 0256 (passed March 25, 1855).
9. Matthew Delmont and Jeanne Theoharis, "Introduction: Rethinking the Boston 'Busing Crisis,'" *Journal of Urban History* 43, no. 2 (March 1, 2017): 193.
10. Charles Sumner, *Argument against the constitutionality of separate colored schools, in the case of Sarah C. Roberts vs. The City of Boston* (Boston: B. F. Roberts, 1849), 3; Anna Mae Duane, "Introduction: When Is a Child a Slave?," in *Child Slavery before and after Emancipation: An Argument for Child-Centered Slavery Studies*, ed. Anna Mae Duane (New York: Cambridge University Press, 2017), 11.
11. Capshaw, *Civil Rights Childhood*, 250; Ruby Bridges, *Through My Eyes* (New York: Scholastic Press, 1999), 4, 12.
12. Liva Baker, *The Second Battle of New Orleans: The Hundred-Year Struggle to Integrate the Schools* (New York: HarperCollins, 1996), 2–3.
13. Bridges, *Through My Eyes*, 20; "Ruby Bridges Goes to School," *The African Americans: Many Rivers to Cross*, Public Broadcasting Service WNET, http://www.pbs.org/wnet/african-americans-many-rivers-to-cross/video/ruby-bridges-goes-to-school/; Bridges, *Through My Eyes*, 20; Capshaw, *Civil Rights Childhood*, 249, 252.
14. Useful sources include Stephen Kendrick and Paul Kendrick, *Sarah's Long Walk: The Free Blacks of Boston and How Their Struggle for Equality Changed America* (Boston: Beacon Press, 2004); Marouf Hasian Jr. and Geoffrey D. Klinger, "Sarah Roberts and the Early History of the 'Separate but Equal' Doctrine: A Study in Rhetoric, Law, and Social Change," *Communication Studies* 53, no. 3 (Fall 2002): 269–83.
15. *Triumph of Equal School Rights in Boston. Proceedings of the Presentation Meeting Held in Boston, Dec. 17, 1855; including addresses by John T. Hilton, Wm. C, Nell, Charles W. Slack, Wendell Phillips, Wm. Lloyd Garrison, Charles Lenox Remond* (Boston: R. F. Wallcut, 1856), 7.
16. See Leigh Radford and Renee C. Romano, introduction to, *The Civil Rights Movement in American Memory*, ed. Renee C. Romano and Leigh Radford (Athens: University of Georgia Press, 2006), xiv–xv; Leslie Theresa Hitchens, "The Beauty of Hatred: The McDonogh Three's Untold Stories" (EdD diss., Hamline University, 2014).
17. Robert Coles, *Children of Crisis: A Study of Courage and Fear* (Boston: Little, Brown, 1964), inside jacket; Capshaw, *Civil Rights Childhood*, 254; Baker, *Second Battle of New Orleans*, 440; Bridges, *Through My Eyes*, 48; Coles, *Children of Crisis*, 76–82.
18. Bridges, *Through My Eyes*, 56; "Ruby Bridges Goes to School."
19. Bridges, *Through My Eyes*, 52; Baker, *Second Battle of New Orleans*, 480; Bridges, *Through My Eyes*, 59–60.
20. Jacquelyn Dowd Hall, "The Long Civil Rights Movement and the Political Uses of the Past," *The Journal of American History* 91, no. 4 (2005): 1262; Miletsky, "Before Busing," 206. Epideictic rhetoric articulates virtue and vice and defines its subjects as worthy of praise or blame. Victoria Gallagher and Kenneth S. Zagacki connect epideictic rhetoric with historical memory in useful ways: "Epideictic discourses of commemoration are ... about asserting those things we should keep in memory and the values that will or ought to help us live in the present." Victoria Gallagher and Kenneth S. Zagacki, "Visibility and Rhetoric: The Power of Visual Images in Norman Rockwell's Depictions of Civil Rights," *Quarterly Journal of Speech* 91, no. 2 (May 2005): 196.

INDEX

AASS. *See* American Anti-Slavery Society
Abiel Smith School, 118
abolitionists: abuse of children by, 58; activism in Boston, 29–30, 33–35, 53; in antebellum Boston, 118; in Beacon Hill neighborhood, 1–2, 5–6, 30; cases following *Aves* and, 65–67, 70–72, 75; Child's documentation of, 108–9; choice of slavery and, 63, 72, 75, 95; in England, 16, 18; Med commemorated by, 76–80; Med replaced by adult icons by, 98–99; Med transformed into adult by, 96–97; Med used and abandoned by, xi, 5, 9–10, 80–82, 125; moral geography and, 77; Nell's writings and, 145n53; newspapers of, 134n44; Shaw condemned by, 96; Slater's criticism of, 58–59; Texas Troubles and, 84–86; tragic flaw of, 63–64; victory claimed for, xi; violence against, 34–35; Wheatley's poetry and, 27; *Zong* massacre and, 132n30. *See also* antislavery movement and community
Abraham (Pinda's husband), 99–102
African Americans: in Beacon Hill, 5–7, 54–55, 64–67; Child's novel's omission of, 108; citizenship and, 88, 90–94, 108, 146n53; military role of, 146n53; PAS advocacy for, 25–26; well-known historical figures, 8–9; Wheatley's poetry and, 27
The Age of Phillis (Jeffers), 132n29
Alabama, 86
Allen, Richard, 30
Alton, Illinois, 7, 85, 143n5
American (Lawrence), 96
American Anti-Slavery Society (AASS), 30, 33, 39, 102–3, 109, 143n5, 148n10
American Revolution, 19, 22–23, 112
Amistad captives, 98
Anne (enslaved child), 70–71, 75
Anson (enslaved child), 72–75, 113
Antigua, 44–45
antislavery Boston and Massachusetts, 9, 26–32, 54–55, 65, 87, 92–97, 101. *See also* abolitionists; antislavery movement and community; Boston Female Anti-Slavery Society; Massachusetts Anti-Slavery Society
The Anti-Slavery Cause in America and Its Martyrs (Wigham), 149n33
Anti-Slavery Fair, third annual, 77–79, 143n4
"Anti-Slavery Landmarks in Boston," 29
antislavery movement and community: Child's novel and, 108–9; Choate and, 137n41; Coffin and, 147n8; *Dred Scott* ruling and, 92–94; in England,

153

antislavery movement and community (*continued*)
15–19, 22–25; free soil principle and, 76–77; Hale and, 110, 149n35; Med and disrupted narrative of, 9–10; Med's haunting of, 5; in Pennsylvania, 25–26; press reports of deaths and, 81; schism in, 103; Slater and Curtis's relationships with, 7; Texas Troubles and suspicion of, 84–86. *See also* abolitionists; American Anti-Slavery Society; antislavery Boston and Massachusetts; Boston Female Anti-Slavery Society; Massachusetts Anti-Slavery Society; New England Anti-Slavery Society

"Anti-Slavery Reminiscence" (Child), 104

Apess, William, 73

An Appeal in Favor of that Class of Americans Called Africans (Child), 27, 33

Arkansas, 72–74

Attucks, Crispus, 92–93, 146n53

August 26 proclaimed as holiday, 77, 143n3

Aves, Thomas, 1–6, 42, 46, 54–55, 82, 129n11

Baltimore Chronicle, 52

Bancroft, George, 79, 143–44n10

Barbadoes, James, 30

Bates, Polly Ann, 37

Bates County, Missouri, 86

Beacon Hill neighborhood in Boston, 1–2, 5–6, 36, 118–19, 129n11

Benito Cereno (Melville), 115, 150n52

Bernstein, Robin, xiii

Betty (enslaved person), 95–96

Betty's Case, 92, 94–96

Bewley, Anthony, 85

BFASS. *See* Boston Female Anti-Slavery Society

Bill of Rights, 37, 39, 78

Billy Budd (Melville), 115, 150n52

Bishop, Mrs., 100

black activism, 29–30

Black Girlhood in the Nineteenth Century (Wright), xiii

Black Heritage Trail, 6, 123

black newspapers, 134n44

Blackstone, William, 15–16

Boston, Massachusetts: abolitionist activism in, 29–30, 33–37; busing crisis, 120–21; Otis School, 117–19; plan of (1835), 5; Samaritan Asylum in, 5, 53, 55–59, 68, 139n4; segregated school system in, 8; Suffolk County Courthouse, 29–30. *See also* antislavery Boston and Massachusetts; Beacon Hill neighborhood

Boston Advertiser, 52

Boston African American National Historic Site, 123

Boston Atlas, 71–72

Boston Centinel, 51–52

Boston Commercial Gazette, 58

Boston Courier, 52, 71–72

Boston Female Anti-Slavery Society (BFASS): annual reports, xii, 7, 33, 76, 79; Bright case and, 66; *Chickasaw* rescue and, 37–38; Child's novel's omission of, 108; *Commonwealth v. Aves* and, vii, xi–xiii, 40–44, 50–51, 148–49n28; enslaved people in transit and, 39–40; investigation of Med's presence on Beacon Hill, 1–2, 6; Med as poster child for, 5, 40; before Med's case, 31; Med commemorated by, 76–80; Med erased by, 76, 79–81; "mob year" (1835) and, 31, 33–35; "mother love" and, 41, 61, 137n38; outcome for Med and, 57–62; quote, vii; Samaritan Asylum and, 56–57; *Somerset's Case* used as precedent by, 28; during the summer of 1836, 35–37; *Third Annual Report*, xii, 76, 79

Boston Herald, 95

Boston Massacre, 93

Boston School Committee, 118–21

Boston Transcript, 38, 52

Boston Women's Memorial, 13

Bradford, Mrs., 100

Bridges, Ruby, vii, 117–18, 121–25

Bright, Elizabeth, 64–68, 75

Bright, Henry (and family), 65–68

British imperialism, 23

British West Indies, 15, 34
Brooks, Joanna, 22
Brooks, Preston, 136n30, 151n4
Brown, Christopher, 24
Brown, Lois, 81–82
Brown v. Board of Education of Topeka, 122–23
Burke, Kenneth, 62
Burns, Anthony, 29, 93
Bush, Earl Benjamin, 122
Bush v. Orleans Parish School Board, 122
Butler, Pierce, 26
Butler v. Hopper, 26

Campbell, John, 89–90
Canada, 100
Capshaw, Katharine, xiii, 122–24
Carpenter, Joseph, 108
Carretta, Vincent, 20
The Case of the Slave-Child, Med (pamphlet), 7–8, 42
Catron, John, 89
Centinel and Gazette, 38
Chaffee, Calvin, 94
Chambers, Lee, xiii, 33
Channing, William Ellery, 25
Chapman, Ann, 139n5
Chapman, Henry, 54–55, 104
Chapman, Maria Weston: *Betty's Case* ruling and, 94; BFASS and, xiii, 33; *Chickasaw* rescue and, 37–38; enslaved people aided by, 37; free soil principle and, 36; investigation of Med's presence on Beacon Hill, 1–2, 6; Jane Johnson and, 86–87; *Liberty Bell* edited by, 33, 61, 94; as "new mother" to Med, 76; Phebe's funeral and, 141n44; "Pinda: A True Tale," 98–104, 148n16; removal of Med from Aves home and, 54–55; Shaw's ruling and, 51
Cheney, James, 71
Chickasaw (ship), 37–38; rescue (1836), 31, 37–38
Child, David Lee, 68, 104
Child, Lydia Maria: on Anti-Slavery Fair and work-bags, 77–79; *An Appeal in Favor of that Class of Americans Called Africans*, 27, 33; on Bancroft, 143–44n10; biography of Hopper, 133–34n42; Chapman and, 33, 148n16; courtroom atmosphere and, 42, 49; *Freedmen's Book*, 106, 108; Garrison on, 33; investigation of Med's presence on Beacon Hill, 1–2, 6; Karcher's biography of, xiii; letter protesting outcome for Med, 58; *Letters*, xi; letter to Mary Aves Slater, 59–62; Med's case revised by, 98, 108; Med's illness and death and, 68–69, 109; as "new mother" to Med, 76; Pinda's escape and tale and, 100, 104; *A Romance of the Republic*, 98–99, 104–9
children: abused by abolitionists, 58; consent and, 31–32, 63–64, 71–74, 121, 140n9; emancipation of, 9–10, 56–57, 75–80, 107; free soil model and, xiii, 9–10, 40, 53, 63–64; voices of, 7–8, 129n14. *See also* enslaved children
Children of Crisis (Coles), 124
Child Slavery before and after Emancipation (Duane), xiii
Choate, Rufus, 6, 42, 44–45, 51, 137n41, 148–49n28
Christianity and slavery, 48
citizenship: African Americans and, 88, 90–94, 108, 110, 146n53; navy sailors and, 110–11
Civil Rights Childhood (Capshaw), xiii
civil rights movement and struggles, 7, 117–24
Civil War, 92, 104
Coffin, William C., 101, 147n8
Coles, Robert, 124
Collected Correspondence (Child), xi
The Colored Patriots of the Revolution (Nell), 146n53
"The Comfort of Enlightenment" (Maysles), 151n2
comity and slavery, 7, 46–47, 49–50, 69, 92
Commentaries on the Laws of England (Blackstone), 15
commission merchant, Slater as, 82, 144n1

Commonwealth v. Aves, 40–53; arguments used for freedom of Med in, 26, 28, 32, 42–49; celebration of ruling, 133n40, 143n3; *Commonwealth v. Fitzgerald* and, 98; *Commonwealth v. Taylor* compared to, 73; *Dred Scott* and, 89, 91; forgotten in Texas, 85–86; Henry Wilson on, 140n28; informal name for, 7–8, 129n13; in legal scholarship, xi, xiii, 123; Pinda's story and, 100, 103; *Sarah C. Roberts v. the City of Boston* and, 119; *Somerset's Case* and, 10, 19, 44–47, 49; status of enslaved people in free jurisdictions and, 5, 105–6, 113; subsequent cases and, 67, 70

Commonwealth v. Fitzgerald, 98, 109, 113–15
Commonwealth v. Holloway, 26
Commonwealth v. Stratton, 71
Commonwealth v. Taylor, 72–74
Compromise of 1850, 7
Connecticut, 57
consent, ability to exercise, 31–32, 63–64, 71–74, 99, 114, 121, 140n9
Constitution, U.S. *See* U.S. Constitution
Constitutional Unionists, 145n23
Cooper, Afua, 28
Cowper, William, vii, 22–25, 48, 77, 132n29, 133n31, 133n40
Craft, William and Ellen, 29
Creole (ship), 106
Cresswell, Tim, 16
"Crime against Kansas" (Sumner), 151n4
Cuba, 31–32, 83, 98
Cugoano, Ottobah, 115
Curtis, Benjamin Robbins: biography of, xiii; Bright case and, 66; *Dred Scott* and, 90–94; Parker's condemnation of, 93–94; relationship with slavery and antislavery, 7, 129n12; role in *Aves*, 6–7, 42, 44–47; Streichler on, 146n55
Curtis, Charles P., 6, 31, 42, 44–45
Curtis, George Ticknor, 90
Custom House, U.S. *See* U.S. Custom House

Daily Advertiser (Boston), 39, 95–96
Daniel, Peter, 89–90
Davy, William, 17, 18

Declaration of Independence, 46, 112, 115
Delmont, Matthew, 120
DeLombard, Jeannine, 150–51n53
democracy, 77–79, 110–12, 123
Democratic Party, 73, 142n56, 145n23
Dependent States (Sánchez-Eppler), xiii
District of Columbia, 35, 143–44n10
Douglass, Frederick, 3, 7, 9, 57, 104, 109, 147n8
Dred Scott v. Sanford, xiii, 7, 86, 88–96, 108
Duane, Anna Mae, xiii, 9, 31–32, 121, 129n14
Dublin (enslaved person), 143n1
Dunning, John, 16–17
Duyckinck, Evert, 109

Eames, Olivia, 70–71
Egypt, 21
Eli Whitney (ship), 99
emancipation: of children, 9–10, 56–57, 75–80, 107; process of, 77, 107, 115
Emancipation Act (1833), 19
emancipation laws, 9–10, 57
Emancipation Proclamation, 84
Emancipator, 39
Emerson, John, 87–88
Emma (enslaved child), 64, 75
England: antislavery sentiment in, 15–19, 22–25; free soil principle in, 16–19, 23–26, 45, 48, 106, 115, 150–51n54; moral geography of, 16, 18, 24, 76–77; P. Wheatley's trip to, 19–21; *Slave, Grace* case in, 44–45; *Somerset* myth, 115; *Somerset's Case* in, 15–19, 44; vernacular law in, 18, 131n13
enslaved children: consent and, 63–64, 71–74, 140n9; free soil model and, 40; gradual emancipation of, 57; parallels with civil rights children, 7; recognition of their status, 3; study of enslavement and, 9. *See also* children
enslaved people: accompanying summer sojourners, 35–36, 43–44; birthdays unknown by, 3; choice of slavery and, 63, 72, 75, 95, 107; as chosen people, 21; legal advocates for, 25–26; in Massachusetts, 18–19, 31–32, 35–37, 63–64, 100, 113–14; moral geography

of England and, 16, 18, 24; in transit, 26, 39–40, 47, 52, 70, 95, 108. *See also* enslaved children; free jurisdictions, status of enslaved people in
enslavement: power dynamics of, 13; reattachment theory of, 45, 89–90, 108; terminology of, 8. *See also* slavery
enslavers: in Egypt compared to America, 21; intent of, 2, 31–32, 40–41, 64–65, 67, 71
epideictic rhetoric, 152n20
equality before the law, 119–20
Equiano, Olaudah, 115, 132n30
Etienne, Gail, 123
Ex parte Simmons, 26
Eyes on the Prize (documentary), 125

"A Farewel to America. To Mrs. S.W." (Wheatley), 20
Fehrenbacher, Don E., xiii, 88–90
Finkelman, Paul, xiii, 46, 90, 92, 113
First Amendment rights, 35
The First Step (Goodman), 117–19
The First Woman in the Republic (Karcher), xiii
Fitzgerald, Edward, 113
flogging, 109–12, 149n35
Forefathers Day, 143n4
Fortier, Michel, 70
Foster, Samuel, 71
Francisco (enslaved child), 31–32, 40, 63
free blacks, protection of, 26
Freedmen's Book (Child), 106, 108
freedom of assembly, 34–35
freedom suits, xi, 5, 10, 18–19, 26, 51, 98. *See also Commonwealth v. Aves*
freedom suit scenario, 62–64, 67–71, 75–76, 96, 114–15, 125, 141n30
free jurisdictions, status of enslaved people in: *Dred Scott* and, 88–90, 92; Med's legal status and, 1, 45–46; Pennsylvania's free soil borderland and, 25–26; *A Romance of the Republic* and, 105–6; Shaw's rulings and, 5, 113, 133n40; *Somerset's Case* and, 17–18, 105–6. *See also Somerset's Case*
free soil fictions, 98–116; Med's replacement by adult icons, 98; "Pinda: A True Tale," 98–104; *A Romance of the Republic*, 104–9; *White-Jacket*, 109–16
free soil of Massachusetts: Bright case and, 67; Chapman's metaphor on, 36; children and, 40; in Child's novel, 106–7; Loring's arguments and, 50–51; Med's case and affirmation of, xi; Shaw's rejection of, 32, 49; *Somerset's Case* and, 19, 26
free soil principle: children's disruption of model, xiii, 9–10, 40, 63; in Child's letter to Slater, 61–62; *Commonwealth v. Aves* and, xi, 9, 49–53, 62; in England, 16–19, 23–26, 45, 48, 106, 150–51n54; enslaved people in transit and, 39–40; history of, in Europe, 16; moral geography and, 16, 18–19, 62, 76–77; Peabody on, xiii; in Pennsylvania, 25–26; Plymouth Rock and, 77–78; *White-Jacket* and, 110–11; work-bags as celebration of, 78. *See also* free soil fictions; free soil of Massachusetts
fugitives from slavery: Chapman's story and, 100–103; in Child's novel, 107–8; *Commonwealth v. Aves* and, 5, 100; Constitution and, 48; distinction from non-fugitives, 26, 70, 108, 147n5; Med's case compared to those of, 8–9; in Nassau, 106; PAS and, 26; Somerset as inspiration to, 17; words of, 7
Fugitive Slave Act (1793), 26, 37
Fugitive Slave Act (1850), 86, 90, 92–93, 96, 98, 107–10, 116
fugitive slave clause in the Constitution, 25, 46–49, 96

gag rule, 35
Gallagher, Victoria, 152n20
Galveston, Texas, 83
Garrison, William Lloyd: as abolitionist, 29–31, 34–35, 104; on Attucks, 92–93, 146n53; on Child, 33; in Child's novel, 108; on *Dred Scott* decision, 92–93; as publisher, 7, 27
Garrisonian immediatism, 29–30, 55, 59
General Colored Association, 30, 148n10
Georgia, 86
Ginsberg, Lesley, 120

Goddu, Teresa, 102
golden rule, 60, 62
Goodman, Susan, 117–19
gospel ground, 60–62, 77–78
Gosse, Van, 19
Gould, Philip, 21
Gove, Asa D., 64
Grace (enslaved person), 44–45
Gradual Abolition Act (1780), 25
gradual emancipation laws, 57
Greenwood v. Curtis, 48
Gregson v. Gilbert, 132n30
Gronningsater, Sarah L. H., 9, 140n9
Grover, Mrs. Simon, 95
Guiana, 100–101
Gunn, Lynda, 151n2

habeas corpus: Anson's case and, 72–73; *Betty's Case* and, 95; *Chickasaw* rescue and, 37; Emma's case and, 64; *In re Francisco* and, 31; Johnson's case and, 87; Lucas's case and, 113–14; Mansfield's ruling and, 17–18, 150–51n54; Pinda's tale and, 99; Rose's case and, 71; Shaw's denial of, 96
Hale, John P., 110, 149n35
Hall, Primus, 30
Hall, Prince, 30, 120
Hallett, Benjamin Franklin, 73, 113, 142n56
Hallowell Free Press, 52
Hargrave, Francis, 16
Harris, Levin H., 2, 6, 42, 53
Hartman, Saidiya, xi
Havana, Cuba, 31–32, 83
Haverhill Gazette, 52
Hayward, Rebecca Hutchinson, 58
Henderson County, Texas, 83
Hester (Douglass's aunt), 3
Higginson, T. W., 109
Hilliard, Francis, 39–40
Hilton, John, 30
Historical Notaries' Indexes in New Orleans, 82
Hogan, Mr. and Mrs. (Pinda's enslavers), 100–102, 104, 148n16
Holden Anti-Slavery Society, 70
Hole, Jeffrey, 110

Holt, John, 15–16
Hopper, Isaac, 133–34n42
Horton, George Moses, 27
Howard, Mrs., 31–32
Huggeford, H. H., 2
human rights, 130n12–13
Hunter, T. K., xiii, 16, 110, 139n7

Illinois, 87, 89–90
In re Francisco, 31–32, 63
interracial marriage, 106, 118

Jackson, Francis, 54–55
Jackson, James, 81
Jacobs, Harriet, 3, 7, 132–33n31, 147n5
Jacobs, John S., 147n5
Jeffers, Honorée Fanonne, 132n29
Johnson, Daniel, 86–87
Johnson, Isaiah, 86–87
Johnson, Jane, 86–87

Kane, John Kintzing, 87
Karcher, Carolyn, xiii, 34, 108
Kaul, Suvir, 23, 133n36
Kentucky, 90
Knapp, Isaac, 7, 27, 56, 58–59, 139n7

Latimer, George, 29, 98
Latimer Committee, 98
Lawrence, Massachusetts, 95
Letters (Child), xi
Levy, Leonard, xiii, 32, 113–14
Lewis, E. B., 117–18
Liberator: Anti-Slavery Fair report in, 77–78; *Betty's Case* and, 95–96; *Commonwealth v. Fitzgerald* ruling and, 114; *Dred Scott* discussed by, 92–93; Emma's case and, 64; Med's case and, 51; Refuge of Oppression column, 58, 140n15; Rose's case and, 71; Samaritan Asylum and, 56; Slater's letter reprinted in, 58–59; Wheatley's poems published by, 27
The Liberty Bell, 33, 61, 94
Lincoln, Abraham, 92
Logan, Mr. (Pinda's enslaver in story), 99–100

Loring, Charles G., 65
Loring, Ellis Gray: BFASS honoring of, 76; Bright case and, 65–67; in Child's novel, 107–8; *Commonwealth v. Aves* and, 6, 25–26, 32, 41–55, 60, 138n60, 148–49n28; at Hogan party, 104; *Lunsford v. Coquillon* and, 70; Med's illness and death and, 68–70, 81; Pinda's escape and, 100–101; Robert Morris and, 119; Rose's case and, 71–72
Loring, Louisa, 68
Louisiana, 45–47, 50, 69–70, 83, 86
Louisiana Supreme Court, 70
Louisville Advertiser, 52
Lovejoy, Elijah, 7, 143n5
L. T. (enslaved person), 36–37
Lucas, Robert, 109, 113–16
Lunsford, Rebecca, 69–70
Lunsford v. Coquillon, 69–70

Mansfield, Lord (William Murray): Loring and Shaw compared to, 76; on odious nature of slavery, 17, 23; *Somerset's Case* ruling and, 16–19, 26, 45, 47, 115, 130n12–13, 150–51n54; *Zong* massacre and, 132n30
March Fifth commemorations, 93
Mardi (Melville), 110
Marie Louise, f.w.c., v. Marot, 70
Martineau, Harriet, 35
The Martyr Age in the United States (Martineau), 35
Mashpee Indians, 73
Mashpee Revolt (1833–1834), 73
MASS. *See* Massachusetts Anti-Slavery Society
Massachusetts: desegregation of public schools, 120, 123; *Dred Scott* ruling and, 92; enslaved people in, 18–19, 31–32, 35–37, 46–47, 100, 113–14; personal liberty law (1837), 70; slavery abolished in, 78–79. *See also* antislavery Boston and Massachusetts; free soil of Massachusetts; *specific city names*
Massachusetts Anti-Slavery Society (MASS): BFASS and, 33, 51; *Commonwealth v. Taylor* ruling and, 73–74; fundraising for, 94, 100, 102–4, 143n4; Logan at sixth annual meeting of, 99; origins of, 30, 148n10
Massachusetts Declaration of Rights (1780), 46–47, 119
Massachusetts General Hospital, 56
Massachusetts Supreme Judicial Court: *Betty's Case* and, 94–96; *Commonwealth v. Aves* and, 5, 49, 51–52, 148–49n28; freedom suits following *Aves* and, 71–74; *Sarah C. Roberts v. the City of Boston*, 119, 121; Shaw's career as chief justice of, 113
Mathews, George, Jr., 70
Maysles, Philip, 151n2
McConnell, John, 29
McDonogh Three, 123–24
McLean, John, 92
Med: cases following that of, 62–75; death of, xi, 9–10, 58, 68–70, 75, 80–82, 87; *Dred Scott* compared to, 87–88; enslaved by Slater family, 3; family life of, 4; at home of T. Aves in Boston, 1–4; as Maria Sommersett, 76–82; mystery of life of, 7–10, 28; naming of, 129n13; outcome for, post-case, 52–62, 68–70; as poster child for BFASS, 5, 40; replaced by adult icons, 98–99; Ruby Bridges and Sarah Roberts compared to, 118, 121, 123, 125; stories prior to that of, 13–28, 31–32, 36–39
Med's case. *See Commonwealth v. Aves*
Med's mother: efforts at convincing Slater to free, 59–61, 68; Med's separation from, 1, 4, 41–43, 49–51, 59, 69, 107; powerlessness of, 50, 61, 139n7; Slater's enslavement of, 3
Melville, Herman, 98–99, 109–16, 150n52
Memoir and Poems of Phillis Wheatley (Odell), 27
Memoir of James Jackson (Paul), 81
Merrill, James C., 64, 141n31
Middle Passage, 13, 15, 28
Middleton, George, 6
Minardi, Margot, 19
Missouri, 87–88, 92
Missouri Compromise (1820), 88, 90–92

Missouri Supreme Court, 88–89
Moby-Dick (Melville), 110, 115
"mob year" (1835), 31, 33–35
Monthly Law Reporter, 74
Monthly Offering, 99, 102
Moorhead, Scipio, 13
moral geography: of England, 16, 18, 24, 76, 133n36, 150–51n54; free soil principle and, 16, 18–19, 40, 50–51, 62, 76–77; gospel ground and, 62, 78; of Pennsylvania, 25; P. Wheatley and, 21; segregation and, 118–19; *White-Jacket* and, 110–11
Morris, John B., 37
Morris, Robert, 119, 121, 123, 151n4
Murray, William. *See* Mansfield, Lord
My Name is Phillis Wheatley (Cooper), 28

NAACP. *See* National Association for the Advancement of Colored People
Nantucket, Massachusetts, 101, 147n8
Narrative (Douglass), 3, 9
Narrative of the Life and Travels of Mrs. Nancy Prince (Prince), 55
Nassau, British West Indies, 106
National Anti-Slavery Bazaar, Twenty-Second, 86
National Anti-Slavery Standard, 99, 103–4, 106
National Association for the Advancement of Colored People (NAACP), 122, 124–25
National Park Service (NPS), 6, 123
Navy, U.S. *See* U.S. Navy
NEASS. *See* New England Anti-Slavery Society
Nell, William Cooper, 93, 104, 123, 146n53
Nelson, Samuel, 89, 92
New Bedford, Massachusetts, 33, 66, 101
New Bedford Mercury, 41
New England Anti-Slavery Society (NEASS), 30–33, 148n10
New Jersey, 57
Newman, Richard S., 25, 30
New Orleans, Louisiana: Anne's case, 70–71; Emma's case, 64; Med's mother in, 1, 4, 41, 43, 50, 82, 139n7; Med's possible return to, 43, 49–50, 53, 58, 69; school desegregation in, 117, 122–24; ships to north from, 139n2; Slater household in, 1–4, 7, 68, 82
New Orleans Public Schools, 123–24
New York, 57
New York Courier and Enquirer, 52
New York Express, 52
New York Observer, 84–85
Northampton, Massachusetts, 68, 107
North Slope of Beacon Hill, 5–6
NPS. *See* National Park Service

Occom, Samson, 21
Odell, Margaretta Matilda, 27
Old Colony Club, 143n4
"On the Death of General Wooster" (Wheatley), 21–22
Otis School (Boston), 117–19
Otter, Samuel, 110–11
Our Nig (Wilson), 57–58

Paley, Ruth, 18
Parker, Mary S., 56, 66, 104
Parker, Theodore, 93
Parkman, George, 141n31
PAS. *See* Pennsylvania Abolition Society
paternalism, 119–21
Paul, Susan, 30, 56, 81
Peabody, Sue, xiii, 16, 18, 62
Pennsylvania: free soil borderland in, 25–26, 134n42; gradual emancipation of children in, 57; Johnson's slave transit case in, 86–87
Pennsylvania Abolition Society (PAS), 25–26, 86–87
personal liberty law (Massachusetts, 1837), 70
Peters, John, 22, 27
Phebe (child in Samaritan Asylum), 68, 141n44
Phillips, Wendell, 96–97, 108
Phillis (ship), 13
Pico, Abigail, 56
Pierce, Franklin, 142n56
Pilgrims, 77–79, 143n5
Pilgrim Society, 143n4

"Pinda: A True Tale" (Chapman), 98–104, 148n16
"Pity for Poor Africans" (Cowper), 24, 132n29
Plessy v. Ferguson, 119
Plymouth Rock, 77–79, 143n5
Poems on Various Subjects (Wheatley), 13, 14, 19, 21
Prevost, Tessie, 123
Prince, Nancy, 6, 30, 54–55
Problem We All Live With, The (Rockwell), 117–18, 123, 151nn1–2
proslavery sentiment and press: cases following Med's and, 63, 99; *Chickasaw* rescue and, 37–38; Child's letter addressing, 60–61; Curtis condemned for, 93–94; Med's death and, 80; Yorke-Talbot opinion, 15. See also *Dred Scott v. Sanford*
Purvis, Robert, 109

Quakers, 23, 133n42

Rachel v. Walker, 89
Racial Innocence (Bernstein), xiii
reattachment theory of enslavement, 45, 89–90, 108
Redburn (Melville), 110
"Remember your Weekly Pledge" collection box, 102
replevin, 70–71
Republican Party, 83
Reynolds, Donald, 84, 86
Rhode Island, 57
Richmond Enquirer, 52
Rise and Fall of the Slave Power in America (Wilson), 148–49n28
Roberts, Benjamin Franklin, 119, 121, 123, 151n4
Roberts, Robert, 30
Roberts, Sarah, 8, 116–21
Robertson-Lorant, Laurie, 111
Robinson, Sophia and John, 65–66
Rockwell, Norman, 117–18, 123, 151nn1–2
Rogin, Michael, 113, 115
A Romance of the Republic (Child), 98–99, 104–9

Rose (enslaved child), 71–72, 75
Rothman, Adam, 83
Ruchames, Louis, 139n7
Rusert, Britt, xi

Salem Register, 71
Samaritan Asylum for Indigent Children, 5, 53, 55–59, 68, 139n4
Samson (biblical), 79
Sánchez-Eppler, Karen, xiii, 9, 81
Sancho, Ignatius, 22
Sarah C. Roberts v. the City of Boston, 119–21
Sargent, Henrietta, 6, 54–55
Schafer, Judith Kelleher, 69
school segregation and desegregation, 8–9, 116–21, 123
Schuyler, Lucy S., 95
Scott, Dred, 8, 87–94, 125
Scott, Eliza, 88, 145n35
Scott, Harriet Robinson, 88
Scott, Lizzie, 88, 145n35
Scott v. Emerson, 88, 92
Sedgwick, Theodore, 48
segregation, 8–9, 116–21, 123
self-emancipation, 10, 20
separate but equal doctrine, 9, 116–22
Services of Colored Americans in the Wars of 1776 and 1812 (Nell), 146n53
Sewall, Samuel: cases following *Aves* and, 64–66, 71–73; *Chickasaw* rescue and, 37–39, 136n30; in Child's novel, 108; *Commonwealth v. Aves* and, 6, 41–42, 51, 148–49n28; *Commonwealth v. Fitzgerald* and, 113; *Dred Scott* ruling and, 93; *In re Francisco* and, 31–32
Sharp, Granville, 16, 18, 20, 76, 132n30
Shaw, Francis, 105
Shaw, Hope Savage, 33
Shaw, Lemuel: on abolition of slavery in Massachusetts, 78–79; *Betty's Case* and, 94–96; BFASS honoring of, 76; *Billy Budd* and, 150n52; Bright case and, 65; celebration of Med's case and, 78, 148–49n28; *Chickasaw* rescue and, 37–38; *Commonwealth v. Aves* ruling, xi, 5–6, 9, 26, 44–46, 49–51; *Commonwealth v.*

Shaw, Lemuel (*continued*)
  Fitzgerald and, 98, 109, 113–15; *Commonwealth v. Taylor* and, 72–74; expansion of Med precedent, 113; fugitives from slavery and, 8–9; *In re Francisco*, 31–32; Lord Mansfield and, 17, 26; Loring's argument on immorality of slavery and, 47, 138n60; *Lunsford v. Coquillon* and, 70; Med's death and, 69, 81; Rose's case and, 71–72; *Sarah C. Roberts v. the City of Boston* and, 119–20; school segregation ruling, 8–9, 116
Shaw, Robert Gould, 104–5
Shipley, Mrs. (BFASS member), 139n5
Sims, Thomas, 8–9, 29, 96, 114–15
Sinha, Manisha, 30
Skyllon, F. O., 150–51n54
Slater, Mary Aves, 1–6, 43, 58–62, 68, 82, 86
Slater, Samuel (son-in-law of T. Aves): as American Stewart, 82–86; household in New Orleans, 1–4; land transactions of, 83, 145n20; letter to the editor, 58–59; Med drama and, 1–2, 4–6, 41, 43, 47, 54–55, 128n2; Med's death and, 82; relationship with slavery and antislavery, 7
Slater, Samuel N. (grandson of T. Aves), 3–4
Slater, Thomas Aves, 3–4
Slave, Grace, 44–45, 89–90, 108
slave insurrection panic (1860), 7, 83–86, 145n23
slave law: in American colonies, 18–19; comity and, 46; in England, 16–18, 45; in Louisiana, 45–46; in Massachusetts, 39, 41–42, 45–50, 100
slavery: abolished in the British Empire, 19; calls for abolition of, 29–30, 33, 35–37, 136n17, 143–44n10; choice of, 63, 72, 75, 95, 107; comity and, 3, 46–47, 49–50, 69, 92; historical amnesia about, 27; immorality of, 45–48, 51, 59–61, 115, 138n60; power dynamics of, 13; twenty-first-century terminology regarding, 8; violence of, 3; Wheatley on hypocrisy of, 21–22. See also antislavery movement and community; fugitives from slavery
slaves. See enslaved children; enslaved people
slave trade, 7, 22–23, 83
slave transit cases, 8; BFASS and, 36–37, 39–40; in Boston (1832), 31; *Commonwealth v. Fitzgerald*, 98, 109; *Dred Scott*, xiii, 7, 86, 88–94; Hunter on, 110; Johnson's case, 86–87; *White-Jacket* and, 110–11
Small, Eliza, 37
Smith, Increase, 67
Smith, John J., 6
Snowden, Samuel, 65, 108
Soifer, Aviam, 95
Somerset, James, 17, 76, 125, 143n1. See also *Somerset's Case*
Somerset's Case: the colonies and, 18–19; Cowper and, 23; human rights and, 130n12–13; Med's case compared to, xiii, 8, 10; moral geography of England and, 76, 150–51n54; precedence of, 28, 44–47, 49, 89–92; status of enslaved people in free jurisdictions and, 17–18, 105–6; Van Cleve on, 130n6; Wheatleyan moment and, 19–20
Sommersett, Maria, 76–82
Stewart, Charles, 16–17, 20, 130n12
Stewart, Maria, 30
Still, William, 86–87
Story, Joseph, 42, 89, 138n60
Stowe, Harriet Beecher, 80–81
Stowell, Lord, 45, 89–90
Strader, 90
Stratton, Samuel, 71
Streichler, Stuart, xiii, 146n55
Suffolk County Courthouse, 29–30
Sullivan, Catherine, 54–55, 68, 139n5
Sullivan, Hephzibah, 56
Sumner, Charles, 119, 121, 123–24, 136n30, 151n4
Supreme Court, U.S. See U.S. Supreme Court
Sweet, Sullivan and Mrs., 95–96

Taliaferro, Lawrence, 88
Taney, Robert B., 88–92, 94
Task, The (Cowper), 23–25
Tate, Leona, 123
Taylor, Diana, 63, 141n30
Taylor, Mary B., 73–74, 113
Tennessee, 95
Texas, Republic of, 83
Texas Troubles, 7, 83–86, 145n23
Thacher, Peter Oxenbridge, 65, 67
Thacher girl (enslaved child), 37
Theoharis, Jeanne, 120
Third Annual Report of the Boston Female Anti-Slavery Society, xii, 76, 79
Thomas, Brook, 115
Thomas Jefferson Semmes school, 123
Thompson, George, 34–35
Thomson, James, 23
Through My Eyes (Bridges), 122–24
Ticknor, Eliza M., 71–72
"The Transatlantic Progress of Sugar in the Eighteenth Century" (Jeffers), 132n29
transportation, segregation of, 118
Treaty of Paris, 23
The Trial of Theodore Parker (Parker), 93–94
Turner, Matthew, 37
Tyler, Texas, Vigilance Committee, 83–86

Uncle Tom's Cabin (Stowe), 80–81
Underground Railroad, 6, 96
United States (ship), 109, 113
Upham, Joshua, 71
U.S. Constitution: citizenship and, 91; fugitive slave clause in, 25, 46–49, 96; school segregation and, 122; slavery and, 47–49
U.S. Custom House, 83
U.S. Navy, 109–13
U.S. Supreme Court, 88, 90, 93–94, 122, 146n55

Van Cleve, George, 130n6
VanderVelde, Lea, 145n35
Vermont Telegraph, 133n40

vernacular law, 18, 131n13
von Frank, Albert J., 90

Waldstreicher, David, 20
Walker, David, 30
Warren, Earl, 122
Washington, Madison, 106
Webster, Daniel, 42
Webster, John White, 141n31
Weston, Anne Warren, 33–34, 37, 66, 100, 139n5, 141n44
Weston, Caroline, 33, 54–55, 59, 67
Weston, Debora, 33, 37, 54–55, 66, 100–101, 139n5, 141n44
Weston, Maria. *See* Chapman, Maria Weston
Weston, Mary, 34
Weston sisters, 33–37, 66, 68, 101
The Weston Sisters (Chambers), xiii
Weyler, Karen, 27
Weymouth, Massachusetts, 33
Wheatley, John, 13, 22, 27
Wheatley, Nathaniel, 19, 21
Wheatley, Phillis: death of, 22; enslavement of, 13–15; "A Farewel to America. To Mrs. S.W.," 20; Jeffers's poetry and, 132n29; legacy of, 27–28; manumission of, and life after, 19–22; Med's experience compared to that of, 15, 22, 28; in Odell memoir, 27; "On the Death of General Wooster," 21–22; *Poems on Various Subjects*, 13, 14, 19, 21; portrait of, 13, 14; revival of poetry of, 26–28, 134n44
Wheatley, Susannah, 13, 21, 27
Wheeler, John H., 86–87
Whipple, Charles, 100
White, Farnum, Jr., 71
White-Jacket (Melville), 98–99, 109–16, 150–51n53
white menace, 122–23
white sentimentalism, 22
Whittier, John Greenleaf, 79
Wiecek, William, 17–18, 45
Wigham, Eliza, 149n33
Wilkins, Shadrach, 8, 29, 96, 114–15

Willard, Solomon, 29
William Frantz school, 117–18, 122
Williams, Kidada E., 28
Williamson, Passmore, 86–87
Wilson, George, 58
Wilson, Harriet, 57–58
Wilson, Henry, 148–49n28
Winter, Steven L., 150n52
Wisconsin Territory, 88
Wise, Steven M., 18
Women's Equality Day, 143n3

Wong, Edlie, xiii, 41, 74
Woodhouse, Barbara, 31, 57
Worcester County, Massachusetts, 70–71
work-bags, 78–79
Wright, Nazera Sadiq, xiii, 63, 128n6

Yorke-Talbot opinion (1729), 15

Zagacki, Kenneth S., 152n20
Zong massacre and lawsuit, 23, 132n30

KAREN WOODS WEIERMAN is professor of English at Worcester State University (MA), where she teaches American literature and first-year writing. She is the former director of the Commonwealth Honors Program and recipient of the George I. Alden Excellence in Teaching Award. She holds a BA in American studies from Georgetown University and a PhD in English from the University of Minnesota. An avid archival detective, Weierman is the past recipient of research fellowships from the American Antiquarian Society and the Massachusetts Historical Society. Her book *One Nation, One Blood: Interracial Marriage in American Fiction, Scandal, and Law, 1820–1870* (University of Massachusetts Press, 2005) explores the taboo against interracial marriage by investigating the traditional link between marriage and property. Weierman was born in Brooklyn, raised on Long Island, and resides in Massachusetts.

www.ingramcontent.com/pod-product-compliance
Lightning Source LLC
Chambersburg PA
CBHW032215230426
43672CB00011B/2562